T0215197

Lecture Notes in Computer Science   9586

Commenced Publication in 1973
Founding and Former Series Editors:
Gerhard Goos, Juris Hartmanis, and Jan van Leeuwen

Services Science

Subline of Lectures Notes in Computer Science

Subline Editors-in-Chief

Subline Editorial Board

More information about this series at http://www.springer.com/series/7408

Alex Norta · Walid Gaaloul
G.R. Gangadharan · Hoa Khanh Dam (Eds.)

Service-Oriented Computing – ICSOC 2015 Workshops

WESOA, RMSOC, ISC, DISCO, WESE, BSCI, FOR-MOVES
Goa, India, November 16–19, 2015
Revised Selected Papers

 Springer

Editors
Alex Norta
Tallinn University of Technology
Tallinn
Estonia

Walid Gaaloul
Télécom SudParis
Evry
France

G.R. Gangadharan
Institute for Development and Research
 in Banking Technology
Hyderabad
India

Hoa Khanh Dam
University of Wollongong
Wollongong, NSW
Australia

ISSN 0302-9743   ISSN 1611-3349 (electronic)
Lecture Notes in Computer Science
ISBN 978-3-662-50538-0   ISBN 978-3-662-50539-7 (eBook)
DOI 10.1007/978-3-662-50539-7

Library of Congress Control Number: 2016938403

LNCS Sublibrary: SL2 – Programming and Software Engineering

Printed on acid-free paper

This Springer imprint is published by Springer Nature
The registered company is Springer-Verlag GmbH Berlin Heidelberg

Preface

This volume presents the proceedings of the workshops that were held in conjunction with the 13th International Conference on Service-Oriented Computing, which took place in Goa, India, November 16–19, 2015.

The workshops provide venues for specialist groups to meet, to generate focused discussions on specific subareas within service-oriented computing, and to engage in community-building activities. These events helped significantly enrich the main conference by both expanding the scope of research topics and attracting participants from a wider community.

The ICSOC 2015 workshop track consisted of seven workshops on a wide range of topics that fall into the general area of service computing:

- WESOA 2015: The 11th International Workshop on Engineering Service-Oriented Applications
- RMSOC 2015: The Second Workshop on Resource Management in Service-Oriented Computing
- ISC 2015: The Second Workshop on Intelligent Service Clouds
- DISCO 2015: The First International Workshop on Dependability Issues in Services Computing
- WESE 2015: Workshop on Engineering for Service-Oriented Enterprises
- BSCI 2015: The First International Workshop on Big Data Services and Computational Intelligence (joined with ISC 2015)
- FOR-MOVES 2015: The Second International Workshop on Formal Modeling and Verification of Service-based systems

The workshops were held on November 16, 2015. Each workshop had its own chairs and Program Committee who were responsible for the selection of papers. The overall organization for the workshop program, including the selection of the workshop proposals, was carried out by Alex Norta, Walid Gaaloul, and G.R. Gangadharan.

We would like to thank the workshop authors, as well as keynote speakers and workshop Organizing Committees, who together contributed to this important aspect of the conference.

We hope that these proceedings will serve as a valuable reference for researchers and practitioners working in the service-oriented computing domain and its emerging applications.

March 2016
Alex Norta
Walid Gaaloul
G.R. Gangadharan

Organization

General Chairs

Aditya Ghose   University of Wollongong, Australia
Srinivas Padmanabhun   Infosys Labs, India

Program Chairs

Alistair Barros   Queensland University of Technology, Australia
Daniela Grigori   Université Paris Dauphine, France
Nanjangud C. Narendra   Ericsson Research, Bangaluru, India

Steering Committee

Boualem Benatallah   University of New South Wales, Australia
Fabio Casati   University of Trento, Italy
Bernd Krämer   FernUniversität in Hagen, Germany
Winfried Lamersdorf   University of Hamburg, Germany
Heiko Ludwig   IBM Research, USA
Mike Papazoglou   Tilburg University, The Netherlands
Jian Yang   Macquarie University, Australia
Liang Zhang   Fudan University, China

Workshop Chairs

Alex Norta   Tallinn University of Technology, Estonia
Walid Gaaloul   Télécom SudParis, France
G.R. Gangadharan   Institute for Development and Research in Banking
                                   Technology, India

Demonstration Track Chairs

Vinay Kulkarni   Technology Service Corporation, USA
Radha K. Pisipati   Infosys Labs, India
Vinod Muthusamy   IBM, USA

Panel Chairs

Florian Daniel   Politecnico di Milano, Italy
Gargi B. Dasgupta   IBM Research, India
Andreas Metzger   University of Duisburg-Essen, Germany

Publicity Chairs

Georgiana Copil   TU Vienna, Austria
Tri Kurniawan   Brawijaya University, Indonesia
Renuka Sindhgatta   IBM Research, India

Organizing Chairs

Karthikeyan Ponnalagu   IBM Research, India
Wagh Ramrao S.   Goa University, India

Publication Chair

Hoa Khanh Dam   University of Wollongong, Australia

Web Chairs

Allahbaksh Asadullah   Infosys Labs, India
Ayu Saraswati   University of Wollongong, Australia

Finance Chair

Bernd Krämer   FernUniversität in Hagen, Germany

Engineering Service-Oriented Applications (WESOA 2015)

George Feuerlicht   HCTD, University of Technology, Sydney, Australia
Winfried Lamersdorf   University of Hamburg, Germany
Guadalupe Ortiz   University of Cádiz, Spain
Christian Zirpins   Karlsruhe University of Applied Sciences, Germany

Resource Management in Service-Oriented Computing (RMSOC 2015)

Cristina Cabanillas   Vienna University of Economics and Business, Austria
Alex Norta   Tallinn University of Technology, Estonia
Nanjangud C. Narendra   Cognizant Technology Solutions, Bangalore, India
Manuel Resinas   University of Seville, Spain

Intelligent Service Clouds (ISC 2015)

Roman Vaculin   IBM T.J. Watson Research Center, USA
Alex Norta   Tallinn University of Technology, Estonia
Rik Eshuis   Eindhoven University of Technology, The Netherlands

Dependability Issues in Services Computing (DISCO 2015)

Javier Alonso Lopez   University of Leon, Spain
Rahul Ghosh   Xerox Research, India
Jogesh K. Muppala   Hong Kong University of Science and Technology,
                             Hong Kong, SAR China

Workshop on Engineering for Service-Oriented Enterprises (WESE 2015)

Khaled Gaaloul   Luxembourg Institute of Science and Technology -
                             LIST, Luxembourg
Imed Boughzala   Telecom Ecole de management, Paris, France
Wided Guedria   Luxembourg Institute of Science and Technology -
                             LIST, Luxembourg
Olfa Chourabi   Telecom Ecole de management, Paris, France

Big Data Services and Computational Intelligence (BSCI 2015)

Zhangbing Zhou   China University of Geosciences (Beijing), China
Patrick Hung   University of Ontario Institute of Technology, Canada
Suzanne McIntosh   Cloudera Inc. and New York University, USA
Vaskar Raychoudhury   Indian Institute of Technology Roorkee, India

Formal Modeling and Verification of Service-Based Systems (FOR-MOVES 2014)

Hanifa Boucheneb   Montreal Polytechnic, Montréal, Canada
Kais Klai   LIPN, University of Paris 13, France

Workshop Introductions

Introduction to the 11th International Workshop on Engineering Service-Oriented Applications (WESOA'15)

George Feuerlicht[1,2,3], Winfried Lamersdorf[4], Guadalupe Ortiz[5],
and Christian Zirpins[6]

[1] Unicorn College, Prague, Czech Republic
[2] Prague University of Economics, Prague, Czech Republic
[3] University of Technology Sydney, Ultimo, Australia
george.feuerlicht@uts.edu.au
[4] University of Hamburg, Hamburg, Germany
lamersdorf@informatik.unihamburg.de
[5] University of Cádiz, Cádiz, Spain
guadalupe.ortiz@uca.es
[6] Karlsruhe University of Applied Sciences, Karlsruhe, Germany
christian.zirpins@hs-karlsruhe.de

The Workshop on Engineering Service Oriented Applications (WESOA) focuses on core service software engineering issues and at the same time keeps pace with new developments such as methods for engineering of cloud services. Our aim has been to facilitate evolution of new concepts in service engineering research across multiple disciplines and to encourage participation of researchers from academia and industry, providing a common platform for exchange of ideas between these groups. Over the past eleven years WESOA has been able to attract high-quality contributions across a range of service engineering topics. The 11th Workshop on Engineering Service Oriented Applications (WESOA'15) was held at the Goa University, in Goa, India on 16 November 2015. The ICSOC workshop day at the Goa University included keynotes by Richard Hull from IBM Research, Aditya Ghose from University of Wollongong and Guido Governatori from NICTA. The WESOA technical sessions included six research papers. Each paper submission was reviewed by at least three reviewers with the following papers accepted for presentation at the workshop and publication in the ICSOC'2015 Workshop Proceedings: *All the Services Large and Micro: Revisiting Industrial Practice in Services Computing* by Gerald Schermann, Jurgen Cito, and Philipp Leitner, *From Choreography Diagrams to RESTful Interactions* by Adriatik Nikaj, Sankalita Mandal, Cesare Pautasso, and Mathias Weske, *A Web Services Infrastructure for the Management of Mashup Interfaces* by Jesús Vallecillos Ruiz, Javier Criado, Antonio Jesús Fenández-García, Nicolás Padilla, and Luis Iribarne, *Establishing Distributed Governance Infrastructures for Enacting Cross-Organization Collaborations* by Alex Norta, *Distributed Service Co-evolution based on Domain Objects* by Martina De Sanctis, Kurt Geihs, Antonio Bucchiarone, Giuseppe Valetto, Annapaola Marconi, Marco Pistore, and Fondazione Bruno Kessler, and *Estimating the Complexity of Software Services using an Entropy based Metric* by George Feuerlicht and David Hartman.

Workshop Organizers

George Feuerlicht	UTS, Sydney, Australia; Unicorn College, PUE, Czech Republic
Winfried Lamersdorf	University of Hamburg, Germany
Guadalupe Ortiz	University of Cádiz, Spain
Christian Zirpins	Karlsruhe University of Applied Sciences, Germany

Program Committee

Marco Aiello	University of Groningen, Netherlands
Vasilios Andrikopoulos	University of Stuttgart, Germany
Muneera Bano	University of Technology, Sydney, Australia
David Bermbach	TU Berlin, Germany
Alena Buchalcevova	Prague University of Economics, Czech Republic
Javier Cubo	University of Malaga, Spain
Florian Daniel	University of Trento, Italy
Schahram Dustdar	Technical University of Vienna, Austria
Thomas Fuchß	Karlsruhe University of Applied Sciences, Germany
Laura Gonzalez	Universidad de la República, Uruguay
Paul Greenfield	CSIRO, Australia
Thai Tran Hong	University of Technology, Sydney, Australia
Agnes Koschmieder	Karlsruhe Institute of Technology, Germany
Mark Little	Red Hat, USA
Leszek Maciaszek	Wroclaw University of Economics, Poland
Marcelo Medeiros Eler	University of São Paulo, Brasil
Massimo Mecella	Univ. Roma La Sapienza, Italy
Daniel Moldt	University of Hamburg, Germany
Rebecca Parsons	ThoughtWorks, USA
Ilja Petrov	Reutlingen University of Applied Sciences, Germany
Andreas Petter	Seeburger AG, Germany
Pierluigi Plebani	Politecnico di Milano, Italy
Wolfgang Reisig	Humboldt-University Berlin, Germany
Norbert Ritter	University of Hamburg, Germany
Eric Wilde	UC Berkeley School of Information, USA
Erik Wittern	IBM Watson Research, USA

Acknowledgements

The organizers of the WESOA'15 workshop wish to thank all authors for their contributions to this workshop and members of the program committee whose expert input made this workshop possible. Finally, we acknowledge the support of the ICSOC'15 workshop chairs Walid Gaaloul, Alex Norta, and G.R. Gangadharan.

Introduction to the 2nd Workshop on Resource Management in Service-Oriented Computing (RMSOC) 2015

Cristina Cabanillas[1], Alex Norta[2], and Manuel Resinas[3]

[1] Vienna University of Economics and Business, Vienna, Austria
cristina.cabanillas@wu.ac.at
[2] Tallinn University of Technology, Tallinn, Estonia
alex.norta@gmail.com
[3] University of Seville, Seville, Spain
resinas@us.es

1 Preface

The Second Workshop on Resource Management in Service-Oriented Computing (RMSOC)[1] was held in conjunction with the 13th International Conference on Service-Oriented Computing (ICSOC'15) and as part of a joint session with the Intelligent Service Clouds (ISC) and the Big Data Services and Computational Intelligence (BSCI) workshops in Goa, India.

The goal of RMSOC was to devise a holistic vision of resource management in Service-Oriented Computing through the analysis of multiple perspectives from several research communities. These perspectives range from the management of human resources in intra-organizational processes in the context of Business Process Management (BPM) to the distribution of work in crowdsourcing scenarios to the management of networked components in the field of Cyber-Physical Systems (CPS). For this reason, the workshop solicited contributions focused on the management of human and non-human resources in both intra- and inter-organizational scenarios. This included topics such as resource assignment, planning, analysis, visualization or composition, amongst others.

After a thorough peer-review process conducted by the workshop's Program Committee, three papers were selected as representative of the multi-perspective approach the workshop aimed at. Following is a brief overview of the contributions.

The full research paper "Extending Generic BPM with Computer Vision Capabilities" by Adrian Mos, Adrien Gaidon and Eleonora Vig presents an approach to enrich business process models with computer vision (CV) capabilities so that cameras are used as resources in the process and the information provided by them is transformed into actionable data for BPM. The approach involves a CV engine where

---

[1] https://ai.wu.ac.at/rmsoc2015/.

various CV patterns such as car detectors are individually described and composed on-the-fly for any business process.

The full research paper "S-PDH: A CPS Service Contract Framework for Composition" by Lie Ye, Kaiyu Qian and Liang Zhang presents a framework for the composition of Cyber-Physical Systems (CPS) based on three-level service contracts, namely, the physical property contract, the dynamic physical behaviour contract, and the hybrid system behaviour contract. This framework enables the compatibility checking of the different resources that compose the CPS.

The full research paper "Towards RAM-Based Variant Generation of Business Process Models" by Ahmed Tealeb, Ahmed Awad and Galal Galal-Edeen deals with the problem of generating variants of a business process that come from changes in their organizational perspective. In particular, the authors use Resource Assignment Matrices (RAMs) as the model in which changes are introduced and present several algorithms to generate consistent process model variants caused by adaptations in them.

We sincerely thank the Program Committee Members of the RMSOC 2015 workshop for their time and support throughout the reviewing process.

Cristina Cabanillas, Alex Norta, and Manuel Resinas
RMSOC 2015 Workshop Chairs

2 Organization Details

2.1 Workshop Chairs

Dr. Cristina Cabanillas. Vienna University of Economics and Business, Austria. E-mail: `cristina.cabanillas@wu.ac.at`

Dr. Alex Norta. Tallinn University of Technology, Estonia. E-mail: `alex.norta@gmail.com`

Dr. Manuel Resinas. University of Seville, Spain. E-mail: `resinas@us.es`

2.2 Program Committee Members

Fabio Casati	University of Trento, Italy
Florian Daniel	University of Trento, Italy
Félix García	University of Castilla-La Mancha, Spain
Lam-Son Lê	HCMC University of Technology, Vietnam
Jonathan Lee	National Taiwan University, Taiwan
Vinod Muthusamy	IBM, USA
Antonio Ruiz-Cortés	University of Seville, Spain
Anderson Santana De Oliveira	SAP, France

Stefan Schönig   University of Bayreuth, Germany
Stefan Schulte   Vienna University of Technology, Austria
Mark Strembeck   Vienna University of Economics and Business, Austria
Dimitrios Tsoumakos   Department of Informatics, Ionian University, Greece

Introduction to the Proceedings
of the Workshop on Engineering
for Service-Oriented Enterprise (WESE) 2015

Khaled Gaaloul[1], Imed Boughzala[2], Wided Guedria[1],
and Olfa Chourabi[2]

[1] Luxembourg Institute of Science and Technology (LIST), Esch-sur-Alzette,
Luxembourg
{khaled.gaaloul,wided.guedria}@list.lu
[2] Telecom Ecole de management, Paris, France
{imed.boughzala,olfa.chourabi}@telecom-em.eu

1 Introduction

The Workshop on Engineering for Service-oriented Enterprise (WESE) is set up as a one-day event in such a way that it attracts academics and practitioners. WESE 2015 is co-located with the ICSOC 2015 conference in Goa, India.

Present day enterprises often become service-oriented enterprises, which are comprised of a dynamic network of organizations that collectively provide services. In this context, we define a service as a self-contained unit of functionality that establishes a meaningful value to enterprises such as service performance, service customer, service producer, service delivery, etc.

Moreover, service-oriented enterprises need to negotiate many challenges, such as changes in the economic climate, mergers, acquisitions, innovation, novel technologies, and regulations. This involves enterprise transformation addressing digital transformation issues which are related to stakeholders' experience, technology in process integration and new digitally-modified business models.

Enterprise engineering is the general term for an engineering based approach to architect, transform or develop service-oriented enterprises. Enterprise engineering is based on rationales of how an enterprise wants to use its organizational socio-technical systems, such as business processes and information systems.

As a first event, this workshop succeeded in attracting different communities from research fields such as Organizational Science, Management Science and Information Science composing the source fields on enterprise engineering. The workshop attracted in total 9 submissions. The submitted papers came from both academics and practitioners who shared their original insights concerning research approaches in EE. Every paper received more than three reviews and was independently discussed with the advisory board. At the end, we decided to accept 4. Papers presentations are opportunities for stimulating meaningful discussions between participants, with the goal of developing approaches for research methodologies in EE; thereby creating synergies and jointly identifying topics for further research in, hopefully, in the next WESE event.

Khaled Gaaloul
Imed Boughzala
Wided Guedria
Olfa Chourabi
WESE 2015 Workshop chairs

Introduction to the Proceedings
of the Workshop on FORmal MOdeling
and VErification of Service-Based Systems
(FOR-MOVES) 2015

Hanifa Boucheneb[1], and Kais Klai[2]

[1] École Polytechnique de Montréal, Montréal, Canada
hanifa.boucheneb@polymtl.ca
[2] Université Paris 13, Sorbonne Paris Cité, Paris, France
kais.klai@lipn.univ-paris13.fr

1 Introduction

The Second workshop on Formal Modeling and Verification of Service-based systems (FOR-MOVES) 2015 was held in conjunction with the ICSOC'15 conference in Goa, India. During the few last years the use of formal approaches for the modeling and the verification of service-based processes is increasingly widespread. On the one hand, formal modeling allows one to define unambiguous semantics for the languages and protocols used for the specification of service oriented systems. On the other hand, formal verification approaches are popular means of checking the correctness properties of these applications, such as safety, liveness, QoS requirements and security. Thus, the aim of FOR-MOVES workshop was to provide a venue for the presentation and discussion of new ideas and work in progress in formal modeling and verification methods, in the field of Service Oriented Computing (SOC). This year, the Workshop Program Committee Members selected two full papers after a thorough peer-review (four reviewers per paper). Following is a brief overview of the contributions.

The full research paper with the title "Toward the formalization of BPEL", by authors Laila Boumlik and Mohamed Mejri, deals with the formalisation using process algebra of a fragment of BPEL. BPEL is considered as an important standard language for web services orchestration. However, many of its features are complex and source of a large misunderstanding due to the absence of formalization. The formalisation of PBEL is a mandatory step for automatic modelling and verification of PBEL Web services.

The full research paper with the title "Expressive Equivalence and Succinctness of Parametrized Automata with respect to Finite Memory Automata", by authors Tushant Jha, Walid Belkhir, Yannick Chavalier and Michael Rusinowitch, deals with the comparison of two formalisms parametrized automata, proposed by the authors, and a class of finite memory automata used to model services. It proves that both classes have the same expressive power, while parametrized automata can be exponentially succinct for some languages and that simulation preorder over parametrized automata is EXPTIME-complete.

We sincerely thank the Program Committee Members of the FOR-MOVES 2015 workshop for their time and support throughout the reviewing period.

Introduction to the Proceedings
of the Workshop on Intelligent Service Clouds
(ISC) 2015

Roman Vaculin[1], Alex Norta[2], and Rik Eshuis[3]

[1] IBM Research, Yorktown Heights, NY, USA
vaculin@us.ibm.com
[2] Department of Informatics, Tallinn University of Technology, 12618 Tallinn, Estonia
alex.norta.phd@ieee.org
[3] TU-Eindhoven, PAV D11, POBox 513, 5600 Eindhoven, The Netherlands
h.eshuis@tue.nl

1 Introduction

The Second Workshop on Intelligent Service Clouds (ISC) 2015 was held in conjunction with the ICSOC'15 conference in Goa, India. The workshop followed the increasing interest in big data, cloud, analytics services, cyberphysical systems and rich combinations with human driven services. The goal of the workshop was to provide a platform for exploring this exciting landscape and the new challenges in the context of intelligent service clouds. It aimed at bringing together researchers from various communities interested in the challenges. We solicited contributions that study fundamental as well as practical aspects. At the fundamental, solution side we sought approaches that study adequate service models addressing the above characteristics, mechanisms for specification, discovery, composition, delivery and scaling of intelligent cloud services, data, computational-, security- and privacy aspects of analytics services, and cloud environments for analytics services, and address specific technical intelligent service-oriented cloud solutions, e.g., analytics; mining, visualization; self-management; security; trust mechanisms; collaboration mechanisms. At the practical, problem side we were interested in case studies in which intelligent service-oriented cloud computing technologies are applied in socio-technical systems/processes like smart logistics, smart manufacturing, healthcare, commerce, public administration, etc. The ISC'15 workshop was a direct successor of the full day first Workshop on Intelligent Service Clouds ISC 2015 which we organized in conjunction with ICSOC 2014, and the full day first Workshop on Pervasive Analytical Service Clouds for the Enterprise and Beyond which we organized in conjunction with ICSOC 2013.

Two full ISC-workshop papers were selected after a thorough peer-review by the Workshop Program Committee Members. Following is a brief overview of the contributions.

The full research paper with the title 'Context-Aware Personalization for Smart Mobile Cloud Services' by authors Waldemar Hummer and Stefan Schulte focuses on the ability of context-aware applications to offer personalized cloud services to support context-aware applications. The proposed solution is based on a three-phase approach with context change analysis, context state management, and context-triggered adaptation actions. The authors use an illustrative scenario from the connected car domain, and they introduce a system model and an approach for context-based personalization of mobile services.

The full research paper with the title 'Information governance requirements for architectural solutions supporting dynamic business networking' by authors Mohammad R. Rasouli, Rik Eshuis, Jos J.M. Trienekens and Paul W.P.J. Grefen is a study of architectural solutions for emerging information governance requirements in dynamic business networks. While in the previous research several different architectural solutions have been developed, in this paper the authors investigate the extent to which the emerging information governance requirements in dynamic business networks are covered by the developed architectural solutions. The main findings indicate that some further developments are needed to enhance information governance requirements, particularly in emerging customer centric business networking scenarios.

We sincerely thank the Program Committee Members of the ISC 2015 workshop for their time and support throughout the reviewing period.

Roman Vaculin
Alex Norta
Rik Eshuis
ISC 2015 Workshop Chairs

Introduction to the Proceedings of the First International Workshop on Dependability Issues in Services Computing (DISCO) 2015

Rahul Ghosh[1], Javier Alonso Lopez[2], and Jogesh K. Muppala[3]

[1] Xerox Research Center India, Bengaluru, India
rahul.ghosh@xerox.com
[2] University of Leon, Leon, Spain
javier.alonso@unileon.es
[3] Hong Kong University of Science and Technology, Hong Kong
muppala@cse.ust.hk

1 Introduction

The First International Workshop on Dependability Issues in Services Computing (DISCO) was held on November 16, 2015, in conjunction with ICSOC 2015 conference in Goa, India. As the name suggests, the workshop was organized to create awareness and share research ideas about dependability issues within the service oriented computing research community. While service-oriented computing is becoming mature and new generation of services are spawning everyday, the need for dependability is becoming even more critical. Recent paradigms of mobile computing, cloud services and Internet of Things offer ubiquitous and large-scale computing services as a utility. The concomitant complexity of these new service-oriented computing environments makes them prone to unexpected failure. Mitigating the effects of such failures via proactive and reactive approaches falls under the purview of dependability. In general, dependability is an umbrella concept that encompasses attributes such as reliability, availability, performability, survivability, safety, integrity, and maintainability. Security related concepts such as confidentiality, availability and integrity can also be brought under the dependability framework. DISCO 2015 workshop was planned keeping in mind the researchers and practitioners whose expertise fall in the intersection of service oriented computing and dependability computing. However, the participation of the audience and their enthusiastic interactions during the day of the workshop proved that the appeal of the workshop reached out to broader services community. Presence of academic faculty members, industry researchers and PhD students from India, Europe and the US made the workshop event truly global. Four full papers were selected after a thorough peer-review by the workshop program committee members. We sincerely thank the program committee members of the DISCO 2015 workshop for their time and support throughout the reviewing period. We also thank all the authors for their contributions and summarize the papers here.

The paper titled 'On Composition of Checkpoint and Recovery Protocols for Distributed Systems' authored by Soumi Chattopadhyay, Ansuman Banerjee and Himadri Sekhar Pal focuses on checkpoint based rollback recovery protocols that are used to increase fault tolerance of critical distributed applications. The authors model the composition of protocol and check whether such composition is consistent with recovery. The specific protocols that are used for such protocols are: (1) coordinated checkpointing and recovery, (2) receiver-based pessimistic message log-based recovery, and (3) quasi-synchronous checkpointing protocol. The authors prove that that after rollback, the states of the processes are consistent with respect to each other.

The paper titled 'Safe Configurations of Replica Voting Processes in Fault-resilient Data Collection Services' authored by Kaliappa Ravidran and Arun Adiththan addresses the challenge of enforcing safe configurations of a replica voting system, when environmental factors change dynamically. Although the authors limit the scope of their paper for data collection by sensor devices, approaches proposed in the paper can be applied to broad variety of distributed settings. The authors present an analytical model to describe the performance of voting systems in presence of voter failures to deliver the data. Numerical results from model evaluation quantify the influence of the device redundancy on the Quality of Service achieved.

The paper titled 'A Proactive Solution to Manage Web Service Unavailability in Service Oriented Software Systems' authored by Navinderjit Kaur Kahlon, Salil Vishnu Kapur, Kuljit Kaur Chahal, Sukhleen Bindra Narang presents a framework to manage the availability of web services. Key components of the proposed framework are workflow manager, service manager, service listener and service repair module. Experimental results are show to demonstrate how the adaptation process of proactive framework get triggered when a web service becomes unavailable at the service provider side.

The paper titled 'A Reusable Architecture for Dependability and Performance Benchmarking of Cloud Services' authored by Amit Sangroya and Sara Bouchenak propose a generic software architecture for dependability and performance benchmarking for cloud computing services. While there are existing approaches to evaluate the performance and reliability of Cloud services, a benchmark essential standardizes the process of such evaluation. The authors present different phases for such benchmarking and evaluate the performance of the proposed tool for several use cases. The proposed tool can also be used during the design phase of the Cloud services to quantify the dependability and performance of a given architecture.

Rahul Ghosh
Javier Alonso Lopez
Jogesh K. Muppala
DISCO 2015 Workshop Chairs

Contents

Engineering Service-Oriented Applications

From Choreography Diagrams to RESTful Interactions

Adriatik Nikaj[1][(✉)], Sankalita Mandal[1], Cesare Pautasso[2], and Mathias Weske[1]

[1] Hasso Plattner Institute at the University of Potsdam, Potsdam, Germany
{adriatik.nikaj,sankalita.mandal,mathias.weske}@hpi.de
[2] Faculty of Informatics, University of Lugano (USI), Lugano, Switzerland
cesare.pautasso@usi.ch

Abstract. Today, business process management is a key approach to organize work, and many companies represent their operations in business process models. Recently, choreography diagrams have been introduced to represent interactions between business processes, run by different partners. While there is considerable work on using process models during process implementation, there is little work on using choreography models to implement interactions between business processes. In this paper, a novel approach to enhance choreography diagrams by execution information is introduced. The approach is based on the REST architecture style, which is the primary way for interacting systems. Using enhanced choreography diagrams allows us to develop REST-based interactions among business partners in an efficient manner. The approach is illustrated by an example of an accommodation reservation service.

1 Introduction

As the number and the complexity of interactions between multiple business partners grow, it becomes important to describe them using precise models which can be refined to a level of detail suitable for their implementation. As more and more services adopt the representational state transfer (REST) architectural style [1] to expose their internal business processes on the Web [2], we identify the opportunity to define and represent interactions among business processes at a suitable level of abstraction with choreography diagrams, specified in the Business Process Model and Notation (BPMN) standard [3].

In this paper we introduce a novel approach to enrich BPMN choreography diagrams with annotations that facilitate capturing information required for an efficient implementation of REST-based information exchanges between two or more interacting business partners. The approach is motivated by an example of a multi-party conversation [4] inspired by Airbnb, a popular accommodation reservation service, which acts as a broker between many partners that are concurrently enacting business processes for offering, selecting and booking suitable accommodations.

The paper is organized as follows. The basics of BPMN choreography diagrams are introduced in Sect. 2, where also a motivating example is discussed.

A. Norta et al. (Eds.): ICSOC 2015 Workshops, LNCS 9586, pp. 3–14, 2016.
DOI: 10.1007/978-3-662-50539-7_1

Section 3 introduces the role of the REST architectural style during business process enactment. RESTful choreography diagrams are in the center of Sect. 4, providing the conceptual basis of the approach introduced. The approach is evaluated in Sect. 5 by applying the identified patterns to the multi-party interaction of the example. Section 6 explores related approaches; concluding remarks complete this paper.

2   Motivating Example

Choreography diagrams were first introduced in the standard BPMN 2.0 [3]. Going by the definition of a choreography, it does not focus on the internal activities of the participants, instead, it focuses on the interaction between the participants. Starting from a process model where each organization participating in the process is represented by separate pools, we can say that the choreography diagram corresponding to the process model will abstract all the work done by the individual pools and only portray the message exchanges between the pools.

The main building block of choreography diagram is a choreography task. A choreography task consists of three bands representing the two participants and the choreography task name. The participant who initiates the message exchange is named as initiator and is highlighted white whereas the other participant who receives the message and optionally sends a response is called the receiver and is highlighted in grey.

The messages sent by the initiator and/or the receiver can be shown explicitly using a message icon associated with the respective sender. The message icon must be unfilled if it is the initiating message of the choreography task. On the other hand, a message icon depicting the response must be highlighted in grey. Several choreography tasks can be modelled using a sub-choreography with more than two participant bands and a 'plus' sign indicating the abstraction.

An example is used both to illustrate choreography diagrams and to motivate our approach. Figure 1 presents a choreography diagram for the accommodation booking process of a fictional company ARS (Accommodation Reservation Service). There are four participants: 1. ARS (the main platform of communication), 2. Guest (who wants to rent an apartment), 3. Host (the owner of an apartment) and 4. Payment Organization (who handles the payment on behalf of ARS).

The conversation starts when the Guest makes a reservation request, represented by the first choreography task in Fig. 1. ARS checks whether the selected offer is still available at this point or not. The latter may happen if, while creating the reservation request, the apartment gets booked by another Guest, or the Host changes his plans. If the offer is not available any more, then ARS sends the Guest a message saying 'Not Possible' and the reservation request fails.

Otherwise, ARS notifies the Host about the request and waits for 24 h for a response. At this point, the Guest also receives an email that the Host has been notified and the Guest can expect an answer within 24 h. The Host can either accept or decline the request within 24 h and the Guest can cancel the request

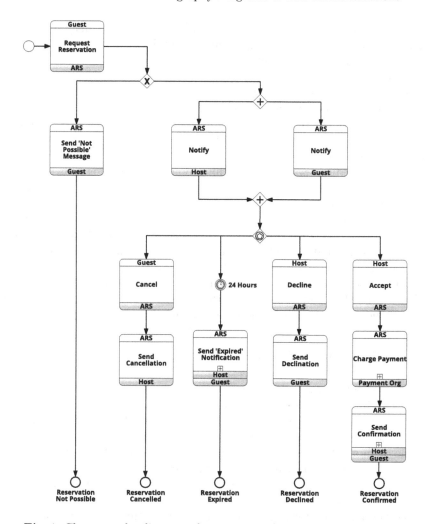

Fig. 1. Choreography diagram of an accommodation reservation service

before he gets a response from ARS. If none of these interactions happen within 24 h, the request automatically expires, and an expiration notification is sent to both Guest and Host.

In case of a cancellation by the Guest or a declination by the Host, the Host or the Guest is notified, respectively, and the choreography comes to an end. But when the Host accepts the request, the Payment Org comes into play. ARS requests the Payment Org to charge the Guest using the payment details entered at the time of creating the reservation request. After payment is completed, the reservation request is confirmed, and ARS sends this confirmation to both Guest and Host. In the example, the interactions between ARS and Payment Org are abstracted using the sub-choreography 'Charge Payment'.

As can be seen in the motivating example, a choreography diagram can have different gateways like exclusive gateways, event based gateways and parallel gateways. These gateways are introduced next.

The exclusive gateway is used in a choreography where based on a decision one of several alternatives can be chosen. Selecting one path deactivates the other options. In the example, when a Guest sends a reservation request to ARS, ARS checks the status of the Host's calendar and then one of two paths is chosen, i.e., either the Guest receives a 'Not Possible' message or the partners are notified about the reservation request.

An event based gateway is a branching point in a choreography where the alternatives are not chosen based on the data, rather, one of the alternatives is followed based on an event occurrence at that point. For example, after ARS sends the notification about the reservation request to the Host, it waits for any of the four events to occur: either the Host accepts the request or declines it within 24 h, the request expires after 24 h, or the Guest cancels the request. The event that occurs first determines the path to be followed.

Parallel gateways are used to represent independent paths that can be executed concurrently. In our example, if the reservation request is possible, then ARS sends notification to both the Host and the Guest concurrently.

3   RESTful Business Processes

The REST architectural style has gained widespread acceptance as the foundation for building Web-based applications and so-called RESTful Web services or RESTful Web APIs. These make full usage of the HTTP protocol not only to exchange messages between the participants (usually one client interacting with one or more Web service following a business process) but also to express properties (e.g., the addressing and identification of the Web resources involved in the interaction) and constraints (e.g., the idempotent request to perform a state transition) of the interactions. The result is a highly decentralized system, whose components are designed to be scalable under the assumption of stateless interactions and mostly read-only operations.

Web resources are uniquely and globally identified through URLs accessed via their Uniform Interface. In case of the HTTP protocol, this corresponds to a limited set of verbs (like GET, POST, PUT, DELETE) that define the effect of the basic interactions on the state of the resource. For example, POST will create a new resource whose identifier is determined by the server, while PUT will update (or create) a resource whose state and identifier are provided by the client. GET will retrieve the current state of the resource, while DELETE will remove it.

Business process models, seen as a collection of individual activities, can be used both to represent the orchestration of one or more Web resource as well as to indicate how the internal state of a resource may evolve. For example, a process may define the behavior of a client which looks for a suitable accommodation by navigating (GET) across multiple offerings, once an accommodation has been found a client submits a reservation request (POST) and waits until either the request has been accepted by the host (PUT) or keeps looking for another accommodation.

Due to their client/server constraint, REST and HTTP do not play well with server-sent notifications of state changes, which typically rely on a publish/subscribe messaging system. Whereas it is possible to reverse the roles of the interaction and have the server call back the client (assuming the client also publishes a RESTful API for incoming notifications) or have the client poll the server by means of a feed subscription.

Concerning typical Web platforms such as ARS, this problem is solved by email-based notifications, whereby authenticated clients are associated with an email address, which is used to send event notifications triggered by state changes of the reservation system, or, more precisely, on the reservation resource. What is important is that the email does not only include information about the new state of the reservation resource, but also embeds hyperlinks so that the recipient may follow them to perform further interactions.

In general, when multiple clients are involved in an interaction with a resource shared between them, it becomes important to reason about their interactions not only from the perspective of individual participants, but also from the global perspective. Hence, we aim at creating RESTful choreography diagrams to reason about all possible valid interactions that lead to a given successful or unsuccessful outcome. These will help us model what interaction each participant may perform depending on the state of the shared resource, which may of course change and evolve as a consequence of the participants interactions.

4 Implementation of Choreographies

RESTful choreography diagrams are an enhancement of BPMN choreography diagram with REST-specific annotations. This section introduces the building elements of RESTful choreography diagrams and their uses, before causality relationship patterns are introduced.

4.1 REST Annotations

Since choreography tasks are the basic units for modeling interactions in a choreography, we use them for modeling the basic RESTful HTTP request/response interaction and email messaging. To properly annotate the choreography task with REST information, we use annotated messages associated to choreography tasks. This is realized by specializing the exchanged messages into HTTP request, HTTP response or email messages (see Fig. 2).

Using annotated messages for expressing REST specific information avoids the introduction of new modeling elements, and hence, avoids changing the meta-model of BPMN choreography diagrams.

Due to the fact that one of the architectural constraints of REST is the client/server communication, we identified two possible usages of the choreography task, which depend on the presence of a recipient's RESTful API.

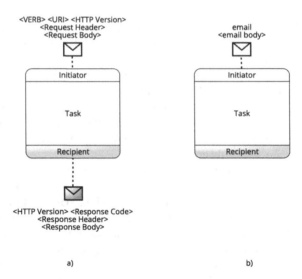

Fig. 2. Enriching choreography tasks by annotations

If the recipient provides a RESTful API then the client plays the role of the initiator, while the server plays the role of the recipient. The initiating message is a HTTP request and the return message is a HTTP response, as shown in Fig. 2(a).

As discussed earlier, the recipient may not always provide a RESTful API (e.g., the Guest and the Host in the example). The problem of notifying a client can be solved via an email-based approach. In this case, the server plays the role of the initiator, whereas the client plays the role of the recipient.

As initiating message, we use an email message, illustrated in Fig. 2(b), which contains further links for the client to follow in the upcoming choreography tasks. In this case, there is no need to model a return message.

The information in the HTTP requests/responses or email messages does not need to be of the same level of detail as that of the implementation, which might include, for instance, text fragments.

However, it is essential to include links which eventually determine the behavior of the entire interaction modeled in a choreography diagram. In the ARS scenario, for example, it is essential to include links in an email message to the Host that allows him to accept or decline the reservation request by following those links.

Sequence flow, per se, does not need any additional enhancement. However, we can make use of conditions, which can be added to conditional sequence flows. In the RESTful choreography diagram, the link can constitute a condition. It perfectly fulfills the requirement of the choreography diagram, which states that the condition should have been previously sent via a message (as links are). Conditional flows can be placed directly after choreography tasks as well as exclusive or inclusive gateways.

4.2   Causality Relationship Patterns

We observed several patterns that reoccur in choreography diagrams concerning the relation between the content of the messages exchanged and the ordering of choreography tasks. In REST-based interactions, links sent between participants pave the way for upcoming interactions. More specifically, the number of links contained in a choreography task impacts the type of the consecutive nodes in a choreography diagram.

In REST-based interaction scenarios, links are the most prominent artifacts, because links allow interaction partners to access and modify shared resources. The patterns introduced below categorize interactions based on the number of links transmitted. These categories provide useful information for checking if a RESTful choreography diagram is feasible.

- **no-link pattern** In case of the no-link pattern, the choreography task incorporates a HTTP response message or an email message without any link. This can be a simple notification, e.g., the information about a resource being deleted. This choreography task is usually followed by an end event or by another choreography task, which does not have the same participants as the former interaction. In any case, the missing link hints to a lack of future conversation between the participants.
- **single-link pattern** In the single-link pattern, the choreography task incorporates a HTTP response message or an email message with a single link. This kind of message, generally, is a notification, which can link to additional information than what is included in the HTTP response body or the email body itself. Typical examples are a HTTP response linking to an updated resource and an email linking to the status of a recently changed resource.
- **multi-link pattern** In case of the multi-link pattern, the choreography task incorporates a HTTP response message or an email message with n ($n > 1$) links. This task can be followed by an exclusive gateway or an event-based gateway. In case of an exclusive gateway, the outgoing sequence flows of the gateway are conditional sequence flows, each of which refers to a link contained in the preceding choreography task. The following choreography task involve the client as initiator, making a request to the resource identified by the link corresponding to the chosen branch.

The validity of the patterns is illustrated as follows. If there is no link transmitted from the participant that provides a RESTful API, then applying the no-link pattern ensures that the other participants make no further interaction with the resource. A typical example of the no-link pattern in an online shopping scenario is a message that informs the customer of a late delivery.

If there is a single link transmitted among interaction partners, the receiver has a handle for further interactions. In an online shopping example, the customer receives an email message with a link to his open orders. Using this link, the customer can use GET messages to retrieve the current status of his orders.

If there is a gateway in a choreography diagram, the outcome of which leads to different resource states, then applying the multi-link pattern will make sure that the links are transmitted beforehand. The customer might decide to cancel the order or update the delivery address, using several links that have been transmitted to him by the online shop.

5   Evaluation

To evaluate the effectiveness of the approach, we enhance the ARS choreography model with REST annotations and proceed one step further to the implementation level.

5.1   RESTful Choreography Diagram

In Sect. 4, patterns of RESTful interactions have been identified. We return to the motivating example described in Sect. 2 and apply the approach to the example; the resulting RESTful choreography diagram is shown in Fig. 3.

The approach is based on identifying the interaction types of choreography tasks, mentioned in Sect. 4. The first interaction type consists of an initiating message (HTTP request) and a return message (HTTP response), represented by the first choreography task in the diagram. The Guest makes a POST request and gets back the status '201 Created' along with a link (*/reservation/id/details*) for further correspondence.

The second type of interaction is an email-based notification sent from server side to the client. We can see this type of interaction when ARS notifies the Host about the reservation request. The Host receives an email with several links from ARS and sends no specific response at this point.

Regarding the causality relationship patterns introduced above, three scenarios can be encountered. If there is no link transmitted in the choreography task, then no further interaction between the participant and the resource is expected. This pattern can be seen in the example where the task 'Send Cancellation', which is implemented by an email based interaction without passing any link, leads to an end event (Reservation Cancelled).

The second pattern describes the choreography task containing a single link, which the participant can use to get further details about the resource. This pattern can be witnessed in several places. For example, when ARS notifies the Host about the reservation request, at the same time the Guest also receives an email with a single link */reservation/id/notified* allowing the Guest to get more details about the reservation at any time.

In general, whenever there is an update to a resource, using the single-link pattern, a link with the details is transmitted from ARS to other participants. This transmission is done either as an HTTP response (e.g., 'Accept') or as an email message (e.g., 'Send Confirmation', 'Send Declination').

The third pattern describes a scenario where a choreography task incorporating more than one link is followed by a gateway. This pattern is found when ARS sends a notification email to the Host containing three links. The task is followed by an event-based gateway. The Host can use the */reservation/id/details* link for

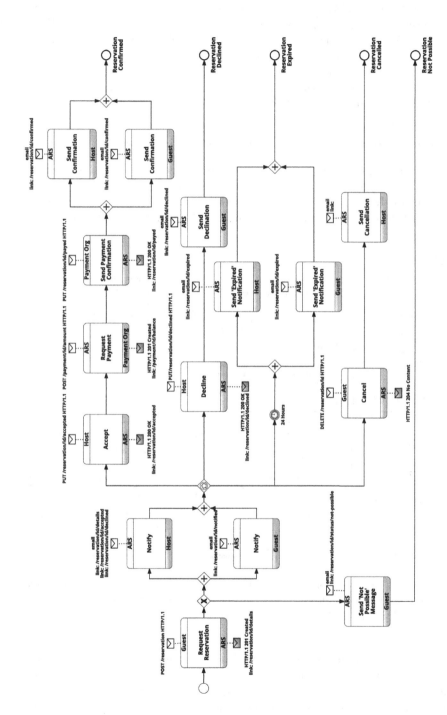

Fig. 3. RESTful choreography diagram for the motivating example

getting the detailed information about the reservation request. The other two links give the Host the options to accept or decline. This is represented in Fig. 3 by the tasks 'Accept' and 'Decline'. At this point, the choreography has two other possibilities: the reservation request can expire after 24 h or the Guest cancels the request. These interactions can be represented by an event-based gateway. In general, the multi-link pattern is used whenever there is an upcoming decision, represented by a branching structure in the choreography diagram.

5.2   From Model Level Towards Implementation Level

The goal of the approach is to mitigate the gap between model level and implementation level. So far, we have enriched models with annotations that provide information for the implementation level. In this section, we come up with a series of messages that can be generated from the RESTful choreography diagram.

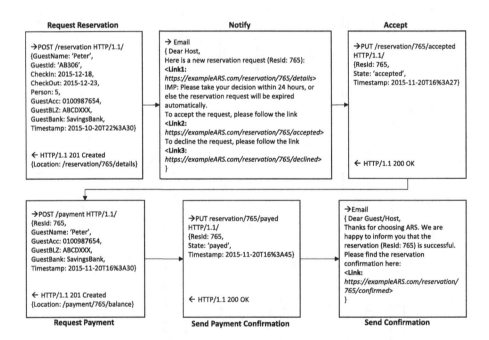

Fig. 4. Messages and their ordering resulting from an interaction between multiple participants, from the sending of a reservation request by a Guest to the message implementing the respective confirmation by ARS.

Figure 4 shows the messages generated from the interactions between ARS and the other three participants for one instance where the reservation is successful. The series of messages identifies with the REST and email interactions starting from the creation of reservation request by the Guest until the reservation is confirmed. Each interaction is represented by a single rectangle containing the generic message template for each REST operation and the corresponding responses. The rectangles are named with the same labels used as choreography tasks in the RESTful choreography model.

The reservation request contains details about the inquired reservation as well as the payment details of the Guest. The reservation details are then stored in the location */reservation/765/details* where 765 is the unique reservation id. The link https://exampleARS.com/reservation/765/details[1] is passed to the Host along with two other links for accepting or declining the request, all included in an email sent by ARS, taking advantage of the multi-link pattern.

In this case, the Host decides to accept the Guest by clicking on the link https://exampleARS.com/reservation/765/accepted. After getting the acceptance from the Host, ARS creates a payment request using the POST operation with the parameters containing the same payment details entered by the Guest at the time of creating reservation request. Finally after a successful payment, an email is sent to both the Guest and the Host with the link https://exampleARS. com/reservation/765/confirmed, using the single link pattern.

In standard BPMN or choreography models, this information cannot be represented. With our approach, it is possible to define this information and to integrate it in the model. Moreover, including implementation information in the model not only helps to come up with the messages for each instance, but also gives a detailed overview of all possible instances.

6   Related Work

Different approaches exist for bridging the gap between the choreographies and their implementation. One notable approach is that of Decker et al. [5], in which the authors extend the BPEL web service composition standard [6] for modeling choreographies. The result is BPEL4Chor, an extended language capable of orchestrating choreographies. That paper uses a bottom-up approach that integrates pre-exisiting BPEL service orchestrations, based on web services standards like SOAP and WSDL [7]. In contrast, the approach presented in this paper uses a top-down approach, starting at the choreography level. In addition, our technological basis is REST as opposed to standard web services techniques, and we incorporate email messaging, which is not addressed in the BPEL4Chor approach.

Another approach, which enhances a modeling language for bridging the gap between modeling and implementation is BPMN for REST [8]. The author introduces an enrichment of BPMN for modeling RESTful business processes. The paper's focus is on the representation of business processes that interact with external resources or where elements of the business processes are published as resources. Conversely, our approach abstracts from business processes or their composing elements and focuses only on the interaction aspect of business processes. Nevertheless, these two approaches are complementary, and thus, can be both used for modeling the same scenario from the two respective perspectives. The mapping between the two representations is left as a future work.

---

[1] exampleARS.com is a fictional website.

7   Conclusions

This paper introduced a novel approach for enriching BPMN choreography diagrams with REST-specific annotations, aiming at easing the transition from choreography models to the implementation of RESTful HTTP conversations. RESTful choreography diagrams still comply with the formal specification of BPMN standard, since only annotations are used to capture the additional information. This approach makes it feasible to use existing modeling tools and the standardized output serialization, which is also defined in the BPMN standard.

This paper provides the conceptual basis of the approach and uses an example that is inspired by a well-known accommodation reservation service. The patterns identified can also be found in other scenarios, including online shopping and e-commerce scenarios [9], where the integration of HTTP request-response interactions and email communication plays an important role.

Future work will include an investigation on methodological aspect of the approach, in particular which stakeholders are involved, to further ease the transition from choreography models to executable REST based implementation.

References

1. Fielding, R.T.: Architectural Styles and the Design of Network-based Software Architectures. Ph.D. thesis AAI9980887(2000)
2. Pautasso, C., Wilde, E.: Push-enabling RESTful business processes. In: Kappel, G., Maamar, Z., Motahari-Nezhad, H.R. (eds.) Service Oriented Computing. LNCS, vol. 7084, pp. 32–46. Springer, Heidelberg (2011)
3. OMG: Business Process Model and Notation (BPMN), Version 2.0, January 2011. http://www.omg.org/spec/BPMN/2.0/
4. Hohpe, G.: Let's have a conversation. IEEE Internet Comput. **11**(3), 78–81 (2007)
5. Decker, G., Kopp, O., Leymann, F., Weske, M.: Bpel4chor: extending bpel for modeling choreographies. In: IEEE International Conference on Web Services, ICWS 2007, pp. 296–303. IEEE (2007)
6. Jordan, D., Evdemon, J., Alves, A., Arkin, A., Askary, S., Barreto, C., Bloch, B., Curbera, F., Ford, M., Goland, Y., et al.: Web services business process execution language version 2.0. OASIS standard 11, 10 (2007)
7. Alonso, G., Casati, F., Kuno, H., Machiraju, V.: Web Services. Springer, New York (2004)
8. Pautasso, C.: BPMN for REST. In: Dijkman, R., Hofstetter, J., Koehler, J. (eds.) BPMN 2011. LNBIP, vol. 95, pp. 74–87. Springer, Heidelberg (2011)
9. Benatallah, B., Casati, F., et al.: Web service conversation modeling: A cornerstone for e-business automation. IEEE Internet Comput. **8**(1), 46–54 (2004)

Estimating the Complexity of Software Services Using an Entropy Based Metric

George Feuerlicht[1,2,3(✉)] and David Hartman[1]

[1] Unicorn College, V Kapslovně 2767/2, 130 00 Prague 3, Czech Republic
george.feuerlicht@gmail.com,
david.hartman@unicorncollege.cz
[2] Prague University of Economics,
W. Churchill Square. 4, 130 67 Prague 3, Czech Republic
[3] University of Technology, Sydney,
Broadway, P.O. Box 123, Ultimo, NSW 2007, Australia

Abstract. Poor design of software services results in unnecessarily complex and inflexible SOA applications that are difficult to maintain and evolve. There is also some evidence that the quality of service-oriented applications degrades and as complexity increases with new service versions that include modifications to rectify problems and improve functionality. Design quality metrics play an important role in identifying software quality issues early in the software development lifecycle. The concept of software entropy has been used in literature to express decline in the quality, maintainability and understandability of software through its lifecycle. In this paper we propose a Service Entropy Metric (SEM) that estimates the complexity of service design based on the complexity of the XML message structures that form the basis for service interfaces. We illustrate the application of the SEM metric using the Open Travel Alliance specification and show that the complexity of the specification as measured by SEM increases over time as new versions of the specification are released.

Keywords: Service design metrics · Service complexity · Software entropy

1 Introduction

Increasing size and complexity of SOA (Service Oriented Architecture) applications presents a challenge to the developers of software services. Large-scale SOA projects typically involve thousands of software services (SOAP and REST [1] services), making the maintenance and evolution of applications implemented using these services highly challenging. It is widely accepted that excessive complexity leads to reduced quality of software and consequently to an increase in the maintenance effort. Predicting the quality of software during the design stage of the SDLC (Software Development Life Cycle), i.e. before the software is implemented, allows early rectification of design defects and can lead to a significant reduction of maintenance costs [2]. Early detection of service design issues requires reliable metrics that access software quality. Software quality can be measured by assessing structural properties of software (i.e. size, complexity, cohesion, coupling, etc.), and various design metrics for

© Springer-Verlag Berlin Heidelberg 2016
A. Norta et al. (Eds.): ICSOC 2015 Workshops, LNCS 9586, pp. 15–23, 2016.
DOI: 10.1007/978-3-662-50539-7_2

object-oriented and component-based software development have been proposed and experimentally verified. [3–5]. Such metrics mostly rely on estimating cohesion and coupling, as maximizing cohesion and minimizing coupling reduces interdependencies between software components allowing individual components to be maintained independently without causing undesirable side effects [6, 7]. However, most of the proposed metrics were originally designed for fine-grained object-oriented software components and are of limited applicability for assessing the quality of coarse-grained, document-centric services that are used extensively in SOA applications. In order to develop a more suitable metric for estimating the quality of software services we focus on analysing the underlying XML message schemas that constitute the basis for service interfaces and directly impact on the quality of SOA applications. In our previous work we have proposed metrics that evaluate interdependencies among a set of XML message schemas by estimating the level of data coupling. Unlike most of the existing service metrics that were derived from metrics for object-oriented software, the DCI (Data Coupling Index) [8] and MDCI (Message Data Coupling Index) [9] analyse the underlying XML data structures to estimate the level coupling and to predict the impact of schema changes on existing SOA applications.

In this paper we focus on estimating the complexity of software services, as a measure of the effort required to develop and maintain software. The concept of *entropy* has been used to measure software complexity for over two decades [10], and more recently it was applied to estimating the complexity of XML schemas [11]. The proposed Software Entropy Metric (SEM) estimates the complexity of a software service based on the complexity of the XML message structures that form the service interface. In the following section (Sect. 2) we review related work that addresses the problem of measuring software quality and complexity. We then describe our approach to estimating the complexity of services and the XSD Analyzer tool that we have developed to compute the SEM complexity metric (Sect. 3). In Sect. 4 we present experimental results obtained by analysing the Open Travel Alliance schemas, and in Sect. 5 we presents our conclusions and outline directions for further work.

2   Related Work

Predicting maintainability of SOA applications using variants of existing metrics has been the subject of recent research interest [2, 12, 13]. Both coupling and cohesions have been used in traditional software design as indicators of software quality [14, 15, 16, 17, 18]. For example Chidamber et al. proposed the Lack of Cohesion in Methods (LCOM) metric for object-oriented software based on evaluating the similarity of methods. This original work has been used as the basis for developing metrics for software services [19, 13, 12]. While there are similarities between object-oriented software and software services, there are also significant differences and that make it difficult to apply similar metrics to both approaches. The underlying assumption for such metrics is that each service has a number of operations and that the interfaces of these operations are formed by input and output messages [12]. However, most SOA applications use coarse-grained (document-centric) services that implement the request/response message exchange pattern and do not involve service operations, making such metrics difficult to apply. Another significant difference is that services are often based on pre-existing XML message schemas developed by various consortia and standards organizations. For example, the travel domain web services are based on the OTA (Open Travel Alliance) specification [20] that defines the structure of messages for travel applications. As the message schemas constitute the basis for service interfaces, it follows that the quality of service design is closely related to the quality of design of the underlying XML schemas. There is evidence that such schemas frequently contain overlaps and inconsistencies and suffer from excessive complexity [21, 22]. Standard XML specifications (e.g. OTA [23], UBL [24], etc.) typically contain hundreds of XML message schemas and thousands of schema elements. As these specifications evolve over time incorporating new requirements, their complexity increases even further. Design of such XML schemas typically follows document engineering [25–27] or a similar methodology that produces XML documents by aggregating data elements based on pre-defined simple and complex types [28]. For example, OTA message level schemas are constructed by aggregation of simple (OpenTravel Simple Types) and complex (OpenTravel Common Types, and Industry Common Types) schema elements [23]. This design approach results in overlapping message schemas and high levels of data coupling reducing the maintainability of services implemented using these specifications [4, 29].

Ensuring XML schema design quality in the context of SOA applications presents a particularly difficult problem as the schemas are often developed in the absence of a domain data model [30]. Current work in this area includes research that focuses on identifying dependencies among schema elements and developing tools for automating the propagation of these changes to all dependent schema components. Necasky, et al. proposed a five-level XML evolution architecture with the top level Platform-Independent Model (PIM) that represents the data requirements for a particular domain of interest. PIM model is mapped into a Platform-Specific Model (PSM) that describes how parts of the PIM schema are represented in XML. PSM then maps into Schema, Operational and Extensional level models. Atomic operations (create, update, and remove) for editing schemas are defined on classes, attributes, and associations, and a mechanism for propagating these operations from PIM to PSM schema is proposed. Composite operations are constructed from atomic operations to implement complex schema changes [21, 31, 32].

Evaluation of the quality of design of XML schemas is another research direction that has attracted recent attention [2, 30, 33]. Numerous XML schema quality metrics have been proposed primarily with the objective to measure various aspects of schema complexity. McDowell et al. proposed eleven metrics and two composite indexes to measure the quality and complexity of XML schemas. These metrics are based on counts of complex type declarations, derived complex types, number of global type declarations, number of simple types, and element fanning (*fan-out* – number of child elements that an element has, and *fan-in* – number of times that an element is referenced) [30]. The authors formulate a *Quality Index* and a *Complexity Index* that estimate the quality and complexity of XML schemas based on weighted values of the metrics. A metric analysis tool is provided for developers to verify the validity of the metrics in the context of specific projects.

The concept of entropy [34] has been adapted for the measurement of complexity of software, and was initially applied to procedural software [35], and later to object-oriented design [36, 37]. Ruellan [38] used an entropy measure to assess the amount of information contained in XML documents (information density) with the objective to reduce the size of XML documents and to improve processing speed of XML messaging applications. Thaw et al. [39] proposed entropy-based metrics to measure reusability, extensibility, understandability of XML schema documents. Basci et al. [2] proposed and validated XML schema complexity metric that evaluates the internal structure of XML documents taking into account various sources of complexity that include recursion and complexity arising from importing external schema elements. The authors used the concept of Schema Entropy (SE) to assess XML schema complexity. SE is evaluated based on the complexity of schema elements as measured by fan-in and fan-out, and the number of simple elements that constitute individual schema elements. The SE metric was empirically validated using publicly available XML schemas, and the authors concluded that the metric provides a useful feedback when comparing schemas with equal number of elements [11]. In [40] Tang et al. apply an entropy-based measure to assessing the structural uniformity (*structuredness*) of XML documents. Two metrics are defined: Path-Based Entropy and Subtree-Based Entropy metrics that attempt to measure the level of diversity of a set of XML documents. Unlike Basci et al. [2, 11], the authors base the entropy calculation on XML documents, rather than XML schemas. Pichler et al. [22] developed a set of metrics to analyse the complexity of business documents with the objective of estimating the effort involved in data element mapping between different business document standards.

In summary, different XML schema features, including the number of schema elements, number of complex types, fan-in and fan-out have been used to measures schema complexity. Our approach (described in the next section) is an adaption of the Class Definition Entropy (CDE) metric for object-oriented design developed by Bansiya et al. [36] that measures schema complexity by estimating entropy based on complex schema elements.

3   Service Entropy Metric (SEM)

In this section we describe our approach to estimating the complexity of services using an entropy-based metric. Software services typically use the request/response message exchange pattern and have an interface that can be described by:

S(M_RQ, M_RS)

where **S** is a service and **M_RQ** and **M_RS** are the request and response messages, respectively. For example, the OTA flight booking service has the following interface:

AirBook(OTA_AirBookRQ, OTA_AirBookRS)

where OTA_AirBookRQ and OTA_AirBookRS are the request and response messages, respectively.

We estimate the complexity of the service **S** as the sum of the entropies of the request and response messages, based on the Message Schema Entropy (MSE) [41]. In our formulation of the MSE metric we adapt the approach of Bansiya et al. [36] who developed the Class Definition Entropy (CDE) metric for object-oriented design.

The CDE metric evaluates the frequency of occurrence of name strings for a given class; our MSE metric computes the frequency of occurrence of complex schema elements in a given XML message schema (e.g. the OTA_AirAvailRQ schema). MSE entropy is computed as:

$$\text{MSE} = -\sum_{j=1}^{N} (P_i \log_2 P_i)$$

where:

N = total number of unique complex elements in the message schema
n_i = number of occurrences of the ith complex element in the message schema
M = total number of (non-unique) complex elements in the message schema
P_i = n_i/M

MSE calculation is based on counting complex schema elements (i.e. elements based on complex types) and represents an approximation, as the complexity of individual element substructures is not taken into account. OTA differentiates between *complex types* that contain multiple data elements, and *simple types* that contain a single data element. In addition to globally defined schema elements (common data types), individual message schemas include locally defined elements. For example, the OTA_AirAvailRQ message that is used to implement the (web) service for flight availability inquiry includes 428 elements with multiple levels of nesting. OTA defines common data types (OTA_AirCommonTypes) for the airline messages that form a global type repository of XML Schema components used in the construction OTA Air messages. While the level of nesting and the number of simple elements that constitute the messages contribute to complexity of the services, their inclusion into the metric calculation involves assigning arbitrary weights and can make the interpretation of the metric more difficult.

As entropy values are additive, we can calculate SEM as the sum of the entropies of request and response messages:

$$\text{SEM}(S) = \text{MSE}(M\_RQ) + \text{MSE}(M\_RS)$$

We have developed a prototype XSD Analyzer tool that calculates the values of the MSE and SEM metrics. XSD Analyzer allows the selection of message schemas and produces an output that includes the total number of non-unique schema elements (M), the number of unique (distinct) schema elements (N), counts of occurrences of individual schema elements, and the values of MSE and SEM, for the selected service interface.

4   Experimental Results Using the OTA Air Message Schemas

In this section we use the SEM metric to estimate the complexity of services based on the OTA Air messages specification. OTA Air messages are a subset of the OTA specification for services that support various business functions related to airline travel, such as checking flight availability, flight booking, etc. For example, the Search and Availability of flights service is implemented using the Air_AvailabilityRQ/RS request/response message pair [42].

Table 1 shows SEM values for a subset of eight OTA Air services for the period of 2006 to 2014. It is evident that complexity of the services as measured by SEM increases as the specification evolves over time. The increase in SEM ranges from 11.2 % for the AirBook service to 24 % for the AirDemandTicket service over the nine-year period.

All services shown in Table 1 increase in complexity over time, indicating that as new elements are added to extend the functionality of the services, existing elements are retained to maintain compatibility with previous versions of the specification. Figures 1 and 2 show the values of SEM for the AirAvailability (AirAvail) and Air-Book (AirBook) services for the period of 2006 to 2014. Complexity of both services increases over time, in particular in the period around 2011 that most likely corresponds to a major revision of the specification.

Table 1. Values of SEM for OTA Air Services (versions 2006-2014)

OTA Air Service	2006	2007	2008	2009	2010	2011	2012	2013	2014
AirAvail	10.66	10.82	11.04	11.12	11.13	11.24	12.60	12.60	12.60
AirBook	13.62	13.84	14.13	14.30	14.59	14.54	15.26	15.19	15.14
AirCheckIn	12.45	12.49	12.74	13.01	13.06	13.06	14.24	14.15	14.10
AirDemandTicket	9.25	9.45	9.52	9.62	9.81	10.88	11.53	11.50	11.47
AirFareDisplay	11.33	11.33	11.54	11.54	11.57	11.57	12.94	12.94	12.94
AirLowFareSearch	11.95	12.15	12.57	12.57	12.57	12.53	14.59	14.59	14.59
AirPrice	11.60	11.83	12.45	12.63	12.63	12.63	13.42	13.42	13.42
AirSeatMap	10.05	10.05	10.05	10.05	10.14	10.43	11.35	11.35	11.35

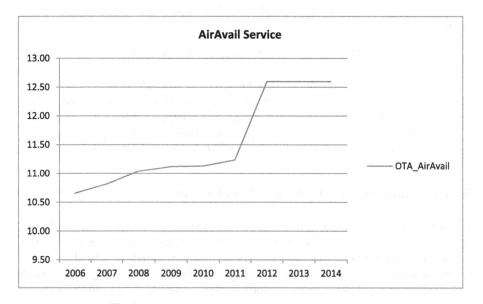

Fig. 1. Increase in complexity of the AirAvail service

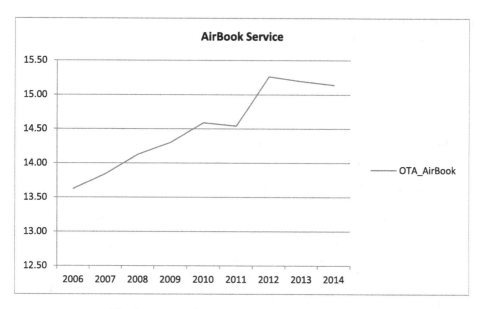

Fig. 2. Increase in complexity of the AirBook service

5 Conclusions and Further Work

The focus of this paper is the estimation of complexity of services based on the analysis of the underlying message schemas. Following a review of related literature in Sect. 2, we have defined an entropy-based service complexity metrics and used the XSD Analyzer tool to compute the values of SEM for eight OTA Air services over a period of nine years (2006–2014). The results indicate an almost monotonic increase in service complexity over the nine-year period, with the increase in SEM ranging from 11.2 % (for the AirBook service) to 24 % (for the AirDemandTicket service). While the exact significance of this increase is difficult to determine without further investigation, it can be argued that an increase in the complexity of the specification leads to a reduction in application development productivity. We note here that we use the OTA specification as an example of a domain specification designed using the document engineering approach, and that we do not imply any criticism of the quality of the OTA specification. Some researchers (in particular in the REST community) argue that large complex schemas are not problematic as long as they have a well-designed extension model and that the resulting coarse-grained services simplify the interaction dialog and have performance advantages in unreliable network environments. We argue that as the reliability of the Internet improves, the impact of excessive complexity on the maintainability of the services will outweigh such performance advantages.

The current version of the SEM metric is purely based on complex element counts and it does not take into account the internal complexity of individual elements (i.e. the sub-structure of complex elements). This makes it relatively easy to interpret the metric, but it also reduces the accuracy of the estimates of service complexity. We are currently working on improving the *sensitivity* of the SEM metric by incorporating a range of structural features (i.e. number of schema levels, number of simple elements, etc.) into the calculation of the metric.

References

1. Fielding, R.T.: Architectural Styles and the Design of Network-based Software Architectures (2000). http://www.ics.uci.edu/~fielding/pubs/dissertation/top.htm
2. Basci, D., Misra, S.: Measuring and evaluating a design complexity metric for XML schema documents. J. Inf. Sci. Eng. **25**(5), 1405–1425 (2009)
3. Bansiya, J., Davis, C.G.: A hierarchical model for object-oriented design quality assessment. IEEE Trans. Softw. Eng. **28**(1), 4–17 (2002)
4. Etzkorn, L.H., et al.: A comparison of cohesion metrics for object-oriented systems. Inf. Softw. Technol. **46**(10), 677–687 (2004)
5. Eder, J., Kappel, G., Schrefl, M.: Coupling and cohesion in object-oriented systems. Technical report, University of Klagenfurt, Austria (1994)
6. Papazoglou, M.P., Yang, J.: Design methodology for web services and business processes. In: Buchmann, A.P., Casati, F., Fiege, L., Hsu, M.-C., Shan, M.-C. (eds.) TES 2002. LNCS, vol. 2444, pp. 54–64. Springer, Heidelberg (2002)
7. Papazoglou, M.P., Heuvel, W.V.D.: Service-oriented design and development methodology. Int. J. Web Eng. Technol. **2**(4), 412–442 (2006)
8. Feuerlicht, G.: Simple metric for assessing quality of service design. In: Maximilien, E., Rossi, G., Yuan, S.-T., Ludwig, H., Fantinato, M. (eds.) ICSOC 2010. LNCS, vol. 6568, pp. 133–143. Springer, Heidelberg (2011)
9. Feuerlicht, G.: Evaluation of quality of design for document-centric software services. In: Ghose, A., Zhu, H., Yu, Q., Delis, A., Sheng, Q.Z., Perrin, O., Wang, J., Wang, Y. (eds.) ICSOC 2012. LNCS, vol. 7759, pp. 356–367. Springer, Heidelberg (2013)
10. Gonzalez, R.R.: A unified metric of software complexity: measuring productivity, quality, and value. J. Syst. Softw. **29**(1), 17–37 (1995)
11. Basci, D., Misra, S.: Entropy as a measure of quality of XML schema document. Int. Arab J. Inf. Technol. **8**(1), 75–83 (2011)
12. Sindhgatta, R., Sengupta, B., Ponnalagu, K.: Measuring the quality of service oriented design. In: Baresi, L., Chi, C.-H., Suzuki, J. (eds.) ICSOC-ServiceWave 2009. LNCS, vol. 5900, pp. 485–499. Springer, Heidelberg (2009)
13. Perepletchikov, M., Ryan, C., Frampton, K.: Cohesion metrics for predicting maintainability of service-oriented software. In: QSIC, pp. 328–335 (2007)
14. Vinoski, S.: Old measures for new services. IEEE Internet Comput. **9**(6), 72–74 (2005)
15. Pautasso, C., Zimmermann, O., Leymann, F.: Restful web services vs. big'web services: making the right architectural decision. In: 17th International Conference on World Wide Web. ACM, Beijing, China (2008)
16. Pautasso, C., Wilde, E.: Why is the web loosely coupled? A multi-faceted metric for service design. In: 18th International Conference on World Wide Web. ACM, Madrid, Spain (2009)
17. Stevens, W.P., Myers, G.J., Constantine, L.L.: Structured design. IBM Syst. J. **38**(2&3), 115–139 (1999)
18. Rumbaugh, J., Blaha, M., Premerlani, W., Eddy, F., Lorensen, W.: Object-Oriented Modeling and Design. Prentice Hall, New Jersey (1991)
19. Chidamber, S., Kemerer, C.: A metrics suite for object oriented design. IEEE Trans. Softw. Eng. **20**(6), 476–493 (2002)

20. OTA: OTA Specifications (2010). http://www.opentravel.org/Specifications/Default.aspx. Accessed 6 May 2010
21. Necaský, M.: Conceptual modeling for XML. Dissertations in Database and Information Systems Series. IOS Press/AKA Verlag (2009)
22. Pichler, C., Strommer, M., Huemer, C.: Size matters!? Measuring the complexity of xml schema mapping models. In: 2010 6th World Congress on Services (SERVICES-1). IEEE (2010)
23. OTA: Open Travel Aliance Specification (2014). http://www.opentravel.org/Specifications/Default.aspx. (cited 6 May 2014)
24. OASIS Universal Business Language (2014). https://www.oasis-open.org/committees/tc_home.php?wg_abbrev=ubl
25. Glushko, R., McGrath, T.: Document Engineering: Analyzing and Designing Documents for Business Informatics and Web Services. MIT Press Books, Cambridge (2008)
26. Glushko, R. McGrath, T.: Patterns and reuse in document engineering. In: XML 2002 Proceedings (2002)
27. Glushko, R.J. McGrath. T.: Document engineering for e-Business. In: Proceedings of the 2002 ACM Symposium on Document Engineering (DocEng 2002), McLean, Virginia, USA. ACM Press, New York (2002)
28. ebXML - Enabling A Global Electronic Market (2007). http://www.ebxml.org/. (cited 9 December 2007)
29. Feuerlicht, G., Lozina J.: Understanding service reusability. In: 15th International Conference on Systems Integration 2007. VSE Prague, Prague, Czech Republic (2007)
30. McDowell, A., Schmidt, C., Yue, K.B.: Analysis and metrics of XML schema (2004)
31. Necaský, M. Mlýnková, I.: A framework for efficient design, maintaining, and evolution of a system of XML applications. In: Proceedings of the Databases, Texts, Specifications, and Objects, DATESO 2010, pp. 38–49 (2010)
32. Necaský, M. Mlýnková, I.: Five-level multi-application schema evolution. In: Proceedings of the Databases, Texts, Specifications, and Objects, DATESO 2009, pp. 213–217 (2009)
33. Visser, J.: Structure metrics for XML Schema. In: Proceedings of XATA (2006)
34. Shannon, C.E.: A mathematical theory of communication. ACM SIGMOBILE Mobile Comput. Commun. Rev. 5(1), 3–55 (2001)
35. Mohanty, S.N.: Entropy metrics for software design evaluation. J. Syst. Softw. 2(1), 39–46 (1981)
36. Bansiya, J., Davis, C., Etzkorn, L.: An entropy-based complexity measure for object-oriented designs. Theory Pract. Object Syst. 5(2), 111–118 (1999)
37. Olague, H.M., Etzkorn, L.H., Cox, G.W.: An entropy-based approach to assessing object-oriented software maintainability and degradation-a method and case study. In: Software Engineering Research and Practice. Citeseer (2006)
38. Ruellan, H.: XML Entropy Study. In: Balisage: The Markup Conference (2012)
39. Thaw, T.Z., Khin, M.M.: Measuring qualities of XML schema documents. J. Softw. Eng. Appl. 6, 458 (2013)
40. Tang, R., Wu, H., Bressan, S.: Measuring XML structured-ness with entropy. In: Wang, L., Jiang, J., Lu, J., Hong, L., Liu, B. (eds.) WAIM 2011. LNCS, vol. 7142, pp. 113–123. Springer, Heidelberg (2012)
41. Feuerlicht, G., et al.: Measuring complexity of domain standard specifications using XML schema entropy. In: SOFSEM 2015. CEUR (2015)
42. Alliance, O.T: OpenTravel™ Alliance XML Schema Design Best Practices (2010). http://www.opentravel.org/Resources/Uploads/PDF/OTA_SchemaDesignBestPracticesV3.06.pdf. Accessed 1 Sept 2010

Establishing Distributed Governance Infrastructures for Enacting Cross-Organization Collaborations

Alex Norta$^{(\boxtimes)}$

Department of Informatics, Tallinn University of Technology,
Akadeemia Tee 15A, 12816 Tallinn, Estonia
alex.norta.phd@ieee.org

Abstract. The emergence of blockchain 2.0 technology enables novel agile business networking collaborations for decentralized autonomous organizations (DAO). Smart contracts are enactable by service-oriented cloud computing and blockchain technology for governing DAOs that engage in business collaborations. The distributed governance infrastructure (DGI) for such governance involves an ecosystem of agents, policies, services, and so on. To the best of our knowledge, a formal investigation of the lifecycle for establishing such a DGI has not been explored so far. This paper fills the gap by establishing a formalized DGI intended for the enactment of smart contracts for electronic communities of DAOs. The evaluation of the DGI-lifecycle is performed by means of model checking and discussing what pre-existing systems and also by means of discussing what pre-existing solutions exist for an application-system implementation.

Keywords: Decentralized autonomous organizations · E-governance · Smart contract · Open cloud ecosystem · Service orientation

1 Introduction

Decentralized autonomous organizations (DAO) [4] engage in the formation of e-communities that are governed by smart contracts [31]. The latter are a computerized transaction protocol [30] for the execution of contract terms. Blockchain technology [13,25] is suitable for achieving non-repudiation and fact-tracking of consensual agreements. By means of cryptographic digests resulting in hash value [23], blockchains are a distributed database for independently verifying the ownership of artefacts. Additionally, service-oriented cloud computing (SOCC) [34] accelerates the seamless, ad-hoc integration and coordination of information- and business-process flow [7] to orchestrate and choreograph [18] heterogeneous legacy-system infrastructures that are involved in DAO eCommunities for business collaborations.

While research results emerge for cross-organizational business collaboration [7,18], a gap exists with respect to a formalized exploration of setting up distributed governance infrastructure (DGI) for subsequently enacting DAO-collaboration lifecycles. This paper fills the gap by investigating the

© Springer-Verlag Berlin Heidelberg 2016
A. Norta et al. (Eds.): ICSOC 2015 Workshops, LNCS 9586, pp. 24–35, 2016.
DOI: 10.1007/978-3-662-50539-7_3

research question how to set up in a dependable way a decentralized governance infrastructure for enacting cross-organizational business collaborations? In this context, dependable [3] means the components that are part of the setup lifecycle are relied upon to perform exclusively and correctly the system task(s) under defined operational and environmental conditions over a defined period of time. Based on this main research question, we deduce the following sub-questions to establish a separation of concerns. What collaboration concepts are used in the design approach? What is the lifecycle for decentralized governance infrastructure establishment? What are the formal system properties that guide an application implementation? Note that the assumption of the collaboration enactment is derived from the smart contract that comprises the machine-readable code for dynamic DGI-establishment.

The remainder of the paper is structured as follows. Section 2 provides additional information relevant for understanding the business-collaboration context with respect to smart contracting [17, 20] and the embedded cross-organizational collaboration model [7]. Section 3 gives the design approach together with the used collaboration concepts to answer the first sub-question. Section 4 shows the formalized lifecycle for establishing a DGI that answers the second sub-question. Section 5 answers the third sub-question and lists the results from model checking that yield deeper insight for implementing a sound DGI-establishment lifecycle with transactionality provisions. Section 6 discusses related work and finally, Sect. 7 concludes this manuscript by summarizing the research work, giving the contributions achieved and showing directions for future work.

2   Conceptual Collaboration Context

For comprehending the DGI-establishment lifecycle in the sequel, the following frameworks are relevant. As contracts are the foundation of business collaboration, we show in Sect. 2.1 concepts and properties for smart contracting and give a corresponding peer-to-peer (P2P) collaboration model of DAOs in Sect. 2.2. Finally, Sect. 2.3 conceptually depicts a setup-lifecycle for a smart contract that is the precursor for the DGI-establishment lifecycle.

2.1   Smart Contract

The depiction in Fig. 1(a) shows the top-level structure of the smart contracting language eSourcing Markup Language (eSML) for which citation [20] gives full details and examples. The bold typed eSML-definitions extend and modify the Electronic Contracting Markup Language (ECML) [2] foundation.

The structure of a smart contract uses the interrogatives *Who* for defining the contracting parties together with their resources and data-use, *Where* to specify the business- and legal context, and *What* for define exchanged business values. Consensus establishment assumes the *What*-interrogative comprises process views that are cross-organizational matched We refer to [20] for more information about the smart-contracting ontology.

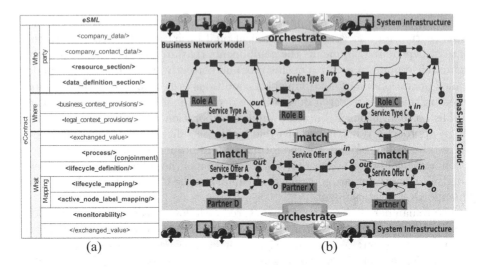

Fig. 1. P2P-collaboration using the eSourcing framework with (a) showing a smart-contracting template [20] and (b) showing a corresponding collaboration model [14].

2.2 P2P-Collaboration Model

The depiction in Fig. 1(b) conceptually shows a DAO collaboration configuration such as a cluster of small- and medium sized enterprises in a cluster for automotive production. The blueprint for forming an eCommunity is a business-network model (BNM) [28]. The latter specifies choreographies for a business scenario and additionally contains template contracts that are service types with assigned roles. The BNMs are located in a collaboration hub for business processes as a service (BPaaS-HUB) [19] that are subset process views [7]. The process views enable a fast and semi-automatical discovery of collaboration parties for learning about their identity, services, and reputation. On the external layer of Fig. 1(b), service offers match with service types contained in the BNM. A collaborating partner must also match [7] with the partner roles of a respective service type.

2.3 Conceptual Setup Top-Level

The lifecycle of Fig. 2 commences with breeding collaboration inceptions that produce BNMs comprising service types and roles. The BNMs that emerge from the breeding ecosystem exist permanently for repeated use in the subsequent populating stage. The validation of BNMs matches the available inserted service offers of potential collaboration partners against service types.

The *populate*-phase in Fig. 2, yields a proto-contract for a *negotiate* step that involves the collaborating partners. The negotiation phase has three different outcome options. An agreement of all partners establishes the eContract for subsequent rollout of a distributed governance infrastructure; a counter-offer

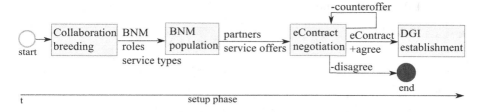

Fig. 2. Conceptual contracting setup-lifeycle for eCommunity establishment.

from a partner that results in a new contract negotiation; finally, a disagreement of a partner results in a complete termination of the setup phase. Note that the setup-lifecycle is formalized and we refer the reader to [17] for further details.

3 Design Approach and Used Concepts

The DAO collaboration lifecycle[1], we formalise with Coloured Petri Nets (CPN) [9], a language for design, specification, simulation and verification of systems. CPN has a graphical representation with a set of modules, each containing a network of places, transitions, arcs and tokens. The modules interact through well-defined interfaces. We use CPN Tools[2] for designing, simulating, performance testing and verifying the models in this paper.

In Table 1, the data elements of the overall DAO-lifecycle are declared for all refinement levels and they correspond to token colours [16] in the CPN-models below. The table shows hierarchic module-refinement availability mentioned in the left column (1 for the top level and 6 for the most detailed refinement). Token colours are present for all lower but not for any higher CPN-refinement-hierarchy levels. The fourth column explains the purpose of a token colour for a lifecycle. The integer-type tokens mostly represent an identification number and string-type tokens are either eContract negotiation outcomes, or eContract proposals. Boolean-type tokens represent decision points in the lifecycle.

4 Decentralized Governance Infrastructure Establishment

The DGI-establishment models below comprises of three parts. First, Sect. 4.1 addresses how the eContract is distributed to respective collaborating parties. As a model-refinement elaboration of the governance distribution, Sect. 4.2 shows how policies are extracted from the local eContracts. Finally, Sect. 4.3 focuses on equipping the DGI with a technical enactment foundation. The sections present on the one hand CPN-models and on the other hand, discusses what pre-existing research and technology exists for an application system implementation.

---

[1] Full CPN-model: http://tinyurl.com/ofae8gn.

[2] http://cpntools.org/.

Table 1. Data properties of the DGI-establishment lifecycle [16].

level	service	data property	description	type
1	eCommunity lifecycle	sO	service offer that fits a service type	integer
		sOs	service offer source for communication channel establishment	
		sOt	service offer target for communication channel establishment	
		pA	partner of an eCommunity	
		rO	role a partner can fill	
		eC	eCommunity identification	
		eCo	eContract based on which partners of an eCommunity transact	
		n,r,k,p,l,q,s	counter variables	
		assigned	service offer assigned to a service type	boolean
		processed	partner prepared for eContract counteroffer re-distribution	
		decision	for negotiated contract proposal (agree|disagree|counter)	string
		outcome	like decision, but input for eCommunity continuation or termination	
2	create	bNM	business network model that get populated with service types and roles	integer
		m	counter variable	
		sT	service type that populates a bNM	
3	populate	ch	channel of communication between services	integer
4	interoperability checking	rOt	role source for communication channel establishment	integer
		rOs	role target for communication channel establishment	
4	contract extraction	spec	specification of extracted eContract	string
4	agreement finalizing	result	whether all eCommunity partners agree on an eContract proposal or not	boolean
		distributed	contract distributed to partner	
4	disagreeing	z	counter variable	integer
		eCo_new	new eContract from a counteroffer to be negotiated	
2	perform	bnma	business network model agent	integer
		sE_l	local service of a respective eCommunity member	
		mO	monitor for observing policy adherance of eCommunity partners	
		sE	electronic service that is enacted	
		lp	local policy extracted from a local contract copy	
		lpnr	counter of local policies	
		s,x	counter variables	
		lC	local contract for respective eCommunity partners extracted from the eContract that coordinates the first	
4	contract establishment	insert	service inserting to local contract	boolean
		extracted	instances of contract copies for negotiation	
5	governance distribution	errorID	error identity	integer
		error	error for synchronizing main contract and local copies	boolean
5	prepare	eP	published endpoint for allowing services to communicate	integer
6	preparation error	prepErr	preparation error in the context of assigning an electronic service to a service offer	integer
		assignErr	assignment error in the actual assignment of an electronic service to a service offer	
		sEr	service error related to concrete electronic servce, e.g., deadlock	
4	operate	tc	termination criteria, either full for eCommunity or partial for disruptive partner change that rolls back to a negotiation stage	integer

4.1   Governance Distribution

The start of this module depicted in Fig. 3, constitutes choosing an agreed upon
eContract that first leads to the distribution of local contract copies and monitors for respective eCommunity-partners. From every local contract follows an
extraction of local policies to which an eCommunity partner must adhere to.

The assigned monitors observe if policy violations occur. Every local contract has a business network model agent (BNMA) attached that utilizes the
monitors to see if eCommunity-partners adhere to local policies and also policies
for behaviour-control of the entire eCommunity. Before the governance distribution completes, an error may be thrown if a synchronization check between the
eContract and the local contracts fail.

Citation [35] recognizes the need for constant evolution of business policies
in service-oriented systems due to changes in the environment. Consequently, a
clear separation exists of policy specification, enforcement strategy and realization drawing on Adaptive Service Oriented Architecture. Furthermore, contractual compliance during business interactions in [11], business policies assure that
represent contractual clauses.

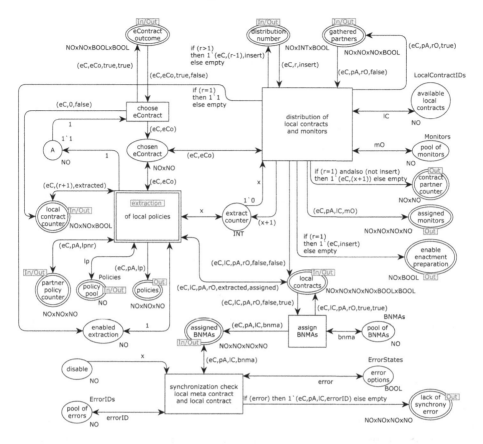

Fig. 3. Policy extraction from local contract copies and assignment of monitors and BNMAs (*governance distribution*) [16].

4.2 Policy Extraction

The model in Fig. 4 is a refinement of a module contained in the governance distribution of Fig. 3 and creates sets of local behaviour-limiting policies that are extracted for every respective eCommunity-partner who is part of later DGI-enactment. Thus, the *extraction*-service of Fig. 4 shows first the choosing of a local contract before enabling the policy extraction for respective eCommunity-partners.

In [27], the authors propose a service-oriented distributed business rules system to manage and eventually deploy business rules to heterogeneous rule engines. In modern service oriented systems, the extracted rules storage medium [1] is the eXchangable Markup Language XML [21] in the form of generated business-rules documents.

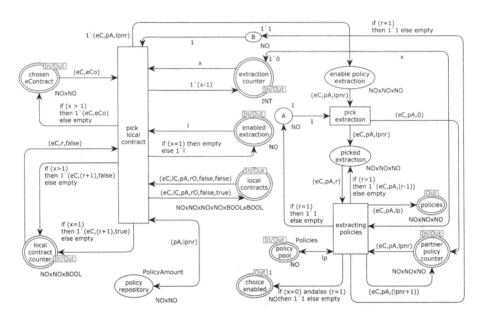

Fig. 4. Extracting from local contract copies a set of required policies (*extraction*) [16].

4.3 Service-Level Preparation

The technical realization of a DGI involves the preparation of concrete local electronic services that fill the respective service offers. The model in Fig. 5 catches and reports exceptions during service-level preparation and service assignment. For each electronic service, the *prepare*-service depicted in Fig. 5 shows the establishment of communication endpoints precede a final check for the operationality of services.

With respect to communication endpoints, in [11] a new programming model supports a compositionality of choreographies based on partial choreographies. The latter mix global descriptions such as on a BNM level with communications among collaborating parties. The essential element for this compositionality of choreographies are process views that are the communication endpoints. Accordingly, citation [7] shows that process views reveal only public, relevant parts of services to partner organizations as abstractions of internal services that are private business process based on different projection relations between them. Several matching relations between the respective process views ensure no structural conflicts such as deadlocks, arise with the internal services that comprise additional activities. For using legacy systems to be part of a larger service-based application system, citation [5] proposes loosely coupled services facilitate the establishment of highly dynamic business relations with means of service-oriented computing [6,24].

During the preparation of an established DGI, errors may occur that the sub-component named *preparation error* of Fig. 5 catches. Error options are for

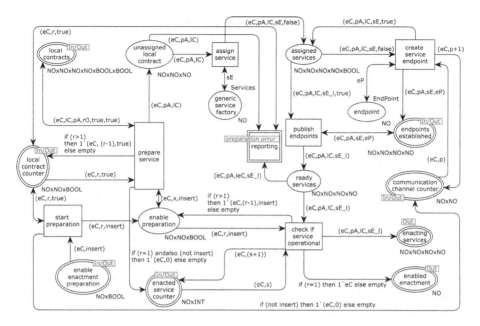

Fig. 5. Electronic service choosing and communication endpoint creation (*prepare*) [16].

the technical preparation of an electronic service, a failure of soundness check [33] and an assignment error between an electronic service and a local contract copy. Further refinements of Fig. 5 are future work.

Next, we discus the enactment the specifics of an established DGI.

5   Model-Checking Results

We used CPN Tools [9] for correctness and performance checking, especially on aspects relevant for system developers: reachability of CPN-modules end states in manual, or fully automated simulation token games as state explosion means full computational verification is challenging for this size of models; detection of loops as a potential source of livelocks that prevent desired termination reachability; loops require specific attention with respect to effectiveness of exit conditions, such as elements of business-level policy control; performance peaks during runtime either for the design of sufficient resources or for restricting the load with business-level policy control; full system utilisation for ensuring that each part of the modelled system actually is used in some scenario; and consistent termination, i.e., consistent home markings that ensure simple testing of a real system.

The model-checking results in Table 2 focus on CPN-modules where the generated state-space is computationally feasible to verify. Loops exist in the enact-module, while not in remaining modules. Performance peaks in Table 2 represent places in the startup-lifecycle that are potential performance bottlenecks. Peaks

Table 2. Model-checking results for the DGI-establishment lifecycle [16].

module	loops	module property			
		performance peaks	liveness	home marking	dead marking
governance distribution and extraction	no	extraction of local policies	D*/NL	no	multiple
prepare	no	assign service, create service endpoint, publish endpoint, check if service operational	D*/NL	no	multiple
enact	yes	enact service, report start error	D*/NL	no	multiple

exist in all listed modules and we give in the corresponding column the labels of occurrence transitions. While no module listed in Table 2 has any home marking, the model-checking results for dead markings show they are all multiple. $D*$ means the model-checking results show the dead markings result from intentional disabling of marking paths for the purpose of focusing in specific marking paths under investigation. The latter means for practitioners the testing of implementations is more demanding as many test cases are required. Finally, pertaining to utilisation tests, Table 2 shows no unused subsets exist in the models. We refer to [16] for full details about the model-checking results.

6   Related Work

It is necessary to cross-organizationally establish collaboration frameworks in a way that does not force companies into disclosing an undesirable amount of business internals [7]. Different research efforts address this issue. In [8], the authors investigate tool support for cross-organizational collaboration design. Similarly in [29], research results present an integrated specification language and a user interface for collaborating government organizations to specify events of common interest, policies, constraints and regulations in the form of different types of knowledge rules, manual and automated services, and sharable workflow processes.

In [15], a framework facilitates the understanding of major cross-organizational collaboration challenges. For example, supporting process-level collaboration, and protection of shared IP and data with various enterprise-level and regulatory policies, including flexible and policy-aware process collaboration among people from different enterprises. Also [22] points out the need for agility of business operations in a collaborative services ecosystem of partners and providers by proposing Work-as-a-Service that a collaboration hub facilitates. A cross-organizational architecture in [8] specifies the features and their composition at a higher level that abstracts the internal implementation mechanisms of the organizations involved.

In [10], the author proposes a very general mathematical model for a governance system of large and heterogeneous distributed systems that assumes the use of policies and so-called law-governed interaction protocols. However, the model does not allow for behaviour simulation comparable to the CPN models in this paper and also the refinement level makes it more challenging to assess a technical feasibility study.

e-Government is a focus in [32] that states computing clouds may lead to considerable cost savings. Still, the research work is not as generally applicable independent of e-Government as the models in this paper that are also suitable for cyberphysical system governance.

Finally, citation [26] discusses the advantages and disadvantages of using distributed governance systems for the internet of things. The authors show that distributed governance poses additional security- and privacy challenges. The assumption in this paper of using process views that hide business secrets internally in larger local services, solves many security- and privacy challenges.

7 Conclusion

The focus of the paper is establishing a decentralized governance infrastructure for enacting cross-organizational business-process aware collaborations. For that, the notion of smart contracts and an affiliated collaboration model is the foundation for deducing a collaboration lifecycle. Assuming an eContract already exists, the lifecycle for establishing and enacting a decentralized autonomous organization we present in combination with additional pre-existing literature discussions that underlines the feasibility of the approach. Finally, the model-checking results allow for a deeper collaboration-system understanding that supports an application-system implementation.

For the lifecycle itself, we choose a formal approach using Coloured Petri Nets that has a graphical notation and also tool support for design, simulation and model checking. We also list the concepts that are embedded in specific parts of the collaboration lifecycle. The latter for decentralized governance infrastructure establishment commences with copying the agreed upon eContract to each respective collaborating party. Next, from each local eContract copy a set of local policies is extracted and monitors and business-network-model agents are assigned to each party. A configuration of local services together with their communication endpoints follows in the lifecycle. When checking the models, the considered properties are loops, performance peaks, liveness, home- and dead markings as they reveal valuable insight for application-system realizations.

For future work, we plan to apply the lifecycle for establishing distributed governance infrastructures in projects for cyberphysical system governance. Additionally, we explore blockchain technology for realizing non-repudiation in process-aware collaboration missions. Furthermore, blockchain technology also promises to enable novel approaches for an effective management of trust, reputation, privacy and security in cross-organizational cyberphysical system collaborations.

References

1. Ali, S., Soh, B., Lai, J.: Rule extraction methodology by using XML for business rules documentation. In: 2005 3rd IEEE International Conference onIndustrial Informatics, INDIN 2005, pp. 357–361, August 2005

2. Angelov, S.: Foundations of B2B Electronic Contracting. Dissertation, Technology University Eindhoven, Faculty of Technology Management, Information Systems Department (2006)
3. Avizienis, A., Laprie, J.C., Randell, B., Landwehr, C.: Basic concepts and taxonomy of dependable and secure computing. IEEE Trans. Dependable Secure Comput. 1(1), 11–33 (2004)
4. Butterin, V.: A next-generation smart contract and decentralized application platform (2014)
5. Di Nitto, E., Ghezzi, C., Metzger, A., Papazoglou, M., Pohl, K.: A journey to highly dynamic, self-adaptive service-based applications. Autom. Softw. Eng. 15(3–4), 313–341 (2008)
6. Hicker, G., Huemer, C., Erven, H., Zaptletal, M.: The web services-businessactivity-initiator (ws-ba-i) protocol: an extension to the web services-businessactivity specification. In: 2007 IEEE International Conference on Web Services (ICWS 2007), pp. 216–224 (2007)
7. Eshuis, R., Norta, A., Kopp, O., Pitkanen, E.: Service outsourcing with process views. IEEE Trans. Serv. Comput. 99(PrePrints), 1 (2013)
8. Hahn, C., Recker, J., Mendling, J.: An exploratory study of IT-enabled collaborative process modeling. In: Muehlen, M., Su, J. (eds.) BPM 2010 Workshops. LNBIP, vol. 66, pp. 61–72. Springer, Heidelberg (2011)
9. Jensen, K., Michael, L., Wells, K.L., Jensen, K., Kristensen, L.M.: Coloured petri nets and cpn tools for modelling and validation of concurrent systems. Int. J. Softw. Tools Technol. Transf. 9, 213–254 (2007)
10. Minsky, N.H.: Decentralized governance of distributed systems via interaction control. In: Artikis, A., Craven, R., Kesim Çiçekli, N., Sadighi, B., Stathis, K. (eds.) Sergot Festschrift 2012. LNCS, vol. 7360, pp. 374–400. Springer, Heidelberg (2012)
11. Molina-Jimenez, C., Shrivastava, S., Strano, M.: A model for checking contractual compliance of business interactions. IEEE Trans. Serv. Comput. 5(2), 276–289 (2012)
12. Montesi, F., Yoshida, N.: Compositional choreographies. In: D'Argenio, P.R., Melgratti, H. (eds.) CONCUR 2013. LNCS, vol. 8052, pp. 425–439. Springer, Heidelberg (2013)
13. Nakamoto, S.: Bitcoin: A peer-to-peer electronic cash system. Consulted 1(2012), 28 (2008)
14. Narendra, N.C., Norta, A., Mahunnah, M., Maggi, F.: Modelling sound conflict management for virtual-enterprise collaboration. In: 2014 IEEE International Conference on Services Computing (SCC), pp. 813–820, June 2014
15. Nezhad, H.R.M., Bartolini, C., Erbes, J., Graupner, S.: A process- and policy-aware cross enterprise collaboration framework for multisourced services. In: SRII Global Conference (SRII), 2012 Annual, pp. 488–493, July 2012
16. Norta, A.: Safeguarding Trusted eBusiness Transactions of Lifecycles for Cross-Enterprise Collaboration (2012). http://tinyurl.com/lghxtrx
17. Norta, A.: Creation of smart-contracting collaborations for decentralized autonomous organizations. In: Matulevičius, R., Dumas, M. (eds.) BIR 2015. LNBIP, vol. 229, pp. 3–17. Springer, Heidelberg (2015)
18. Norta, A., Grefen, P., Narendra, N.C.: A reference architecture for managing dynamic inter-organizational business processes. Data Knowl. Eng. 91, 52–89 (2014)

19. Norta, A., Kutvonen, L.: A cloud hub for brokering business processes as a service: A "rendezvous" platform that supports semi-automated background checked partner discovery for cross-enterprise collaboration. In: SRII Global Conference (SRII), 2012 Annual, pp. 293–302, July 2012

20. Norta, A., Ma, L., Duan, Y., Rull, A., Kõlvart, M., Taveter, K.: econtractual choreography-language properties towards cross-organizational business collaboration. J. Internet Serv. Appl. **6**(1), 8 (2015)

21. OASIS. eXtensible Markup Language (SOAP) 1.1 (2006). http://www.xml.org/

22. Oppenheim, D., Bagheri, S., Ratakonda, K., Chee, Y.M.: Agility of enterprise operations across distributed organizations,: A model of cross enterprise collaboration. In: SRII Global Conference (SRII), 2011 Annual, pp. 154–162, March 2011

23. Panikkar, B.S., Nair, S., Brody, P., Pureswaran, V.: Adept: An iot practitioner perspective (2014)

24. Papazoglou, M.P., Georgakopoulos, D.: Service-oriented computing. Commun. ACM **46**(10), 24–28 (2003)

25. Patron, T., Revolution, T.B.: An Internet of Money. Travis Patron

26. Rodrigo, R., Zhou, J., Lopez, J.: On the features, challenges of security privacy in distributed internet of things. Comput. Netw. **57**(10), 2266–2279 (2013). Towards a Science of Cyber Security and Identity Architecture for the Future Internet

27. Rosenberg, F., Dustdar, S.: Towards a distributed service-oriented business rules system. In: Third IEEE European Conference on Web Services, ECOWS 2005. p. 11, November 2005

28. Ruokolainen, T., Ruohomaa, S., Kutvonen, L.: Solving service ecosystem governance. In: 15th IEEE International Enterprise Distributed Object Computing Conference Workshops (EDOCW), pp. 18–25. IEEE (2011)

29. Su, S.Y.W., Xiao, X., DePree, J., Beck, H.W., Thomas, C., Coggeshall, A., Bostock, R.: Interoperation of organizational data, rules, processes and services for achieving inter-organizational coordination and collaboration. In: 2011 44th Hawaii International Conference on System Sciences (HICSS), pp. 1–10, January 2011

30. Swan, M.: Blockchain thinking: The brain as a dac (decentralized autonomous organization). In: Texas Bitcoin Conference, pp. 27–29 (2015)

31. Szabo, N.: Formalizing and securing relationships on public networks. First Monday **2**(9) (1997)

32. Tripathi, A., Parihar, B.: E-governance challenges and cloud benefits. In: 2011 IEEE International Conference on Computer Science and Automation Engineering (CSAE), vol. 1, pp. 351–354, June 2011

33. van der Aalst, W.M.P., van Hee, K.M., ter Hofstede, A.H.M., Sidorova, N., Verbeek, H.M.W., Voorhoeve, M., Wynn, M.T.: Soundness of workflow nets: classification, decidability, and analysis. Formal Aspects Comput. **23**(3), 333–363 (2011)

34. Wei, Y., Blake, M.B.: Service-oriented computing and cloud computing: Challenges and opportunities. IEEE Internet Comput. **14**(6), 72–75 (2010)

35. Weigand, H., van den Heuvel, W.J., Hiel, M.: Business policy compliance in service-oriented systems. Inf. Syst. **36**(4), 791–807 (2011). Selected Papers from the 2nd International Workshop on Similarity Search and Applications (SISAP) 2009

All the Services Large and Micro: Revisiting Industrial Practice in Services Computing

Gerald Schermann[✉], Jürgen Cito, and Philipp Leitner

University of Zurich, Zurich, Switzerland
{schermann,cito,leitner}@ifi.uzh.ch

Abstract. Services computing is both an academic field of study looking back at close to 15 years of fundamental research and a vibrant area of
industrial software engineering. Industrial practice in this area is notori-
ous for its ever-changing nature, with the state of the art changing almost
on a yearly basis based on the ebb and flow of various hypes and trends
(e.g., microservices). In this paper, we provide a look "across the wall"
into industrial services computing. We conducted an empirical study
based on the service ecosystem of 42 companies, and report, among other
aspects, how service-to-service communication is implemented, how service discovery works in practice, what Quality-of-Service metrics practitioners are most interested in, and how services are deployed and hosted.
We argue that not all assumptions that are typical in academic papers
in the field are justified based on industrial practice, and conclude the
paper with recommendations for future research that is more aligned
with the services industry.

1 Introduction

Since the inception of standardized XML-based service definition, description
and discovery languages and approaches [6] (i.e., the WS-* stack) around the
year 2002, academic research has zealously embraced the ideas of service-oriented
computing and Service-Oriented Architecture (SOA) to build and organize
large-scale distributed applications. However, services computing is not a static field. Over the years, various new industry-driven technological trends (e.g.,
REST [16], enterprise service buses or ESBs [17], cloud computing [4], or most
recently, microservices [12,14]) have appeared, and became integrated into how
academic researchers think about services. The disadvantage of this integrative
approach is that, by now, the term "service-based application" (SBA) can mean
any number of things, ranging from dynamic SOAP- and WSDL-based applications built using the traditional triangle of publish-find-bind [11], WS-BPEL-
based compositions of public Web services, large-scale, heterogenious, enterprise
services connected via an ESB, all the way to microservices-based cloud applications (or any combination thereof).

Orthogonally, but relatedly, a sometimes voiced criticism of current academic
services research is that it is too removed from industrial practice. To give just
one example, Prof. Anthony Finkelstein (University College London) has in a

© Springer-Verlag Berlin Heidelberg 2016
A. Norta et al. (Eds.): ICSOC 2015 Workshops, LNCS 9586, pp. 36–47, 2016.
DOI: 10.1007/978-3-662-50539-7_4

blog entry remarked that research in service discovery deals with a problem that very few practitioners actually have[1]. However, non-anecdotal data about the practical impact and relevance of services research is hard to come by.

In this paper, we aim to provide the academic community with a glance "across the wall" into industrial services computing. We conducted a small-scale survey of the state of practice in services computing, with the primary goal of understanding what practitioners mean when they talk about services, how they technically implement and host services, and what issues they struggle with. Our study has been set up with a specific focus on the recent trend of microservices. We hope to contribute to services research by painting a clearer picture of how service-based applications actually look like in practice, which issues require better approaches, and which traditional research areas in the field are simply not all that relevant in practice. Note that we focus specifically on *technical* issues of services computing in this paper. To keep the size of the research managable, we excluded economic and cultural topics in this study. Further, we limit our research to technical services, and exclude questions on human-provided services, workflows and business processes.

It should be noted that the goal of this workshop paper is to provide a starting point for fruitful discussion, not to critize individual researchers or the community at large. The third author of this paper has himself published on all individual research ideas that are going to be put into question in the following. Further, given that our sample size is not overly large, we do not claim to have all the answers. There is certainly potential for more large-scale and more rigorous follow-up research. We primarily follow an empirical approach. Using a Web-based survey, we questioned 42 companies with one or more service-based products. Our results show that most service ecosystems are of quite managable size. While public Web services are in use, most services are actually internally developed and operated. REST and HTTP are almost ubiquitious, while SOAP is falling out of favor fast. Most companies do not make use of a centralized composition engine or service bus. Instead, most service interactions follow what researchers would call a service choreography style. Cloud computing and QoS monitoring is indeed of large industrial relevance today.

2 Study Setup and Method

We conducted our research as a quantitative, Web-based survey. We targeted developers and companies that self-identify as building a service-based product or making use of a service-oriented architecture. To acquire participants, we advertised our study on multiple programming-related Web sites, as well as through personal contacts and social media. We were able to acquire 42 participants, which were close to equally distributed over companies of all sizes, ranging from 1–20 employees up to global enterprises with more than 1000 employees. About 50 % of our study participants are working as software developers. The bulk of the remaining participants where either team leads, DevOps engineers,

---

[1] http://blog.prof.so/2012/06/bottom-10-software-engineering.html.

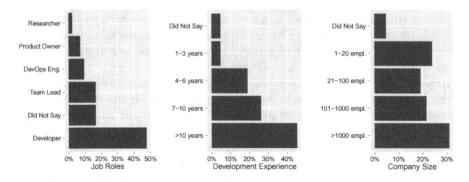

Fig. 1. Demography of study participants. Most participants are experienced and work as software developers in large enterprises.

or product owners. Most of our participants are experienced software developers, with close to three quarters reporting seven years of experience or more. This data is summarized in Fig. 1.

Our study consisted of 25 questions, designed as either multiple choice, single choice, or open-ended free text questions. When designing our study we strived for a good compromise between keeping the study short for the participants and collecting enough material that is related to a wide range of currently "hot" topics in academic services research. Finally, and after discussions with our industrial partners and internal testing of the survey, we decided to ask questions about technical fundamentals, middleware, service discovery, QoS monitoring, and cloud deployment, leading to a Web-based survey that took our participants less than 10 min in the median to complete. A complete list of questions, as well as all resulting data, is available as part of the online appendix[2].

3   The State of Practice in Service-Based Applications

We now discuss the outcomes of our research. For reasons of brevity, we only summarize the most important outcomes.

3.1   Fundamentals

First, we discuss the technical fundamentals of services. What is the typical size and complexity of services, to what extent are external services used, and what are the common programming languages for developing services?

Services Vary in Size, but Few are Truly "Micro". An evergreen question in services computing is the "optimal" size of individual services. Erl refers to services as "coarse-grained entities" [7], implying that each service should carry substantial business logic. The current microservices trend emphasizes tiny services, with "10 to 100 lines of code" (LOC) each[3]. We asked our participants

---

[2] http://wp.ifi.uzh.ch/leitner/?p=743.
[3] http://guidesmiths.com/blog/the-granularity-of-a-micro-service/.

about the typical size of services within their organization in LOC. We observed that services in the range of 1'000 to 10'000 LOC are dominant, as stated by 51 % of our participants, followed by 100 to 1'000 LOC chosen by 43 %. Services following the microservices rule of thumb (less than 100 LOC) are rare (3 %), as are very large services with more than 10'000 LOC.

Services are Dedicated. Another interesting question is how many separate concerns an individual service covers. Following most literature, services are supposed to be dedicated to a single task. As a metric to measure this, we asked our participants how many public operations a service typically provides. The resulting data shows that services seem to indeed typically be dedicated to relatively narrow tasks, exposing between 1 to 9 (46 %) or 10 to 20 (45 %) public operations. The remaining 19 % of our participants operate services with relatively large public interfaces (between 20 and 50 operations).

Most Service Ecosystems are Actually Not Very Large. Much academic research in services computing is motivated by a presumed large number of services to compose applications from. To this end, we have asked our participants how many services they actually have access to within their organization, including in-house and usable external services. Our respondents stated to, in the median, only have access to 30 services. However, the individual answers to this question varied enormously in a range of 7 to 20'000 services. This is because the background of the study participants also varied. Clearly, developers in globally operating enterprises typically have access to substantially more services than startup employees. However, only 25 % of all participants actually deal with service ecosystems of substantial size (more than 100 services) on a regular basis.

Most Companies use External Services. A similar common assumption in academic research is that companies often make use of external services to implement their business goals. According to our responses, almost two thirds (64 %) of our participants indeed make use of external services. However, 68 % of all services that they use are actually internally developed. That is, most companies use external services, but the majority of services in use are still developed and operated internally.

Java is Still the Most Common Way to Implement Services. To conclude technical fundamentals, we were interested in how services are actually developed. The microservices trend often emphasizes a heterogenity of programming languages within an organization ("the right tool for the job"). This was not confirmed in our research. Indeed, we found that 45 % of respondents use at most two programming languages, followed by 25 % using three or four and 20 % using five or six programming languages. The remaining 10 % seem to have a strongly heterogeneous service architecture, as they implement their services in more than 6 different programming languages.

Further, we asked our participants what concrete programming languages they use for developing their services. As illustrated by Fig. 2, Java was selected by 67 % of our participants. Besides Java, we identified a strong focus on scripting

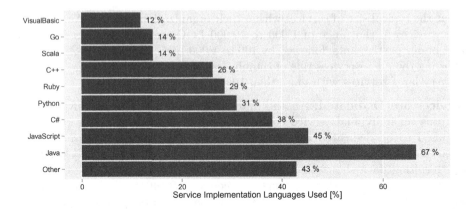

Fig. 2. Java is used to implement most services, followed by JavaScript and C#. Multiple selections were possible.

languages, such as JavaScript, Python, and Ruby, excelling prominent compiled languages such as C++, C#, and Visual Basic. Finally, it should be noted that WS-BPEL or any other service composition language has not been mentioned as a typical service implementation language by any participant.

Key Points. Services vary substantially in size, but true "micro" services are rare. Many companies use some external services, but most services in use are internal. Java and JavaScript are the most common service implementation languages today.

3.2 Communication Between Services

In this section, we focus on how services communicate with each other. Are services more commonly implemented using SOAP/WSDL, or is REST by now more relevant?

HTTP and REST are Ubiquitous. The selection of a communication protocol or technology strongly depends on whether synchronous or asynchronous service-to-service communication is preferred. Almost all participants (95 %) operate synchronous services that are based on HTTP and REST. The dominance of HTTP and REST fits well with the characteristic of microservices being built on top of lightweight communication mechanisms. However, services that communicate via message queues (e.g., AMQP), an asynchronous, event-based communication style, are also used by 57 % of our participants. Interestingly, every participant that stated to use message queues for service-to-service communciation also operates at least one REST service. Only 21 % still rely on RPC-based communication technologies, such as RMI or XML-RPC.

JSON is More Common than Plain XML, SOAP is Less Common than Either. In terms of data exchange formats, we have seen that JSON has widely superseded XML as the primary service data exchange format. As summarized in Fig. 3, 90 % of our participants stated to use JSON as data exchange format, while plain XML was the choice of 57 %. This can partially be

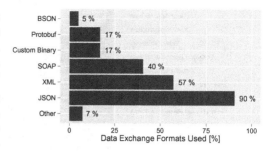

Fig. 3. JSON has replaced XML as primary data exchange format. SOAP is not overly common. Multiple selections were possible.

explained with the increasing importance of JavaScript-based frameworks, such as Node.js. SOAP is not overly wide-spread in our study (40 %). Google's Protobuf is on the rise, but still relatively rare with 17 % usage across participants.

Dedicated Service Middleware is Not Often used. Finally, our study has shown that centralized, heavy-weight middleware (e.g., ESBs or composition engines) are not overly common. Rather, 45 % are not using any middleware at all (excluding simple messaging middleware), which is an interesting fact and highlights the tendency to a more decentralized, choreographed approach rather than a central orchestration point. 31 % of our participants use ESB technology for communication between services. The vast majority of those participants are employed at companies with 100 employees or more. API gateways (e.g., Swagger, Tyk, or Strongloop) are only in use at 19 % of our respondents.

Key Points. HTTP and REST are used by 95 % of our participants' companies. JSON has replaced XML as the most common data exchange format. Half of our of participants does not use any middleware at all, there is a trend towards a more choreography-style of managing service coordination.

3.3   Monitoring and Quality-of-Service

Measuring and monitoring Quality-of-Service (QoS) [13] has historically been considered an important and valuable field of research, but to what extent do practitioners care about QoS?

Standard QoS Attributes are Indeed Widely Monitored and used. As indicated in Fig. 4, our study participants indeed monitor and use a broad spectrum of infrastructure (e.g., CPU utilization, network traffic) and application metrics (e.g., response times, failure rates). However, those metrics are rarely used to select services. Rather, metrics are used at runtime to monitor the health and performance of services. Our study participants use a wide range of monitoring tools, the most common of which are Logstash, Nagios, and NewRelic.

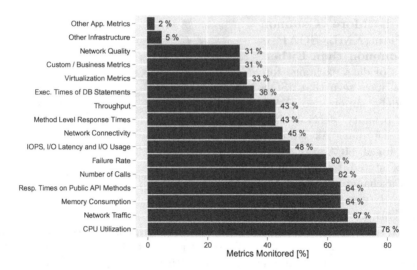

Fig. 4. Participants reported a wide range of QoS metrics being monitored, including system-level and application-level metrics. Business metrics are only used by 31 % of all participants. Multiple selections were possible.

Business Metrics are Rare. A more interesting result is that only 31 % of participants monitor any custom or business metrics[4]. Given that various microservices proponents regularly emphasize the importance of business metrics as basis for development and business decisions, this number was behind our expectations. It seems that for most companies, standard performance metrics are sufficient today.

Key Points. Companies monitor a wide range of standard metrics on application and infrastructure level. These metrics are used to observe the health state of the application rather than to select services. Business metrics are used less than expected.

3.4   Service Discovery

Assuming a service ecosystem with hundreds or thousands of services, discovering the right service is challenging. How do companies handle service discovery in practice, do they use service registries and how do they find out how to invoke services?

Registries are Not Commonly used in Practice. Even though actively researched in the previous 15 years, service registry and discovery concepts such as UDDI have never gained much attention in industrial practice. This is also reflected in our participants' responses when we asked them how they know if certain functionality is available as a service. Only 18 % stated that they have a middleware for registering and querying services. 28 % of participants are

---

[4] http://www.klipfolio.com/resources/articles/what-are-business-metrics.

manually maintaining a list, website, or WIKI page of available services. 25 % stated that service discovery is a minor issue as they do not have that many services and just know what is available. Similarly, 18 % mentioned that there is a contact person within the organization to ask about what services are available.

Client-Side Dynamic Binding of Services is Not Typically used. We have not seen a strong indiciation that practitioners actually follow the "SOA triangle" of publish-find-bind in any real way. 70 % of our participants rely on a documented fixed configuration which does not change, or use server-side approaches (e.g., DNS) to manage service binding. Our participants generally do not make use of client-side dynamic binding approaches, such as QoS-aware service selection.

Key Points. 28 % of our participants manually maintain a list of available service functionality. Documented, fixed configurations are the most common way to bind clients to services.

3.5   Service Hosting and Deployment

Finally, we were interested in how services in the wild are actually hosted and deployed. The academic literature has widely embraced the notion of cloud computing as means to house and provision services, but to what extent does this reflect industrial practice?

Cloud Computing is Mainstream. Our study results, which are also depicted in Fig. 5, indicate that by now cloud computing has indeed found its way into the mainstream of industrial services computing. Two thirds of all participants use either public or private cloud systems to host their applications. Only 50 % of all participants even still have services that are hosted in-house on non-virtualized infrastructure. A third of our respondents are still using long-term external hosting providers. Despite cloud computing being sometimes branded as primarily interesting to startup companies [9], there is no significant difference between the data of small companies and large enterprises in our study.

Interestingly, even though recent study results indicate that elasticity and automated scaling are primary drivers in cloud adoption [5], most services (70 %) are currently actually *not* scaled automatically. However three quarters of participants use the cloud to redundantly deploy their services, mostly to improve fault tolerance. Half of our respondents even deploy their cloud services redundantly over three or more nodes.

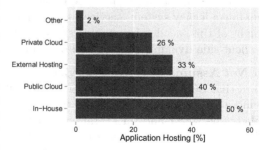

Fig. 5. 66 % of all participants use public or private cloud services. Only 50 % still use in-house hosting. Multiple selections were possible.

Application Packages are Still Widely used. Another interesting outcome of our research is that building and copying application archive packages (e.g., Java JAR or WAR files) is still the most common way (64 %) to provision the implementation code of cloud services, presumably as part of a Continuous Integration toolchain (e.g., Jenkins). Container technologies (e.g., Docker or LXC) are on the rise, but currently only in use at 34 % of all participants. 21 % use virtual machine formats (e.g., Amazon Machine Images or VMWare Images). Small minorities of respondents used UNIX packaging mechanisms or provisioned code directly out of the version control system onto cloud instances (e.g., they clone the code from Git as part of provisioning).

Key Points. Cloud computing is already widely adopted in practice. However, most cloud services are not scaled automatically. Provisioning is still mostly done by building and deploying application packages as part of a Continuous Integration toolchain.

4   Recommendations for Research

The main goal of our study was to survey the state of practice to guide future services computing research. Hence, we now (somewhat provocatively) discuss some implications of our results for a number of common research themes in the field.

***Do Not* Assume that Service Ecosystems are Huge.** Many academic works on service selection are motivated by a presumed extensive number of services to choose from. This is typically not the case, except within a few international corporations. Most service ecosystems are quite easy to track even manually (e.g., via WIKIs). One aspect of this is also that public, external Web services are not quite as prevalent as some research works seem to assume.

***Do Not* Assume that there are Many Alternative Services to Choose From.** In our study we have not seen any particular indication that practitioners indeed commonly need to choose from a list of functionally comparable services. As most services are internal, there is typically exactly one (in some cases two, including a legacy system) service that implements any particular business need. In light of this, academics should reflect whether more attention to approaches for client-side dynamic binding and dynamic service selection is warranted.

***Do Not* Assume that Web Services Always use SOAP.** Our results have shown that SOAP is certainly not a de-facto standard in the Web services field anymore. If a research work needs to assume a specific service style, it should probably be REST and HTTP rather than SOAP. Consequently, the importance of WSDL should also be reconsidered.

***Do* Research on Choreography Rather than Orchestration.** Our participants largely do not make use of centralized composition engines or service buses. Particularly, in smaller service ecosystems, services are composed in an ad-hoc, decentralized, choreography style. We argue that these kinds of service compositions deserve more research attention, particularly in the light of the current microservices trend.

Do **Research on QoS, But for Monitoring Rather than Service Selection.** Our results show that QoS is indeed a "hot topic" in practice. Even though the state of practice in this area is quite mature, it is our impression that there are still interesting research questions to be addressed. However, academics should not assume that QoS is primarily used as a distinguishing factor between functionally comparable services.

Do **Research on Cloud Computing, but *Do Not* Assume that Every Cloud-Deployed Service is Elastic.** Cloud computing is indeed often used in practice, and we argue that the current research attention is warranted. However, there seems to be a trend among current research works to equate cloud computing with elasticity. Our results have shown that there are many, heterogenious reasons why practitioners use the cloud. Academics should not assume that every service deployed to the cloud is necessarily elastic.

5   Related Work

Quantitative empirical research methodologies, such as the one used in our study, are not overly common in the services field. A small number of empirical studies are available, but those are typically focused on a single product (e.g., IBM Jazz [2], SAP [1]) or domain (e.g., telecommunications [8], the financial industry [10]). While many publications present (more or less sophisticated) case studies (e.g., [18–20]), we are not aware of any recent academic publication that systematically validated some of the long-standing assumptions of the research area on a larger and more heterogenious sample of practitioners. Consequently, the research roadmaps of the field (e.g., [15]), as well as reference architectures (e.g., [3]), have historically been driven primarily by academic interests and opinions rather than quantified industrial needs. We argue that this has led to a positive feedback loop for some topics, where many published papers on the topic signified relevance to academics, leading to even more papers on the topic being published, despite little actual industry uptake. It is our hope that our research can serve as a reality-check for researchers that allows them to evaluate whether their assumptions are plausible for industrial practice. However, ultimately, more and more rigorous empirical data will be necessary to move services computing forward.

6   Conclusion

The goal of this study was to provide a peek into the current state of practice in services computing. We surveyed 42 practitioners working in companies of widely varying size. Our results indicate that most service ecosystems are small and consist mostly of internal services. The REST paradigm is very popular. Service choreography is more commonly used than central orchestrators. Cloud computing is of large industrial relevance, but not everybody who uses the cloud does so because of elasticity.

Our goal with this paper was primarily to motivate researchers working on services computing to reflect on the practical relevance of their work, and to occasionally revisit long-standing and often-repeated assumptions. We argue that the services computing field would benefit from more empirical studies being conducted to ground the basic research. Due to the small sample size and large scope, our work can only serve as a first step into this direction.

Acknowledgment. The authors would like to thank all participants of our survey. The research leading to these results has received funding from the European Community's Seventh Framework Programme (FP7/2007-2013) under grant agreement no. 610802 (CloudWave), and from the Swiss National Science Foundation (SNF) under project Whiteboard (no. 149450).

References

1. Akkiraju, R., Ivan, A.: Discovering business process similarities: an empirical study with SAP best practice business processes. In: Maglio, P.P., Weske, M., Yang, J., Fantinato, M. (eds.) ICSOC 2010. LNCS, vol. 6470, pp. 515–526. Springer, Heidelberg (2010)

2. Anderson, L., et al.: Enhancing collaboration with IBM's rational jazz^{tm}. In: Maglio, P.P., Weske, M., Yang, J., Fantinato, M. (eds.) ICSOC 2010. LNCS, vol. 6470, pp. 501–514. Springer, Heidelberg (2010)

3. Arsanjani, A., Zhang, L.-J., Ellis, M., Allam, A., Channabasavaiah, K.: S3: a service-oriented reference architecture. IT Prof. **9**(3), 10–17 (2007)

4. Buyya, R., Yeo, C.S., Venugopal, S., Broberg, J., Brandic, I.: Cloud computing and emerging it platforms: Vision, hype, and reality for delivering computing as the 5th utility. Future Gener. Comput. Syst. **25**(6), 599–616 (2009)

5. Cito, J., Leitner, P., Fritz, T., Gall, H.C.: The making of cloud applications an empirical study on software development for the cloud. In: Proceedings of the 10th Joint Meeting of the European Software Engineering Conference and the ACM SIGSOFT International Symposium on Foundations of Software Engineering (ESEC/FSE), ACM, New York (2015)

6. Curbera, F., Duftler, M., Khalaf, R., Nagy, W., Mukhi, N., Weerawarana, S.: Unraveling the web services web: An introduction to SOAP, WSDL, and UDDI. IEEE Internet Comput. **6**(2), 86–93 (2002)

7. Erl, T.: Service-Oriented Architecture (SOA): Concepts, Technology, and Design. Prentice Hall, Upper Saddle River (2005)

8. Griffin, D., Pesch, D.: A survey on web services in telecommunications. IEEE Commun. Mag. **45**(7), 28–35 (2007)

9. Gupta, P., Seetharaman, A., Raj, J.R.: The usage and adoption of cloud computing by small and medium businesses. Int. J. Inf. Manag. **33**(5), 861–874 (2013)

10. Lawler, J., Li, Z., Javed, N., Anderson, D., Hill, J., Howell-Barber, H.: A study of web services projects in the financial services industry. IS Manage. **22**(1), 66–76 (2005)

11. Leitner, P., Rosenberg, F., Dustdar, S.: Daios: Efficient dynamic web service invocation. IEEE Internet Comput. **13**(3), 72–80 (2009)

12. Lewis, J., Fowler, M.: Microservices, March 2014. http://martinfowler.com/articles/microservices.html
13. Daniel, A.: Menascé.: Qos issues in web services. IEEE Internet Comput. **6**(6), 72–75 (2002)
14. Newman, S.: Building Microservices. O'Reilly, Sebastopol (2015)
15. Papazoglou, M.P., Traverso, P., Dustdar, S., Leymann, F.: Service-oriented computing: State of the art and research challenges. Computer **40**(11), 38–45 (2007)
16. Pautasso, C., Zimmermann, O., Leymann, F.: Restful web services vs. "big" web services: Making the right architectural decision. In: Proceedings of the 17th International Conference on World Wide Web, WWW 2008, pp. 805–814. ACM, New York (2008)
17. Schmidt, M.-T., Hutchison, B., Lambros, P., Phippen, R.: The enterprise service bus: Making service-oriented architecture real. IBM Syst. J. **44**(4), 781–797 (2005)
18. Stein, S., Kühne, S., Drawehn, J., Feja, S., Rotzoll, W.: Evaluation of OrViA framework for model-driven SOA implementations: an industrial case study. In: Dumas, M., Reichert, M., Shan, M.-C. (eds.) BPM 2008. LNCS, vol. 5240, pp. 310–325. Springer, Heidelberg (2008)
19. Tsai, W.T., Wei, X., Chen, Y., Xiao, B., Paul, R., Huang, H.: Developing and assuring trustworthy web services. In: Autonomous Decentralized Systems, ISADS 2005, Proceedings, pp. 43–50, April 2005
20. van der Aalst, W.M.P., Reijers, H.A., Weijters, A.J.M.M., van Dongen, B.F., Alves de Medeiros, A.K., Song, M., Verbeek, H.M.W.: Business process mining: An industrial application. Inf. Syst. **32**(5), 713–732 (2007)

Distributed Service Co-evolution Based on Domain Objects

Martina De Sanctis[1]([⊠]), Kurt Geihs[2], Antonio Bucchiarone[1],
Giuseppe Valetto[1], Annapaola Marconi[1], and Marco Pistore[1]

[1] Fondazione Bruno Kessler, Via Sommarive, 18, Trento, Italy
{msanctis,bucchiarone,valetto,marconi,pistore}@fbk.eu
[2] University of Kassel, Kassel, Germany
geihs@uni-kassel.de

Abstract. Service evolution is a critical ingredient of the service life-cycle. The more our society depends on large-scale, complex service environments including cloud and mobile services, the more pressing becomes the question of how to evolve a service on the fly at runtime, without bringing whole systems to a halt, due to unintended percolation of evolution effects through service inter–dependency chains. Thus, there is an urgent need for coordinated service evolution (co-evolution). This paper contributes a conceptual solution for dynamic, on-the-fly co-evolution of services, as well as a framework that supports the engineering of such co-evolution support. Our solution is built on top of the Domain Objects architectural concept and service-oriented computing model. We also analyze the types of changes that might happen in a service and their potential impact on dependent clients and servers, and discuss the benefits of our approach on those service co-evolution scenarios.

Keywords: Service evolution · Adaptive software · Service-oriented computing

1 Introduction

Our business and private lifes increasingly depend on service-oriented computing applications. In particular, the Internet of Services has become an essential ingredient of the infrastructure of the information society. The variety of available services is virtually unlimited. The advent of cloud computing and the Internet of Things have reinforced this trend even more. The downside of this trend is the ever increasing complexity of service landscapes. This complexity is due to the sheer size of these systems, the manifold interdependencies, the inherent multi–ownership, the heterogeneity of their hardware and software building blocks, the different levels of service abstractions, always-on requirements, etc., and makes service management as a whole a substantial challenge for service providers.

© Springer-Verlag Berlin Heidelberg 2016
A. Norta et al. (Eds.): ICSOC 2015 Workshops, LNCS 9586, pp. 48–63, 2016.
DOI: 10.1007/978-3-662-50539-7_5

Actively used software must be evolved continuously in order to maintain its utility and quality [14]. Adding new features and removing obsolete features, fixing bugs, closing security holes, improving performances, all require updating a software product from time to time. This is also true for services provided via a communication network. In addition, for heavily used services in business-critical applications, upgrade-related downtime is not acceptable in most cases. Hence, the ultimate objective is on-the-fly (i.e., zero downtime) service evolution, which becomes increasingly critical with the proliferation of – and our reliance upon – service-oriented computing systems [17].

Services seldom work in isolation in a stand-alone fashion. Besides direct service provisioning relationships with client software, they are typically part of business processes, in which several services use each other's functionality and construct a hierarchy (or chain) of service interdependencies. That makes service evolution a particularly challenging problem, in particular when several services have to co-evolve together in order to retain their compatibility and bindings. Our goal is to provide a model and a software infrastructure that support *coordinated decentralized service co-evolution.*

In this paper we analyze the requirements of service co-evolution, and present our decentralized solution approach, which is built on a known service-oriented computing model called *Domain Objects.* The paper is structured as follows: Sect. 2 motivates the need for service co-evolution and discusses challenges and requirements. In Sect. 3 we analyze the types of changes that can occur and what their impact on service chains may be. Section 4 presents our solution. In Sect. 5 we evaluate our solution using the real-life SmartCampus project as a case study. Section 6 discusses relevant research, points to future work and offers conclusions.

2   Motivation, Challenges and Requirements

The goal of this Section is to elaborate the requirements and challenges of service co-evolution in the domain of large-scale service-oriented applications. We provide a scenario drawn from our experience in service–oriented development and provisioning for smart cities, and – within the domain – services for smart urban mobility.

2.1   Motivating Scenario

Citizens access their urban smart mobility environment by means of applications (typically mobile Apps), which connect to and leverage an eco–system of services offered by autonomous service providers. The functionality of multiple services often need to be composed to satisfy end–user needs; moreover, service providers may themselves make use of other services, thus creating a service dependency graph. Service providers are independent from each other, and take decisions in

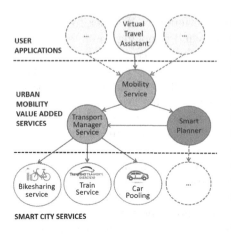

URBAN
MOBILITY
VALUE ADDED
SERVICES

USER
APPLICATIONS

SMART CITY SERVICES

Fig. 1. Service dependency graph.

an independent and decentralized manner. Figure 1 illustrates a service dependency graph extracted from the case study we use for evaluation in Sect. 5. Although small and simplified, this graph is appropriate to exemplify the issues, concepts and principles of service co-evolution. The Virtual Travel Assistant (VTA) is an application developed on top of the Mobility Service (MS), which uses two other services, i.e., Transport Manager Service (TMS) and Smart Planner (SP), to offer multi-modal transport solutions to end users. SP also uses TMS to compute transportation alternatives. In turn, TMS accesses various 3rd–party transport services. Based on this dependency graph, let us now look at some simple cases of service co-evolution.

1. A new version of SP is introduced; it returns route maps in a new graphic format, say, *kml* instead of *jpg*. Thus, the type of the corresponding result parameter in the interface of SP changes. MS does not process itself the map from SP, but it forwards any format *as is* to its clients. Thus, the evolution of SP implies a type change of the corresponding result parameters in the interfaces of MS, but no internal implementation changes. That evolution can be accomplished on-the-fly. However, VTA must itself evolve, to adapt to the new interface of MS. Assuming that VTA already uses viewer components suitable for the *kml* format, this evolution can also be done on the fly as a local adaptation, without the need for software maintenance and development effort.
2. A new regulation (i.e., a new value added tax (VAT) rate) requires the evolution of all services that calculate fees and e-payments at the same time as a consistent, distributed change.
3. Let us assume that the Bike-Sharing Service (BSS) is a replicated service used by TMS in a replication–transparent way. Now, one instance of BSS needs to evolve its service protocol for some important reason. This implies that all other instances of BSS have to change as well in order not to break the transparency property.

2.2 Requirements and Challenges

The crucial research question in service co–evolution we want to address is: *To what extent can we achieve on-the-fly, automated service co-evolution for a graph of interdependent services?* Adhering to the basic concept of encapsulation and information hiding, implementation changes inside a service that have no effect at all on existing client bindings remain out of scope; we consider only those kinds of changes that become externally visible to the immediate clients of an evolving service and beyond.

For example, in case 1 from the scenario above a change in the interface of SP causes change propagation not only to the first–level dependencies but also to a second–level dependency. Many other kinds of structural co-evolutionary changes exist; in Sect. 3, we consider them and their potential implications; we also consider the more difficult cases of behavioral changes. Service co–evolution cases arise also from quality of service (QoS) and service level agreements (SLA) concerns, which may be violated by the evolution of a single service within a dependency graph.

Before we look at the implications of those change types, and at the solution we propose to address them, we state below the principal requirements that such a solution must respect to be realistically viable in complex service provisioning landscapes. We assume, for each service, the availability of a service version graph, that represents the evolution of its versions and their dependencies. We adopt the service version graph model of [15], and forgo a detailed discussion here.

- **Requirement 1.** The evolution support needs to be service–type agnostic, to be effective in a heterogeneous service landscape.
- **Requirement 2.** Services that have dependencies on other services, potentially over multiple dependency arcs, must be able to conduct negotiations with those other services, to ensure they all evolve in a coordinated fashion.
- **Requirement 3.** Since service evolution cannot be fully automated in every case, we need an approach that acknolwedges the need for offline maintenance activities, and facilitates developers in recognizing when the development of a new service version is necessary because of co-evolution needs.
- **Requirement 4.** The need for business continuity requires support for the non-disruptive evolution of services. That is, we need an approach that will not introduce unnecessary service downtime when migrating from one version to another.
- **Requirement 5.** Decision making cannot rely on global knowledge. Given the decentralized nature of service provisioning, all the techniques and tools should rely solely on the knowledge the service has of itself and of its immediate co-dependencies.
- **Requirement 6.** Some service providers may not have the processing capacity to engage in complex evolution coordination protocols, i.e., in case of mobile services, or low-end sensors. Therefore, the evolution solution should not demand that all the required functions and protocols be deployed to the service itself, and should foresee that resource–intensive computations may need to be outsourced to more capable devices.
- **Requirement 7.** Support for distributed service evolution should be robust against partial or temporary inconsistency.
- **Requirement 8.** Service developers and owners must be able to comprehend the dynamics and consequences of service co-evolution capabilities, which calls for novel light-weight analysis, testing, and verification techniques.

While our approach tries to take into account all of the requirements above, they pose a number of difficult research questions, and we are aware that we cannot tackle them all at the same time. Thus, the scope of this paper is on Requirements 1 to 5; the implications of Requirements 6 to 8 have been considered only preliminarily, and are left for future work.

3   Classification of Changes

Service evolution has been studied by several researchers. Papazoglou et al. distinguish between *shallow changes* and *deep changes* [1,17]. The problem of shallow changes in service evolution, i.e., small-scale, incremental changes that are localized to a service and/or are restricted to the consumers of that service [1] is considered solved. However, none of the existing approaches has solved the problem of deep changes, i.e., the multi-step co-evolution in a graph of interdependent services, which is the focus of our work.

Leitner et al. proposed a classification of changes for service evolution [15]. Other authors have adopted the same viewpoint. We agree with [15] but propose a slightly adapted and extended classification; our terminology is consistent with the one used in [1]. We present that classification, together with examples, in Table 1. The differences with respect to [15] are:

- We skipped optional operation parameters since that kind of change does not add any new concern to our focus on service co-evolution.
- We added details on behavioral changes, which can be either changes in the service protocol (i.e., the invocation sequence), or changes in the effect of an operation.
- We singled out business-related changes, that is, changes that originate from, i.e., new legislative constraints imposed upon the business domain; we consider such change out of scope of our co-evolution support and will not consider them further in this paper, because they always require manual intervention by developers.

Another difference vis-a-vis Leitner et al. concerns the effects that the different change types have on the evolution of dependent services (see the third column in Table 1). We distinguish three types of effects, inspired from Cicchetti et al. [6], who have studied the effects of the evolution of meta-models in model-driven software development. In our classification, a change request from a service provider to a service consumer can be: (i) *compatible* (green): the change in the service provider does not affect the service consumer at all; (ii) *not compatible & resolvable* (yellow): the change request from the service provider requires a change in the service consumer, but this change can be resolved automatically by local adaptation; (iii) *not compatible & not resolvable* (red): the change request from the service provider requires a change in the service consumer that cannot be resolved on the fly, but requires manual intervention by the service developer.

For simplicity, in Table 1 we use a color code, which is assigned to the examples. Notice how a 1:1 assignment of color to type of change is not always possible, because the effect of a particular change may depend also on how a service interface is used by the service consumer, i.e., whether all service operations are invoked or just a subset.

Table 1. Evolutionary changes

Category	Type of change	Effect	Example/Comment
Structural	add operation	g	the new interface extends the previous one; this corresponds to type co-variance
	delete operation	g	the service consumer does not use the deleted operation
		r	otherwise
	change operation name	y	a name translation solves the problem
	change operation type	y	a type mapping function is available that maps the old type onto the new type
		r	otherwise
	add parameter	y	the additional parameter is not needed by the service consumer and can be filled with a default value
		r	the service consumer must provide additional information when invoking the service, i.e., additional credentials
	delete parameter	y	the deleted parameter is an output parameter which is not used by the consumer and the operation invocation can continue as before
		r	otherwise
	change parameter name	g	the parameter's name is not relevant when invoking the service
		y	a name translation solves the problem
	change parameter type	y	a type mapping function is available that maps the old type onto the new type
		r	otherwise
Behavior	service protocol	y	the requested new protocol sequence can be achieved automatically, i.e., by skipping a service call or by adding a newly requested initialization call to the invocation sequence
		r	otherwise
	operation effect	g	the service provider fixes a bug in the service implementation but the service consumer had never noticed this bug (note that nevertheless the bug fix is an externally visible change)
		y	the service consumer can automatically adapt to the change, i.e., the service provider switches from one cryptographic scheme to another one which is known and available in the consumer
		r	otherwise
Policy-induced	violation of SLA	y	an SLA is violated and a dynamic negotiation protocol can establish a new agreement
		r	otherwise
	business-related	—	not considered

4   Solution

Compositional adaptation, also termed architectural adaptation, is a form of dynamic adaptation in which software applications are regarded as ensembles of components. Several alternative architectural configurations of components, called variants, can realize the same application, that is, provide the same application functionality, but with different context-dependent non-functional properties. Compositional adaptation strives to modify the software into the configuration that has the best utility [10] in a given operational context. The problem of service co-evolution presents some analogies with compositional application adaptation, but also some important differences:

1. Service co-evolution may require changes in the service consumers; architectural adaptation assumes instead that the client of a component remains unaffected.
2. Although the need for service co-evolution can be anticipated, how it is going to be enacted cannot in general be foreseen; in compositional adaptation, instead, the set of adaptations is typically limited, since all possible architectural variants are known *a priori* at design time. Only a few attempts towards unanticipated architectural adaptation have been made [11,12].
3. Service co-dependency chains add substantially to the complexity of service co-evolution in large-scale service environments; compositional adaptation assumes that available application variants can be installed without further negotiations.
4. Service co-evolution may require code maintenance in the affected services.
5. Service co-evolution requires a language to describe evolutionary changes; architectural adaptation links variants to context, via some built-in reasoning facility (like rule-sets).

Thus, frameworks for compositional adaptation cannot fully solve the service co-evolution problem. However, automation support for service co-evolution can borrow from such technologies.

4.1   Evolution Agent

A central role in our solution is played by the evolution management agent (EVA), a software agent for service evolution. Each service is equipped with an EVA that is responsible for (1) steering the local service evolution and (2) coordinating distributed evolution with other EVAs. An EVA may manage and instantiate multiple versions of the same service at the same time in order to accommodate different clients that may have different needs with respect to the service. The actions of an EVA are controlled by specified evolution rules and constraints, which respond to the requested change and determine the possible service re-configurations. The design of EVA (see Fig. 2) is inspired by the adaptation manager and configuration manager in MUSIC [10], and an EVA combines the functionality of both; more details on the EVA design and its prototype implementation can be found in [21].

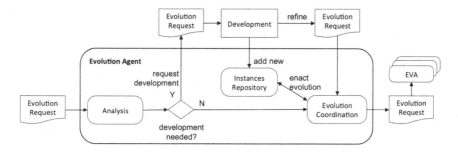

Fig. 2. EVA internal structure

When an evolution request arrives at an EVA, it is passed to the Analysis component, which decides whether the evolution can be achieved automatically, i.e., without the need for developers intervention. If so, the request is passed to the Evolution Coordination component, where the evolution is enacted, possibly involving coordination activities with the EVAs of other services. If manual evolution is needed, the evolution request is forwarded to the development team, which carries out the task, then adds the new service version to the Instances Repository and notifies Evolution Coordination.

The coordination of service evolution among a group of EVAs that need to evolve together as part of a single evolutionary step uses a well-defined choreography. This coordination task may require multiple interactions among the involved EVAs, to understand whether the distributed evolution is proceeding as desired. For example, an EVA might need to cope with situations in which the co-evolution is momentarily not feasible because the partner EVA's services are not in an evolvable state, or because the evolution of the partner service requires further off-line development. If needed, a two-phase commit protocol is used to achieve agreement among the EVAs about consistent service updates (as shown by an example in the paragraph below). Note that this is not the general consensus problem [18], because the EVAs cannot choose any proposed value but only agree to the proposed new version or not. Moreover, the consequences of a temporary version inconsistency will in general not be catastrophic but lead to the rejection of some service requests coming from clients. Notice also that most middleware architectures check the version numbers of caller and callee for compatibility.

Let us briefly explain the collaborative activities of the EVAs with the help of the examples from Sect. 2.1. In the first example, the SP-EVA sends an "interface parameter type change" request to the EVA of the MS. Let us assume that in the MS a new version is available already, which is able to deal with the new parameter type. The MS-EVA adapts MS to the new version and sends an "interface parameter type change" request to the VTA-EVA; that will trigger the application to adapt, and use another viewer for the new map format from that moment onward. In the second example, one of the service EVAs would act as resource manager and trigger a two-phase commit protocol among all dependent

EVAs, in order for everyone to evolve together to the new VAT rate. In the third example (replicated services), the EVA of the evolved BSS tells the TMS-EVA about the evolution. The TMS will be adapted (either by manual intervention or automatically, if possible) and will forward the evolution request to the other BSS replicas. Note that in this case a potential, temporary inconsistency between the replicas and corresponding error messages could occur, and could be tolerated, as long as one TMS-BSS pair is functional.

EVAs may receive evolution requests from a service manager (i.e., a human maintainer who adds a new service version to the EVA Instance Repository) or from other EVAs. Those requests are expressed in a domain-specific Evolution Description Language (EDL), whose specifications remain outside the scope of this paper for the sake of space. The analysis of an incoming request uses local knowledge about the different available service versions and the existing service bindings. In addition, an EVA is aware of the dependencies that the various service versions might have towards other services, since the EVA maintains a dependency graph that records knowledge about local service bindings, as well as notifications from other EVAs about their own bindings.

4.2   Co-evolution Infrastructure

To provide infrastructural support to service co-evolution, we integrate EVAs within an architectural concept called Domain Object (DO). A DO models an *entity*, in terms of its internal *behavior* and its exposed *services*, in a standard, open, and uniform way.

A DO is structured as shown in Fig. 3. A DO has two layers, namely the *Services Layer* and the *Core Layer* which, in turn, exposes an interface, called the *Notification Interface*. In detail, the core layer contains the behavior of a DO and its internal state. Its notification interface is used at design time to configure the relations/connections between DOs. It enables to pre-define DOs hierarchies, which facilitate service reuse, and the provisioning of value-added services on top of lower-level services. This interface is made of *ports*; the DOs connections follow a *publish-subscribe style*, which is implemented by means of *notifications of events* made by a DO on its ports, and *subscriptions* declared by a DO on ports of others DOs.

The services layer exposes externally usable services. The exposed services are modelled as *fragments*. Each fragment is a process representing the protocol which has to be performed to execute the service, in a customizable and portable way.

The concrete service implementation is realized in the core layer, and remains transparent for other DOs using a service, as they only interact with the service protocol specified by its fragment. The strength of the fragments consists in the possibility to define service functionality partially, through the use of *abstract activities*. An abstract activity is defined at design-time, only by specifying the goal that it needs to achieve. Its refinement, instead, is postponed to invocation time, by executing a planning task, which results in a composition of one or more other fragments (from the same DO or other available DOs) that satisfy the stated goal. Therefore, the service layer of DOs defines a dynamic lattice of service dependencies that – in contrast with dependencies form the notification interface – are entirely calculated and established at run time. Our previous work [5] offers to the interested reader full details on the DO concept, and the dynamic and incremental refinement process of an abstract activity in a fragment.

The DO approach offers to developers two complementary ways to define composite service based-applications. With the notification interface, they can configure complex value-added services, and package them as reusable units of functionality in a stable and intuitive way. With the service interface and fragments they can instead avoid the hard-coding of service compositions at design time, delaying their full definition until the execution phase, if that flexibility is desirable in – or mandated by – the domain and the environment.

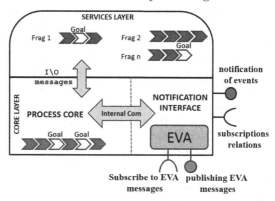

Fig. 3. Structure of a domain object.

When DOs hierarchies are established at design-time through the notification interfaces, those service inter-dependencies are susceptible to changes due to the evolution of services taking part in the hierarchy. We manage that through an EVA contained in the Core Layer, which orchestrates evolution for each service exposed by a DO as described in Sect. 4.1, and leveraging the DO's publish/subscribe messaging facilities.

4.3   Effects of Changes with Domain Objects

The DO architectural construct can be either used to develop new services, or to wrap pre–existing services (legacy or third–party). It thus provides a uniform representation for the design of distributed service-based applications, which brings about several advantages for the management of service co-evolution.

Let us consider the evolution changes that are externally visible to the clients of a service. They can map in two different ways onto the structure of a DO, and either impact the *notification interface*, or the *services layer* of DOs, because we can have service dependencies through both of them. In the former case, those dependencies are defined at design time as publish/subscribe bindings through the DO notification interface, while in the latter case they are established on the fly at run time through fragments and abstract activities.

We can analyze the effects of different service co-evolution changes, depending on what part of a DO specification is involved. Our analysis makes the following *assumptions*: (i) in regard to fragments, we only consider the effect of changes on "new" clients that consume the fragment after its evolution has occurred; we do not consider the possible transitory effect of fragment evolution on pre–exisiting, running consumers. The management of those cases is in the purview of the EVA, and is a shallow evolutionary change, which can be solved with existing, complementary techniques (see for example [20], which deals with long-running service business protocols). (ii) For each abstract activity, there is always at least one fragment composition that can provide a valid refinement. If after an evolution, there are no viable fragments that can refine an abstract activity, we consider this an issue of service availability within the service ecosystem, and not an evolution issue. (iii) Any contracts related to SLA with any service providers have already been defined at the time of third–party service wrapping via DOs.

Structural changes may impact either on the services layer or on the notification interface of a DO. In the former case, such changes never affect the service consumer. This happens thanks to the runtime refinement approach with fragments and abstract activities, which allows the designer to defer their dynamic, on-demand resolution to run time. A detailed example on fragments composition and refinement can be found in [5]. When structural evolutionary changes affect the inter–dependencies established at design time through the publish/subscribe notification interfaces of DOs, they cause – in the worst case scenario – the same effects as in Table 1, unless the evolution agent (EVA) resident in the affected DO is able to resolve them automatically. For all the changes marked with a "red" effect in Table 1, the EVA can – at a minimum – notify and coordinate the service developers, which can lead to a reduction of the downtime due to manual interventions. For example, looking at our scenario, if the TMS has a direct dependency with the train service, and the train service changes the data format for train timetables, the EVA within the train service DO can notify the TMS about the change some time before the new version of the train service is put on-line.

As for *behavioral changes*, they impact only on the services layer of a DO, and do not affect the notification interface, since behavioral specifications are encapsulated by means of the fragment concept. Thus, analogously to structural evolution, and for the same reason, behavioral evolution never affect the service consumer.

Finally, the DO construct remains neutral with respect to *policy-induced changes*. This is because DOs do not have the concept of SLA contract, and also since we assume that any such contracts have already been defined at the time of service wrapping.

5   Evaluation

We discuss hereby the merit of our approach, using a case study drawn from the SmartCampus (SC) project[1], an open development and execution Platform-as-a-Service framework, which aims at facilitating the implementation of service-based applications, in particular in the Smart Cities domain, by providing components, libraries, and services. We focus here on only a portion of the SC platform, the one related to the management of smart mobility services, which

---

[1] http://wiki.smartcommunitylab.it/wikidev/doku.php?id=start.

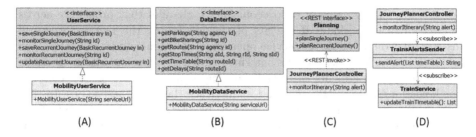

Fig. 4. Excerpts from the SmartCampus class diagram.

represents an instantiation of our motivating scenario of Sect. 2. The complete design of that area of SC is represented in a class diagram, which we cannot include here for the sake of space, but is available online[2] as part of the SC documentation. Across that full design, there are many instances of service dependency chains, where a change in one service would induce some co-evolution, according to the various cases classified in Table 1. Below, we consider some examples, drawn from excerpts of the SC design, which are reported in Fig. 4, and are also marked with letters from A to D in the full class diagram.

5.1 Qualitative Evaluation

By means of the examples in Fig. 4, we can show how DOs can help to avoid establishing at design time a number of permanent service dependencies that are susceptible to service co-evolution, while those which must be still pre–defined can be more efficiently managed, and cause lesser impact. We consider both *structural* and *behavioral* evolution, and we focus on the most critical cases, i.e., the ones color-coded either yellow or red in Table 1. There are several significant examples of *structural changes* that are mapped on the interface of SC services (in grey in the class diagram). For instance, consider the *change operation type* structural change marked as red in Table 1. We can map this change on the design excerpt with label A in Fig. 4, by supposing that in the *saveRecurrentJourney()* operation the return type changes from *BasicRecurrentJourney* to *SavedBasicRecurrentJourney*, which has a different data structure with extra information. This change impacts on the mobile apps developed on top of the SC platform, since they must be able to handle the new data type. Another example can be the *change parameter name*, marked as yellow in Table 1, which could be mapped on the excerpt with label B. Suppose, for instance, that one of the parameters of the *getStopsTimes()* operation changes its name. This will impact on the *MobilityDataService* class code.

When using DOs, all operations in those service interfaces are modeled and exposed as fragments, which are dynamically selected by the consumers of those services via planning, as described in [5]. We focus here on the mobile applications developed on top of the SC platform, since changes impacting on them

---

[2] at https://das.fbk.eu/sites/soa.fbk.eu/files/cdwithlabel_0.png.

represent interesting cases of deep evolutionary changes that propagate across a service invocation chain. If the SC platform adopted the DO architectural construct, it would expose all service operations as fragments (for instance, the *MobilityUserService* class and its interface (label A) can be seen as a single DO exposing the fragments *saveSingleJourney, monitorSingleJourney, etc.*; the same holds for the *SmartPlanner* and its interface (label C), and so on). In that case, mobile applications would not need to be tied to those service interfaces at design time, but they could select the corresponding fragments on-the-fly at run time. All those dependency chains and their evolutionary impact could thus be inherently resolved by the fragment mechanism of DOs.

Furthermore, structural changes can also be mapped onto classes that *implement the service interfaces* (in yellow in the class diagram). For instance, consider the excerpt with label D. To monitor users' itineraries, the *JourneyPlannerController* subscribes to the *sendAlert* method of the *TrainsAlertsSender* which in turn subscribes to and forwards notifications about changes in train timetables, which occur in *TrainService*. Any structural change type listed in Table 1 that involve, for example, the *updateTrainTimetable()* method of the *TrainService* class can cause an impact on the chain of subscribing classes. Those classes model a chain of event-based monitoring and notification relations among services. In the full SC design we can find many of these chains of event-based interactions. When using the DOs, these kind of relations are modelled as connections between the DOs notification interfaces. These are set up at design time precisely to propagate events that are not meant to be part of the externally exposed services, but which are part of their business logic. To alleviate the impact of co-evolution in cases like this, we can rely upon the EVA in each DO. Through EVAs, DOs can define and enact communication and cooperation mechanisms to deal with the effects of this type of service co-evolution, which propagates ortogonally to service interfaces.

To discuss the impact of behavioral evolution we use a simple service protocol example among SC smart mobility services, i.e., the *journey planner service protocol*. Suppose that the protocol is as follows: the *Client* interacts with the *Planning* interface, by sending a *getItinerary()* request. Then, there is a *SmartPlanner* class which implements this interface, and which in turn forwards the request to the *JourneyPlanner* interface of the *JourneyPlannerEngine*, by calling the *plan()* method. An example of behavioral change involving this service protocol could be the following: the *JourneyPlanner* interface changes so that it always requires a (separate) initial invocation of operation *setPreferences()* before *plan()* is invoked. Accordingly, a new operation *setPreferences()* must be added to *JourneyPlanner*. This change also impacts on the *Planning* interface which must now allow passing user preferences when an itinerary is requested, so that the *SmartPlanner* can then invoke the new mandatory *setPreferences()* operation. With DOs, the behavioral specifications of services are represented as fragments in the services layer; there are no fixed dependencies and invocation sequences that need to be pre–defined at design time, but they are established dynamically at run time. For this reason, behavioral evolutionary changes do not pose problems when using DOs.

6   Related Works and Conclusions

Researchers have spent significant effort on investigating methods and techniques for the management of software evolution. In particular, research into the evolution of component-based systems, such as [13], can be seen as a precursor for research on service evolution. However, traditional component-based evolution works under a "closed–world" assumption, which tends to limit evolution to a few entities, and in a centralized fashion. This is not feasible for service evolution scenarios since service–oriented computing happens in an "open world" [2], and calls for the distributed, coordinated evolution (*co-evolution*) of multi-party applications.

We have discussed how research (such as [17]) has classified evolutionary change types in terms of their scope and effects, and pointed out how they pose different challenges and impact in different ways the maintenance of service–oriented applications.

There are several approaches supporting the maintenance and evolution of service–oriented software. For instance, Ryu et al. [20] describes an approach to handle long-running clients instances when the business protocol of the service provider needs to change. In [22], the authors propose an approach that allows service providers to break their backwards compatibility for evolution purposes, by managing the conflicts with the service consumers using a set of refactorings addressing complex changes. *WSDLDiff* [19], instead, analyzes the types and the frequency of changes affecting WSDL interfaces, and provides recommendations to service consumers; its aim is to prevent reliance by those consumers that are particularly unstable because they often undergo evolutive maintenance.

The works above offer support to different facets of the evolution problem. However, they do not directly address deep changes [1], and co-evolution across that chain. This remains largely an open problem, which is of increasing importance because of the ever–growing complexity of contemporary service landscapes. *WSDarwin* [7] is an Eclipse plug-in that attacks the problem of deep evolutionary changes, since it automates the adaptation of the service clients across the co-evolution chain, when structural or behavioral changes are made, to the service interface specifications. However, WSDarwin is a maintenance support tools that operates exclusively at development time.

Our DO-based approach emphasizes the decentralized, dynamic and collaborative management of service co-evolution; it focuses on alleviating the runtime impact of deep evolutionary changes, by using automation and operating on-the-fly whenever the semantics of the changes permits. DOs build upon the openness and flexibility of service–oriented computing, and leverage some of its fundamental tenets, as service dynamic discovery and binding, and advanced results in automated service composition [3, 4, 16]. DOs focus on structural and behavioral changes, and do not address at this stage changes deriving from business policies or regulatory compliance issues.

The level of evolution automation we obtain with DOs is similar to what is advocated by research in self–adaptive software systems, in particular compositional (a.k.a. architectural) adaptation approaches, such as RAINBOW [8] and

MUSIC [10]. MUSIC, in fact, has been inspiring for the design of our service co-evolution framework, since it already supports service-based adaptation [9], although in a context of anticipated adaptation, with strategies that aim at improving the utility of the system, in response to a repertoire of known situations. In conclusion, the need for advancements in service evolution support is undisputed, just as for all software. We have presented a solution for service co-evolution, based on the Domain Object concept, which can provide substantial support to deep changes across a service dependency graph, through the decentralized collaboration of evolution agents. Drawing from a well-accepted classification of externally noticeable service changes and their potential implications on dependent services, we have then shown how our approach can automate several types of changes at run time, and facilitates the coordination of manual maintenance activities in a number of others.

Although our contribution is a significant step towards on-the-fly service co-evolution, we are not there yet. A number of open questions remain, including scalability, transactionality of updates, security, dependability guarantees, etc. Those issues delineate a rich research landscape, which we intend to explore, starting from our results.

Acknowledgment. This work is partially funded by FP7 EU-FET project 600792 ALLOW Ensembles.

References

1. Andrikopoulos, V., Benbernou, S., Papazoglou, M.P.: On the evolution of services. IEEE Trans. Softw. Eng. **38**(3), 609–628 (2012)
2. Baresi, L., Di Nitto, E., Ghezzi, C.: Toward open-world software: Issue and challenges. IEEE Comput. **39**(10), 36–43 (2006)
3. Bleul, S., Zapf, M., Geihs, K.: Flexible automatic service brokering for soas. In: IM (2007)
4. Bucchiarone, A., Marconi, A., Pistore, M., Raik, H.: Dynamic adaptation of fragment-based and context-aware business processes. In: ICWS. IEEE (2012)
5. Bucchiarone, A., De Sanctis, M., Pistore, M.: Domain objects for dynamic and incremental service composition. In: ESOCC (2013)
6. Cicchetti, A., Di Ruscio, D., Pierantonio, A.: Managing dependent changes in coupled evolution. In: Paige, R.F. (ed.) ICMT 2009. LNCS, vol. 5563, pp. 35–51. Springer, Heidelberg (2009)
7. Fokaefs, M., Stroulia, E.: WSDarwin: Studying the evolution of web service systems. In: Bouguettaya, A., Sheng, Q.Z., Daniel, F. (eds.) Advanced Web Services, pp. 199–223. Springer, New York (2014)
8. Garlan, D., Cheng, S., Huang, A., Schmerl, B., Steenkiste, P.: Rainbow: Architecture-Based Self-Adaptation with Reusable Infrastructure. Computer **3**(10), 46–54 (2004)
9. Geihs, K., Evers, C., Reichle, R., Wagner, M., Ullah Khan, M.: Development support for QoS-aware service-adaptation in ubiquitous computing applications. In: SAC, March 2011

10. Hallsteinsen, S.O., Geihs, K., Paspallis, N., Eliassen, F., Horn, G., Lorenzo, J., Mamelli, A., Papadopoulos, G.A.: A development framework and methodology for self-adapting applications in ubiquitous computing environments. JSS **85**(12), 2840–2859 (2012)
11. Keeney, J.: Completely Unanticipated Dynamic Adaptation of Software. Ph.D. thesis (2005)
12. Khan, M.U.: Unanticipated Dynamic Adaptation of Mobile Applications. Ph.D. thesis (2010)
13. Kramer, J., Magee, J.: The evolving philosophers problem: Dynamic change management. IEEE Trans. Softw. Eng. **16**(11), 1293–1306 (1990)
14. Meir, M.: Lehman: programs, life cycles, and laws of software evolution. Proc. IEEE **68**, 1060–1076 (1980)
15. Leitner, P., Michlmayr, A., Rosenberg, F., Dustdar, S.: End-to-end versioning support for web services. In: IEEE SCC (1), pp. 59–66. IEEE Computer Society (2008)
16. Marconi, A., Pistore, M., Traverso, P.: Automated composition of web services: the astro approach. IEEE Data Eng. Bull. **31**(3), 23–26 (2008)
17. Papazoglou, M.P.: The challenges of service evolution. In: Bellahsène, Z., Léonard, M. (eds.) CAiSE 2008. LNCS, vol. 5074, pp. 1–15. Springer, Heidelberg (2008)
18. Pease, M., Shostak, R., Lamport, L.: Reaching agreement in the presence of faults. J. ACM **27**(2), 228–234 (1980)
19. Romano, D., Pinzger, M.: Analyzing the evolution of web services using fine-grained changes. In: IEEE 19th International Conference on Web Services, Honolulu (2012)
20. Hwan Ryu, S., Casati, F., Skogsrud, H., Benatallah, B., Saint-Paul, R.: Supporting the dynamic evolution of web service protocols in service-oriented architectures. TWEB (2008)
21. Tran, H.T., Baraki, H., Geihs, K.: An approach towards a service co-evolution in the internet of things. In: Giaffreda, R., et al. (eds.) IoT 2014. LNICST, vol. 150, pp. 273–280. Springer, Heidelberg (2015). doi:10.1007/978-3-319-19656-5_39
22. Webster, D., Townend, P., Xu, J.: Restructuring web service interfaces to support evolution. In: SOSE (2014)

A Web Services Infrastructure
for the Management of *Mashup* Interfaces

Jesús Vallecillos, Javier Criado, Antonio Jesús Fernández-García[⊠],
Nicolás Padilla, and Luis Iribarne

Applied Computing Group, University of Almeria, Almeria, Spain
{jesus.vallecillos,javi.criado,ajfernandez,npadilla,
luis.iribarne}@ual.es
http://acg.ual.es

Abstract. In the technological world of today, user interfaces (as an essential part of many software applications) are constantly changing in order to meet the needs of different users and adapt to their environment. Accordingly, there is a need for mechanisms to carry out these change processes. This article describes a structure of web services which support the adaptation which constructs mashup type web user interfaces. These interfaces are constructed using third party component architectures, called COTSgets.

Keywords: CBSE · MDE · Web service · Component · Architecture · Mashup

1 Introduction

In today's world it is uncommon for software applications to be static and unchanging. Rather, as is increasingly necessary, applications are adapted, modified and updated over time in response to the demands of users. With user interfaces being an essential part of some software applications, it is necessary that they can also adapt as users change their preferences or modes of use. This has led to new projects and6 proposals in recent years which allow the construction of custom user interfaces through configuration of their interface. In these proposals, the user typically has a Graphical User Interface (GUI) which can be configured to create a bespoke desktop or workspace. The interfaces are made from coarse-grained components (*i.e.* components with fairly complicated functionalities) in order to create *widget*-based *mashup* applications [20]. Examples of these types of interfaces can be found in MyYahoo, Ducksboard or Netvibes [17].

When considering this idea it is often useful to have a software system to manage these user interfaces. Examples of functionalities which can make use of this type of management are: initialising the interface according to either the user's profile or last interaction with the components; saving all the events and actions performed on the interface, or serving as an intermediary in the communication process between components. With these in mind, this article

© Springer-Verlag Berlin Heidelberg 2016
A. Norta et al. (Eds.): ICSOC 2015 Workshops, LNCS 9586, pp. 64–75, 2016.
DOI: 10.1007/978-3-662-50539-7_6

describes a web service infrastructure which allows the dynamic management of component based user interfaces.

The proposed work uses four principal concepts as foundations. Firstly, the research is applied to the domain of *mashup* user interfaces described by component architectures [11]. Secondly, *Component-Based Software Engineering* (CBSE) [8] techniques are used to construct the user interfaces which allow the applications to be custom built for each user and to change over time. User interfaces are based on third-party components, named as COTSgets (from the combination of COTS and widgets). Thirdly, *Model Driven Engineering* (MDE) [9] techniques are used to produce abstraction mechanisms on the *mashup* interfaces and allow their formal representation. Finally, cloud computing concepts [13, 19] are used enabling the component architectures to be managed by web services.

The proposed service infrastructure is based on an architecture with three layers: (a) the client layer, (b) the server side layer which is platform dependent, and (c) the server side layer which is platform independent. The client layer is made up of a user interface constructed from a set of components as described in a component architecture. The platform dependent layer provides the client layer with the services it needs to operate (*e.g.* services related to component communication). It also interacts with the platform independent layer, providing it with some services (*e.g.* services relating to component instantiation) and receiving others (*e.g.* services relating to creating sessions for each user to interact with the interface). The platform independent layer provides a set of services and operations that are common to all possible platforms and can therefore be extended to interfaces other than web *mashup* types. This article will look at the infrastructure which defines the independent layer's set of services. The development of this service infrastructure is focused on the dynamic and flexible management of the component architectures that make up the system. Additionally, the service infrastructure establishes persistence mechanisms for storing and handling these architectures.

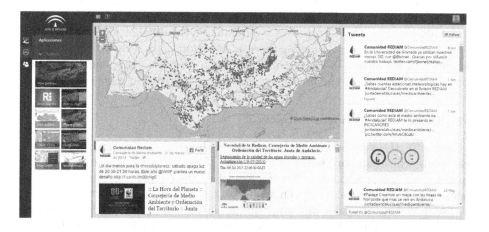

Fig. 1. Web application for ENIA

As an application domain, this service infrastructure has been used to manage a *mashup* user interface of a Geographic Information System (GIS) in the ENIA research project [10], an intelligent Environmental Information Agent. One of the most commonly used data types in these interfaces is obtained from OGC web services developed by the Andalusian Environmental Information Network (REDIAM) [16]. Figure 1 shows an example *mashup* user interface of this GIS [10]. There are a range of services and components on the left side of the interface that can be added to the right side, where the user interacts.

The rest of this article is structured as follows. Section 2 defines the proposed service infrastructure for managing architectures of *mashup* interface components. It then details the three infrastructure levels (databases, drivers and modules) and the public/private services implemented. Section 3 details the implementation of public web services. Section 4 discusses related work, and Sect. 5 presents the conclusions and future work.

2   Multi-service Infrastructure in *mashup* Interfaces

A series of web services, located in the platform independent layer of the Cloud infrastructure, have been created in order to support the component-based architectures of *mashup* interfaces. These services have been organised into two levels according to privacy, see Fig. 2. Public Services are found on the first (highest) level. These include: *Session Web Service, Interaction Web Service, Communication Web Service* y *Component Web Service*. The Public Services are used to provide functionality, persistence and support to applications which have been built from a component-based architecture [18]. Private Services are found on the second level. These include: *Architectural Model Web Service, User Web Service* y *Register Web Service*. These are used to perform certain management tasks such as those related to architectural models, users and the system's available components. Both levels are described in Sect. 2.2.

The *Modules*, *Controllers* and *Databases* levels are found below the two web services levels. The *Modules* level is used by web services and implements all of their functionality. The *Controllers* level manages the different databases which control the environment. Finally, there is the *Databases* level which contains the different databases used to store architecture models, components for user applications, etc. Next, the final three levels are described in more detail.

2.1   Basic Web Services Support

As stated in the previous section, and as can be seen in Fig. 2, there are several levels which support web services. The *Modules* level is the centre of the environment and is responsible for implementing the offered functionality to the user applications by means of web services.

The following modules make up this level: (a) *Lifecycle and Relationships Management Module* (LRMM). This module is responsible for handling the abstract representation of the interface by managing the components and the relationships between them. It is also responsible for handling the component states; (b) *Display Management Module* (DMM). This module is responsible for handling the component visualisation by adapting the device it is working on; (c) *Transaction Management Module* (TMM). This module allows the exchange of messages and the coordination between components to be controlled. This communication between components is synchronised, *i.e.* all the messages sent by one component are instantly received by the others; (d) *Interaction Management Module* (IMM). This module provides an environment where the user interaction on the interface can be managed. Although the IMM module cannot access user events within the components, the events occurring in the environment (*e.g.* move the component) are saved to learn about user behaviour and adapt the interface; (e) *User Management Module* (UMM). Used for administering users in the environment, processing their registration and modifications in the core of our infrastructure (named as COScore). It can also check to see if a user can log in; (f) *COScore Session Management Module* (COSSessionMM). For each user application running in the environment, the COScore creates the LRMM, IMM, TMM y DMM modules. These modules continue their execution as long as the user session is open.

The modules make use of a series of controllers (*Controllers* level) from the following databases which manage the environment all of them implemented in PostgreSQL: (a) *Architectural Models and Users*. This database stores both the applications' architecture models and the environment's users. It is handled by the *ManageArchitecture* controller by means of the mapping framework Hibernate (http://hibernate.org/) which manages the interface's architecture models as objects; (b) *Interaction*. This database saves the interactions which

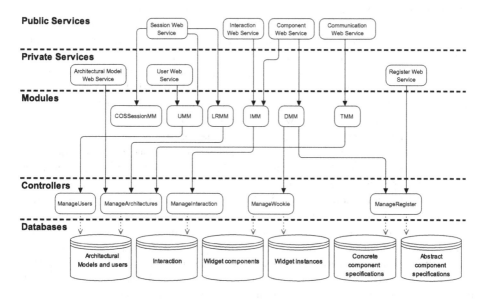

Fig. 2. Web services infrastructure (COScore)

occur in the environment, such as; adding and removing components, changes in size or position as well as communication processes; (c) *Widget components*. Stores all the Widget components which may be needed by the Web applications. These components then generate the instances which are embedded in the user interface. This repository is supported by a server of widget components called Wookie (http://wookie.apache.org/), which follows the W3C standard [15]; (d) *Widget instances*. This repository stores the instances of Widgets that are associated with each user's Web application; (e) *Concrete component specifications*; (f) *Abstract component specifications*. Registers the abstract component specifications, independent of the platform.

2.2   Private and Public Services

As previously stated, the services provided by COScore are organised in two levels. The first level contains the public services, which can be directly used by the user applications; the second level contains the private services, which perform certain management tasks within the COScore, but cannot be accessed by applications.

The **private services** are: *Architectural Model Web Service, Register Web Service* and *User Web Service* (Fig. 2). The purpose of the *Architectural Model Web Service* is to handle the component architectures used to describe the *mashup* user interfaces. The system uses two different architecture models to manage these architectures, the abstract architecture model and the concrete architecture model. Using *Model Driven Architecture* (MDA) as a basis, the architecture models are used to define of the user interface at different levels of abstraction. The abstract architecture models allow a platform independent user interface to be defined in terms of the existing types of interface components and the relationships that exist between these components. These models correspond to the *Platform Independent Model* (PIM) in MDA. Furthermore, concrete architectural models allow a user interface to be defined based on the concrete components used in a given platform. Likewise, these architecture models correspond to the *Platform Specification Model* (PSM) in MDA. The web service allows us to add or remove an abstract or concrete model in order to manage these models. Another private web service is the *Register Web Service*, which allows abstract and concrete components to be registered and removed in the system. Finally, there is the *User Web Service*. This service manages the users and carries out basic functions such as adding and removing users, and checking and modifying users' information.

The **public services** (*Session Web Service, Component Web Service, Communication Web Service* and *Interaction Web Service*) support the *mashup* user interfaces. *Session Web Service* manages user sessions in the environment. One of its tasks is to check whether a user belongs to the system (*Login* operation), initializing the modules for that user. Another of the tasks carried out by this service is the initialization of the user interface. This task reads the component model, generates routing tables, creates component instances and returns the user interface code which has been generated. Finally, by means of the *Logout* operation, this service allows the session to be closed and eliminates the components pertaining to the user. The *Component Web Service* manages the handling of the components in the user interface, i.e., adding and removing components. The *Communication Web Service* manages the communication between components. It receives a message from a component and gets which other components the information should be sent on to. The *Interaction Web Service* is responsible for storing information on how the user interacts with the application. This interaction relates to changes in component position and component size, adding and removing components to the user interface and registering the communication processes between components.

3   Implementation of Public Web Services

This section will explain some operations connected with the public services found in the proposed structure. To describe these services, Business Process Model Notation (BPMN) diagrams will be used to show their operation and the flow of information which takes place. Figure 3 shows the *Login* and *Init User Architecture* operations of the *Session Web Service*.

As described below, both operations are related. The *Login* operation also involves executing the initialization operation. When the *Web application* location is accessed from the browser, the first action is obtaining the HTML code of that application (by using *Request web application*). Next, the user is logged in. This requires the application to communicate with the *JavaScript Server* by using *Process Login request*. Subsequently, the JavaScript server invokes the *Login* operation of *Session Web Service*. This operation makes use of tasks involving the UMM and COSSessionMM modules. Once it has been checked that the user is registered in the system, the user ID is sent to the application. During this process the *Login* response function (in the *JavaScript Server*) invokes the web service's *Init User Architecture* operation. As this initialization interface is executed, the model associated with the user is read (by *Read concrete architectural model*), and the structure for communication between the architecture components is generated (by *Generate routing structure*). The component instances are then created (by *Generate web concrete components instances*) and the necessary code to generate the user interface is returned (by *Generate code for user instances*). The modules involved in this initialization process are TMM, LRMM and DMM. Once the code has been sent to the Web application, the widget instances that have been created (and located in the Wookie server) are embedded in the web page.

Figure 4 shows another example operation (*Add component*). This belongs to the *Component Web Service*. The BPMN diagram shows that the request to add a component to the user interface comes from the *Web application*. The requests are first processed by the *JavaScript Server*. This invokes the operations which correspond to *Component Web Service*. Subsequently, the DMM module executes the task responsible for adding components to the architecture (*Process to add component*). For this, the module communicates with the *ManageArchitectures* controller, which accesses the *Architectural model* database to

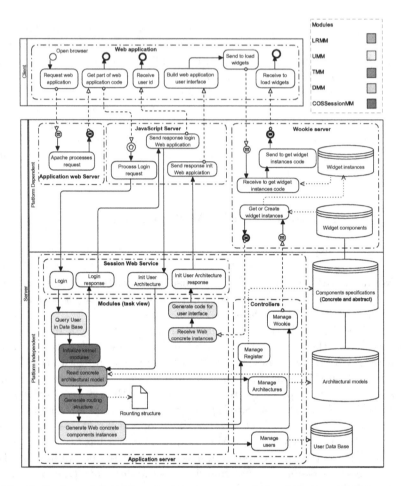

Fig. 3. *Login* and *Init User Architecture* operations of *Session Web Service*

modify the corresponding Architectural model. The operation of adding components involves storing the interaction with the interface requiring the use of the *Interaction Management Module*. By way of *Store Interaction*, this module stores this interaction using the controller *ManageInteraction*. Once these operations have been done, the task *Process to add component* responds by sending the component to be added to the user interface.

In order to demonstrate how the functionality of the web services has been developed, the following example shows the implementation details. The operation *Add component* of the *Component Web Service* is described. Figure 4 shows that for this operation *Add component* is executed first (task 1). Since the user interface is a Web application, this task is implemented using the JavaScript language. Task 1 of Table 1, lines 3–5 show the code which corresponds to the beginning of this operation. Subsequently, the information is sent to the JavaScript

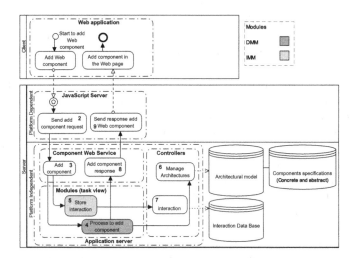

Fig. 4. *Add Component* operation of *Component Web Service*

Table 1. A piece of the code of the Add component operation

tasks		code
1, 10	1	`<html> <head>`
	2	`<script> ...`
	3	`function addComponent(componentId) {`
	4	`  websocket.emit('addComponent', {userID: uid, componentId: componentId}); }`
	5	`  websocket.on('addComponent', function(data) { $('\#main').append(data);});`
	6	`  ...`
	7	`</script> </head> ...`
	8	`</html>`
2, 9	1	`socket.on('addComponent', function(data) {`
	2	`  var argsAddComponent = {userID : data.userID, componentId : data.componentId};`
	3	`  callWS('http://...', 'addComponent', argsAddComponent, function(wsResponse) {`
	4	`    wsResponse.forEach(function(value, index) {`
	5	`      io.sockets.in(data.userID).emit('addComponent', value.codeHTML); }); });`
	6	`});`
3, 8	1	`public class COSWSImpl implements COSWS { ...`
	2	`  public List<ComponentData> addComponent(String userID, String componentId,`
	3	`                                          String componentName) {`
	4	`    List<ComponentData> result = null;`
	5	`    Context initialContext = new InitialContext();`
	6	`    COSSessionMM cossmng = (COSSessionMM)initialContext.lookup("...");`
	7	`    DMM dmm = (cossmng.getUserEJB(userID)).getDMMS().get(0);`
	8	`    IMM imm = (cossmng.getUserEJB(userID)).getIMM();`
	9	`    result = dmm.addComponent(componentId);`
	10	`    imm.setCAM(dmm.getCAM());`
	11	`    imm.loadInteraction(dmm.getCAM().getCamID(), userID, componentId,`
	12	`                        componentName, 'addComponent');`
	13	`    return result;`
	14	`  } ...`
	15	`}`
4	1	`public class DMM { ...`
	2	`  public ConcreteComponent addComponent(String componentId) {`
	3	`    ComponentComponent result = null;`
	4	`    ManageArchitectures ma = new ManageArchitectures();`
	5	`    result = ma.addComponent(componentId);`
	6	`    return result;`
	7	`  } ...`
	8	`}`
5	1	`public class IMM { ...`
	2	`  public boolean registerInteraction(String modelId, String componentId,String userId,`
	3	`          String interactionMoment, String action, String property, String value) {`
	4	`    ManageInteraction mi = new ManageInteraction();`
	5	`    boolean insert = true;`
	6	`    insert = mi.store(modelId,componentId,userId,interactionMoment,action,property,value);`
	7	`    return insert;`
	8	`  } ...`
	9	`}`

server, which acts as a mediator between the client and the platform independent layer. The JavaScript server invokes the corresponding web service using *Send add component request* (task 2 of Fig. 4) by means of the code shown in task 2 of Table 1.

The response to the client application containing the code of the component is also included in task 9 of Table 1, line 4. This is carried out by the task *Send response add web component* (task 9). The information is then received by the web service. The web service and its modules are implemented with Java. The code of the *Add component* task (task 3) is shown in Table 1, "tasks #3 #8". Once the task information has been received, *Process to add component* (task 4) and *Store interaction* (task 5) are invoked. These tasks belong to the IMM y DMM modules. The method shown in the task 8 is returned by the *Add component* operation.

The implementation of the task which stores the interaction (*Store interaction*) is detailed in task 5. It invokes the *registerInteraction* method of the IMM module, which then executes tasks to save the interaction. Subsequently the interaction is stored in the *Interaction Data Base* repository by means of the *Manage Interaction* task. We can see the implementation of the *Process to add component* task 4, which is used to add components. Later, the state of the user architecture is saved in the *ArchitecturalModel* database using the *Manage Architectures* task (task 6). Finally the component to be embedded in the user interface is returned by the *Process to add component* task using the return method shown in task 4.

4   Related Work

By using *mashup* user interfaces it is possible to carry out modifications to user interfaces, adapting them to the user's needs. The project OMELETTE [4] is an example based on the use of *mashup* application technologies to allow users to create their own collaboration platforms. This is achieved by providing a set of tools and components (based on W3C widgets) that support the development of telco *mashup*. They also make use of models to manage the user workspaces. The project differs with regard to this article in that in our environment the focus is on the development of individual applications and desktops are not shared for collaborative tasks. Furthermore, in OMELETTE components use Apache Rave to communicate, which restricts the possibility of communication processes between components other than widgets. In our case, we have used a JavaScript server to interconnect different types of components using Web Sockets. DashMash [3] and ServFace [14] are other examples of similar projects.

A framework is proposed in [5] which allows users to build component based *mashup* interfaces (widget type) to suit their needs. As in our case, they make use of MDE to represent the environment although they are more focussed on supporting web platforms. Our proposal supports multiple platforms.

In [1] an environment called *NaturalMash* is created which allows the construction of *mashup* user interfaces by means of widget type components chosen from a pallet. These components can be dragged and dropped in the workspace allowing users to design their own manipulation environment. The system includes a way to select implemented components using natural language. Nevertheless, the proposal has some limitations such as the possibility for the components forming the environment to communicate. This limits the interoperability between the components.

With respect to using web services to handle *mashup* user interfaces, there are works such as [2] where they are used to provide applications with the opportunity to share workspaces built with *mashup* user interfaces on different devices. Different model types are used to carry out this process of sharing workspaces. In the process, one model is used to compose the user interface patterns, defining the components that form the workspace. Another model describes the current state of the user interface and another visual template model integrates the representative data with graphic elements. These models are provided by web services using *mashup* applications. In contrast to the work in this paper, a hierarchy of services to control the environment is not performed nor are the services intended to handle any elements other than the models i.e. interaction processes or user management.

Other works such as [12] exist where the focus is on the use of components and *mashup* user interfaces to construct applications appropriate to the user's needs. This is done by users creating their own environments from a collection of components. Service Oriented Architectures (SOA) are used for processing the user environment adaption and communicating between the widgets. As such, they use services to control the user interface management processes and the communication between components in a similar way as in this paper although the proposal is not focussed on handling anything other than web type environments. As such, the ability to apply them to other applications is limited.

5   Conclusions and Future Work

This work describes a web services structure, which has been implemented to offer consistency and functionality to architectures, based on COTSgets components, of *mashup* interfaces. This has been achieved using *Component-based Software Engineering* (CBSE), *Model-Driven Engineering* (MDE) and *Cloud computing*. This structure has been organised into two levels of services (public and private) which use a combination of models and controllers to implement all the functionalities and access the database.

As future work, the environment could be extended to support more client applications based on other types of components (*e.g.* built with Java). This would require the creation of new types of component repositories and a different approach to creating the user interface during the login process. Furthermore, dedicated services could be added to the transformation [7] and regeneration [6] processes. The transformation process could be used to allow the architectures to change at an abstract level. By combining these changes with a regeneration process, real components stored in the component repositories, could be associated with abstract components of the abstract model produced as a result of the transformation process.

Acknowledgments. This work was funded by the EU ERDF and the Spanish Ministry of Economy and Competitiveness (MINECO) under Project TIN2013-41576-R, and the Spanish Ministry of Education, Culture and Sport (MECD) under a FPU grant (AP2010-3259), and the Andalusian Regional Government (Spain) under Project P10-TIC-6114. This work was also supported by the CEiA3 and CEIMAR.

References

1. Aghaee, S., Pautasso, C., De Angeli, A.: Natural end-user development of web mashups. In: Proceedings of the 2013 IEEE Symposium on Visual Languages and Human Centric Computing, pp. 111–118. IEEE (2013)
2. Ardito, C., Bottoni, P., Costabile, M.F., Desolda, G., Matera, M., Picozzi, M.: Creation and use of service-based distributed interactive workspaces. J. Vis. Lang. Comput. **25**(6), 717–726 (2014)
3. Cappiello, C., Matera, M., Picozzi, M., Sprega, G., Barbagallo, D., Francalanci, C.: DashMash: a mashup environment for end user development. In: Auer, S., Díaz, O., Papadopoulos, G.A. (eds.) ICWE 2011. LNCS, vol. 6757, pp. 152–166. Springer, Heidelberg (2011)
4. Chudnovskyy, O., Nestler, T., Gaedke, M., Daniel, F., Fernández-Villamor, J.I., Chepegin, V., Fornas, J.A., Wilson, S., Kögler, C., Chang, H.: End-user-oriented telco mashups: the omelette approach. In: Proceedings of the 21st International Conference Companion on World Wide Web, pp. 235–238. ACM (2012)
5. Cinzia, C., Maristella, M., Matteo, P.: A UI-centric approach for the end-user development of multidevice mashups. ACM Trans. Web **9**(3), 11–40 (2015)
6. Criado, J., Iribarne, L., Padilla, N.: Resolving platform specific models at runtime using an MDE-based trading approach. In: Demey, Y.T., Panetto, H. (eds.) OTM 2013 Workshops 2013. LNCS, vol. 8186, pp. 274–283. Springer, Heidelberg (2013)
7. Criado, J., Rodríguez-Gracia, D., Iribarne, L., Padilla, N.: Toward the adaptation of component-based architectures by model transformation: behind smart user interfaces. Practice and Experience. Wiley Online Library, Software (2014)
8. Crnkovic, I., Larsson, M.: Challenges of component-based development. J. Syst. Softw. **61**(3), 201–2012 (2002)
9. Crnković, I., Sentilles, S., Vulgarakis, A., Chaudron, M.: A classification framework for software component models. IEEE Trans. Softw. Eng. **37**(5), 593–615 (2011)
10. ENIA Project: Environmental Information Agent. Applied Computing Group, Ref.P10-TIC-6114, Junta Andalucia (2015). http://acg.ual.es/enia
11. Florian, D., Maristella, M.: Mashups: Concepts, Models and Architectures. Springer, New York (2014)
12. Hoyer, V., Gilles, F., Janner, T., Stanoevska-Slabeva, K.: SAP research rooftop marketplace: putting a face on service-oriented architectures. In: IEEE World Conference on Services-I, pp. 107–114. IEEE (2009)
13. Lee, C.A.: A perspective on scientific cloud computing. In: Proceedings of the 19th ACM International Symposium on High Performance Distributed Computing, pp. 451–459. ACM (2010)
14. Nestler, T., Feldmann, M., Hübsch, G., Preußner, A., Jugel, U.: The ServFace builder - a WYSIWYG approach for building service-based applications. In: Benatallah, B., Casati, F., Kappel, G., Rossi, G. (eds.) ICWE 2010. LNCS, vol. 6189, pp. 498–501. Springer, Heidelberg (2010)
15. W3C: Widgets family of specications. Web Application Working Group, Technical Report, W3C (2012). http://www.w3.org/2008/webapps/wiki/WidgetSpecs

16. REDIAM: Andalusian Environmental Information Network. (2015). http://www. juntadeandalucia.es/medioambiente/site/rediam
17. Sire, S., Bogdanov, E., Palmér, M., Gillet, D.: Towards collaborative portable web spaces. In: 4th European Conference on Technology Enhanced Learning (EC-TEL), Workshop on Mash-Up Personal Learning Environments (MUPPLE 2009) (2009)
18. Vallecillos, J., Criado, J., Padilla, N., Iribarne, L.: A component-based user interface approach for Smart TV. In: 9th International Conference on Software Engineering and Applications. (ICSOFT-EA), 29-31 Aug 2014, pp. 455–463, IEEE. (2014)
19. Whaiduzzaman, Md., Haque, M.N., Rejaul K.C., Gani, A.: A study on strategic provisioning of cloud computing services. Sci. World J. **2014**, 16 (2014)
20. Yu, J., Benatallah, B., Casati, F., Daniel, F.: Understanding mashup development. IEEE Internet Comput. **12**(5), 44–52 (2008)

Resource Management in
Service-Oriented Computing

S-PDH: A CPS Service Contract Framework for Composition

Lin Ye, Kaiyu Qian, and Liang Zhang$^{(\boxtimes)}$

Shanghai Key Laboratory of Data Science, School of Computer Science,
Fudan University, Shanghai, China
{11110240021,14210240018,lzhang}@fudan.edu.cn

Abstract. Cyber-Physical Systems (CPSs) are complex systems in which physical processes are tightly interacting with networked computing components. Some pilot researches suggest that Service-Oriented Architecture (SOA) by promising to guide the development of CPSs, but most of them neglect continuous physical behaviors for coinciding with traditional SOA. Consequently, developed CPS services cannot properly support the tight interaction between physical processes and computing. In this paper, we propose a novel framework S-PDH, in which a CPS service is characterized by a three-level of service contracts, namely, the *physical property contract*, the *dynamic physical behavior contract*, and the *hybrid system behavior contract*. Based on the framework, we study CPS service composition. This study introduces a novel SOA solution to CPS development, and promotes service computing to a new frontier.

Keywords: Service-Oriented Architecture (SOA) · Cyber-Physical System (CPS) · Modeling · Service contract · Service composition

1 Introduction

Cyber-Physical Systems (CPSs) are emerging systems that will reshape the way our modern society perceives the physical world, lives, moves, and interaction in it [1]. In CPSs, computers monitor and control the physical processes via networks in the manner of feedback loops where physical processes affect computations as well [2]. Due to the historical ties to embedded systems, most CPSs so far are designed as *monolithic* ones. The situation gravely impedes CPSs reaching more broad and complex territory. CPSs are seeking more effective paradigms to leverage their development [1].

Meanwhile, Service-Oriented Computing (SOC) has been proved to be an elegant paradigm to deal with complex distributed systems [3]. Corresponding Service-Oriented Architecture (SOA) can guide us to integrate heterogeneous components and make the system scale upwards easily. Therefore, SOC is a promising paradigm to bail the CPS out.

In fact, there have been many studies about CPS services. Researchers have analyzed physical properties [4–6], studied device behaviors [7,8], or probed

© Springer-Verlag Berlin Heidelberg 2016
A. Norta et al. (Eds.): ICSOC 2015 Workshops, LNCS 9586, pp. 79–90, 2016.
DOI: 10.1007/978-3-662-50539-7_7

time-spatial features [9,10]. However, most of them neglect continuous physical behaviors for coinciding with traditional SOA. This compromise expressiveness or verification capability. In CPS, as we know, improper treatment of physical behaviors might lead to low efficiency, serious functional errors or even disasters.

To fill the gap, we propose a method to characterize CPS services, and leverage their composition, in accordance with the roadmap of SOC research [3]. Physical behaviors in CPS are described by three successive levels, from bottom to top, physical properties, dynamic physical behaviors, to hybrid system behaviors.

Our technical contributions include:

- a framework S-PDH which provides a comprehensive model to characterize CPS intrinsic features, and supports CPS services composition;
- the capability of precise control of efficiency and safety in CPSs;
- leveraging the SOC to deal with interacting dynamic systems with both discrete and continuous behaviors.

The paper is organized as follows. Section 2 identifies the necessity of physical behavior characterization and the compositional construction of CPSs via a running example. Section 3 sketches the S-PDH framework, and highlights the rationale underpinning our idea. Section 4 discusses composition facilities in S-PDH. Section 5 outlines the prototype implementation and a case study. In Sect. 6 we review related work. Finally, we conclude the study in Sect. 7.

2   Motivating Example

Let us consider a smart crossing scenario. In its simplest setting, there is a one-way street with a crosswalk (Fig. 1(c)). There are three kinds of participants: cars, traffic lights, and pedestrians. An intent CPS service, named SmartCrosswalk, tries to meet two goals: efficiency and safety. By efficiency, we mean it should let cars and pedestrians pass the crossing as many as possible. By safety, we must be sure that there is no any collision of cars or pedestrians.

In this context, some design issues are:

- How to model participants and their interactions effectively? Can we improve the system performance with the help of the dynamic physical behavior such as cars acceleration?
- Can we develop scalable facilities to support large-scale CPS services, e.g. constructing complex CPS services like Fig. 1(d), or (e) effectively and efficiently by composition?

CPS service approaches so far solve the problem 2 partially, but fail to handle the problem 1. In a word, the CPS services cry for innovations.

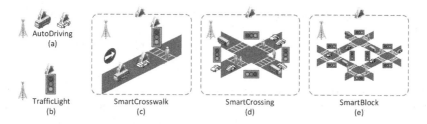

Fig. 1. Constructing complex CPSs progressively. (a) The AutoDriving CPS, (b) The TrafficLight CPS, (c) Constructing SmartCrosswalk from the AutoDriving and the TrafficLight, (d) Constructing SmartCrossing from the SmartCrosswalk, and (e) Constructing SmartBlock from the SmartCrossing or the SmartCrosswalk

3 The S-PDH Framework

In order to capture rich features in CPSs, we propose the S-PDH framework as Fig. 2, which characterizes CPS services progressively through physical properties, to dynamic physical behaviors, until hybrid system behaviors, in accordance with the service foundation dimension [3].

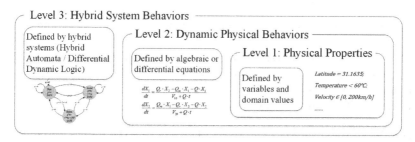

Fig. 2. S-PDH, a three level framework to characterizing CPS services

3.1 Modeling Physical Properties

Physical properties are captured by property variables that reflect the snapshots of physical behaviors of a CPS. The variable range, normally in $\mathbb{R}$, represents physical status, performance, etc. Basically, a physical property is a tuple

$$\alpha_{l1} ::= \langle pname, ptype, pvtype, pvcons, pvunit \rangle,$$

where:

- *pname*: string, the physical property name;
- *ptype*: string, taking from a set of predefined types, e.g. time, dimension, position, energy, temperature, etc.;
- *pvtype*: string, the physical property value type, it can be a simple type such as integer, float, double, boolean, string, etc. or complex type defined by schema such as ranging in $\mathbb{R} \times \mathbb{R}$;

- *pvcons*: the physical property constants or constraint values corresponding to pvtype;
- *pvunit*: the unit of physical property measurement, which is important for unit matching.

Physical properties are supported by traditional CPS service approaches [4–10]. But this facility alone cannot support CPS effectively. Taking the CPS AutoDriving (Fig. 1(a)) as an example, the velocity of a car could be as high as 150 km/h, but if there is another car ahead, the braking distance will impose restriction on the real velocity, e.g. at most 70 km/h at certain moment. Hence, in order to describe physical behaviors precisely, it is required to characterize richer features in CPS service contracts, following SOA priniples.

3.2 Modeling Dynamic Physical Behaviors

Most physical behaviors can be represented formally by the combination of differential and algebraic equations [11]. In our running example, cars running and acceleration behaviors can be expressed by

$$\dot{s} = v, \dot{v} = a. \tag{1}$$

where s represents the passage within time t with the velocity v, and a is the acceleration.

The dynamics of the physical components is an equation of time t. We use linear differential equations and linear algebraic equations, i.e. ako linear time invariant (LTI) [11] to describe all dynamic physical behaviors based on modern control theory. To do so, we have

- **Input Variables**: the set of variables that describe the inputs of the dynamics, e.g. a in the Eq. (1).
- **Controlled Variables**: the set of variables that describe the result of the dynamics, e.g. s, v in the Eq. (1).
- **Output Variables**: the set of controlled variables that we are pursuing, e.g. s in the Eq. (1). We may call the rest of controlled variables **Intermediate Variables**, e.g. v in the Eq. (1).

Now a physical dynamic system can be modeled as Fig. 3.
Generally, the model of a system is a function in the form [11]

$$F : X \rightarrow Y, X = Y = \mathbb{R}^{\mathbb{R}} \tag{2}$$

To conclude, the dynamic physical behavior description is a tuple

$$\alpha_{l2} ::= \langle inpvar, intvar, outvar, func \rangle,$$

Fig. 3. A physical dynamic system   **Fig. 4.** The car's acceleration behavior

where:

- the first three elements represent input variables, internal variables and output variables, respectively. Note that each element in the tuple is still a tuple in the form $\langle pname, ptype, pvtype, pvcons, pvunit \rangle$, and each variable could be a function of time t;
- $func$: the algebraic or differential equations of the variables.

As an example, for the Eq. (1), its model is depicted as Fig. 4.

3.3   Modeling Hybrid System Behaviors

The intertwining of discrete and continuous dynamics is the intrinsic feature of a CPS [12]. An excellent formal model to support the intertwining is the so-called *hybrid system*, in which there are system flows (by differential equations) and jumps (by difference equations) [13]. We will use hybrid automaton or hybrid program [14] interchangeably for intuitive or expressive power purposes.

In this way, the hybrid system can be modelled as a hybrid automaton or a hybrid program. Furthermore, we choose Differential Dynamic Logic ($d\mathcal{L}$) [14] to characterize the hybrid system behavior.

Example 1. The hybrid behavior of an AutoDriving CPS service for the auto-driving of multiple cars is depicted by Fig. 5.

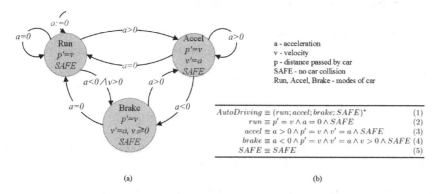

Fig. 5. Hybrid automaton (a) and hybrid program (b) for AutoDriving hybrid system

Accordingly, we have

Hybrid Programs [14]:

$$\alpha, \beta ::= x_1 := \theta_1, \cdots, x_n := \theta_n | x_1' := \theta_1, \cdots, x_n' := \theta_n \& \chi | ?\chi | \alpha \cup \beta | \alpha; \beta | \alpha^*$$

where α, β are hybrid programs, θ_i are d$\mathcal{L}$ terms, $x_i \in \Sigma$ are state variables, and χ is a hybrid formula of first-order logic over reals.

Here, the d$\mathcal{L}$ terms and hybrid formula are defined as:

d$\mathcal{L}$ **Terms** [14]:

$$\theta ::= x | f(\theta_1, \cdots, \theta_n).$$

where $\theta_1, \cdots, \theta_n$ are terms, f is a function symbol of arity n, and $x \in \Sigma$ is a logical variable.

Hybrid Formulas [14]:

$$\phi, \psi ::= p(\theta_1, \cdots, \theta_n) | \neg\phi | (\phi \wedge \psi) | (\phi \vee \psi) | (\phi \rightarrow \psi) | \forall x \phi | \exists x \phi | [\alpha]\phi | \langle\alpha\rangle\phi$$

where ϕ, ψ are d$\mathcal{L}$ formulas, θ_i are terms, p is a predicate symbol of arity n, $x \in V$ is a logical variable, and α is a hybrid program.

Note that $\alpha \cup \beta | \alpha; \beta | \alpha^*$ in the hybrid programs definition are composition of hybrid programs, which will be used in the next section.

Then, the hybrid system behaviors description in S-PDH is the tuple

$$\alpha_{l3} ::= \langle HybridPrograms\rangle.$$

It is not obligated that every CPS service populates all its three levels of contracts. We could choose suitable S-PDH levels in application to fit specific contexts so long as it meets the requirement that the higher level depends on the lower levels.

4 CPS Service Composition in S-PDH

Along another dimension of SOC research roadmap in [3], we use composition as the means to develop new coarser grained services for value-added purpose.

CPS Service Composition: A composition of CPS services is a pair $\langle \mathcal{C}, \mathcal{U}\rangle$, standing for the constitution part and the utility part, respectively, where,

$$\mathcal{C} ::== \alpha | \mathcal{C} || \mathcal{C}, \qquad \mathcal{U} ::== p(\mathcal{C}) | v(\mathcal{C}) | d(\mathcal{C}) | h(\mathcal{C}) | s(\mathcal{C}).$$

The constitution part reflects the fact that the composition is closed, i.e. the composite service is still a CPS service. More specifically,

- α is a triple $\langle \alpha_{l1}, \alpha_{l2}, \alpha_{l3}\rangle$, where elements α_{l1}, α_{l2}, and α_{l3} are defined in the last section, along the S-PDH framework;
- $\mathcal{C} || \mathcal{C}$ represents the parallel composition of two CPS services who are mutually compatible at the same level in S-PDH.

On the other hand, the utilities about $\mathcal{C}$ have following meaning:

- $p(\mathcal{C})$ checks compatibility on physical properties;
- $v(\mathcal{C})$ takes actions on variables. Three operations are: recognizing shared variables, initializing variables function, and evaluating variables function;
- $d(\mathcal{C})$ takes actions on dynamic physical behaviors. There are two important operations: initializing dynamic physical behavior function, and evaluating dynamic physical behavior function.
- $h(\mathcal{C})$ takes actions on hybrid system behaviors. There are two important operations: recognizing hybrid system behavior states, and evaluating hybrid system behavior states.
- $s(\mathcal{C})$ takes the synchronization actions as needed. There are four operations: synchronizing physical properties, synchronizing variables, synchronizing dynamic physical behaviors, and synchronizing hybrid system behavior states.

In composing CPS services, we need to guarantee the compatibility of contracts at all the three levels.

4.1 Compatibility Checking for Physical Properties

At the property level, i.e. α_{l1},

- for $\mathcal{C}||\mathcal{C}$, we analyze the intersection of variable domains to compose two physical properties without resource contention. We could use $p(\mathcal{C})$ and $s(\mathcal{C})$ to conquer the nondeterministic;
- $p(\mathcal{C})$ evaluates physical properties, which can be $pvtype, pvcons$, and $pvunit$.
- $v(\mathcal{C}), d(\mathcal{C})$, and $h(\mathcal{C})$ are not available at this level;
- $s(\mathcal{C})$ takes the synchronization operations on physical properties at this level.

Example 2. For the AutoDriving case in Example 1, the car's location is at $latitude = 31.163514, longitude = 121.579742$. So the following car can check whether the location conflicts if it is going to get that place.

4.2 Compatibility Checking for Dynamic Physical Behaviors

We use the control theory [11], i.e. transfer functions and block diagram models, to develop composition analysis rules as Table 1.

Based on these rules, we propose an algorithm (Algorithm 1 below) to check the compatibility at the dynamic physical behavior level without any information lost. More specifically, the $\mathcal{C}||\mathcal{C}$ represents the parallel composition of two α_{l2}.

- $v(\mathcal{C})$ takes the steps 1–8 of Algorithm 1.
- $d(\mathcal{C})$ takes the steps 9–17 of Algorithm 1.
- $h(\mathcal{C})$ is not available at this level.
- $s(\mathcal{C})$ takes actions on demand.

Table 1. Transformation with equivalent diagram

Transformation	Original Diagram	Equivalent Diagram
1. Cascade Combining		
2. Parallel Combining		

Algorithm 1. Composition analysis for dynamic physical behaviors analysis

Input: $\langle inpvar1, intvar1, outvar1, func1 \rangle, \langle inpvar2, intvar2, outvar2, func2 \rangle$
Output: $ComposedFunc$
1: **if** $(inpvar1 \cup intvar1 \cup outvar1) \bigcap (inpvar2 \cup intvar2 \cup outvar2) == \emptyset$ **then**
2:     **return false**
3: **else**
4:     $SharedVar = (inpvar1 \cup intvar1 \cup outvar1) \bigcap (inpvar2 \cup intvar2 \cup outvar2)$ {Check for common variable domain area}
5:         **if** $Evaluate(SharedVar) == \emptyset$ **then**
6:             **return false**
7:         **end if**
8: **end if**
9: $TranFunc1 = Laplace(func1), TranFunc2 = Laplace(func2)$
10: **if** $Typeof(SharedVar) == [inpvar1, inpvar2]\|[intvar1, intvar2]\|[outvar1, outvar2]$ **then**
11:     $ComposedTransFunc = TranFunc1 + TranFunc2$
12: **else if** $Typeof(SharedVar) == [inpvar1, intvar2]\|[inpvar1, outvar2]\|[inpvar1, outvar2]$ **then**
13:     $ComposedTransFunc = TranFunc1 \cdot TranFunc2$
14: **end if**
15: $ComposedFunc = UnLaplace(ComposedTransFunc)$
16:
17: **return** $ComposedFunc$

Example 3. In Example 1, the AutoDriving car has a brake-distance function $brakedistance = \frac{v^2}{2g\mu}$. However, it is affected by current velocity and road condition. We now can get a more compact safe distance between two cars by evaluating their brake-distance, much better than other approaches that merely use the physical properties, e.g. *max brake-distance*.

4.3   Compatibility Checking for Hybrid System Behaviors

With the help of d$\mathcal{L}$ [14], we can check the compatibility of hybrid system behaviors systematically. More specifically, hybrid programs form a regular-expression-style Kleene algebra with tests. Along this line, $\mathcal{C}\|\mathcal{C}$ represents the parallel composition of two α_{l3}, which is supported by $\alpha \cup \beta, \alpha; \beta, \alpha^*$.

– $p(\mathcal{C}), v(\mathcal{C}), d(\mathcal{C})$ are checked as above;
– $h(\mathcal{C})$ will conduct the state reachable analysis for hybrid systems, and system condition verification, etc.
– $s(\mathcal{C})$ is in charge of synchronizing the variables, states in certain conditions.

In our study, we use KeYmaera [15] to verify the hybrid system behaviors.

5   Prototype Implementation and Evaluation

To validate the feasibility and the effectiveness of the S-PDH framework, we implement a prototype around the motivating example in Sect. 2.

We use JAX-WS in SOAP style, and extend ⟨ComplexType⟩ in WSDL 2.0 to support the three level contracts in S-PDH. We also use Mathematica as a differential equation solver to meet the requirements of the d$\mathcal{L}$ with the KeYmaera [15].

We choose JAX-WS instead of more sophisticate WS-* standards because it is a lightweight solution to Web Services and is bundled within JDK.

To validate the feasibility of the S-PDH, we conduct a case study against the motivating scenarios. The atomic CPS services TrafficLight and AutoDriving are straightforward as depicted in above examples.

What's really interesting is that we can compose CPS services to a new CPS service, and let the process progress iteratively. Note the corresponding in S-PDH between a CPS service and a CPS, this capability implies a new approach for CPS development. For example, the CPS service SmartCrosswork (Fig. 1(c)) can be constructed by two autonomous CPS services, say AutoDriving and TrafficLight, by integrating all the three levels of contracts as Fig. 6.

Based on the SmartCrosswalk service, we can further get SmartCrossing (Fig. 1(d)) and SmartBlock Service (Fig. 1(e)) by composition such as Fig. 7.

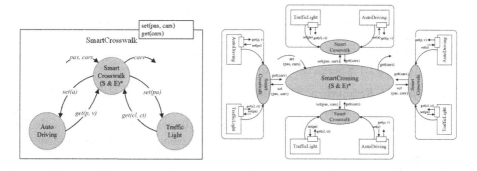

Fig. 6. SmartCrosswalk service   **Fig. 7.** SmartCrossing service

To make our approach more concrete, we apply it on digilent's ZRobots. By embedding our prototype into the ZedBoard (running ARM-based Linux), we get AutoDriving Service. Please refer to [16] for implementation details. The test shows that by acquiring the motion equations of front car provided by its AutoDriving service, the following car can evaluate the distance change curve with fully braking by Mathematica, which demonstrates the precise control of safety and efficiency with S-PDH by introducing physical behaviors in service contracts.

6   Related Work

Over last five years, more and more researchers have pursued SOA-based CPSs. We review them by categories.

Contract-Based Services Modeling. Contract-based services modeling was introduced in [17], and developed by [18]. In [19], the author claimed that it will bring huge advantages of exploiting behavioural information for service discovery and composition, which inspires us to utilize the contract-based services modeling approach in constructing CPS services.

Physical Resource / Physical Property Focused Model. Typical SOA-based extensions for CPS take into consideration of the physical resource constrains, which differs from traditional software services [20–23]. Physical property model utilizes the semantic methods [4,5] or context model [6] to examine the compatibility of different physical properties. They evolve the service constrains with physical resources and some related physical properties, and utilize QoS to fulfill the requirement of CPS service.

Our work encloses the physical resources and physical properties into S-PDH Level 1, and focuses on more comprehensive physical behaviors at higher abstraction levels, i.e. the Level 2, and the Level 3.

Virtual Device Operating Methods. Some researchers study how to capture device operating and results [7,8]. They wrap the physical part as virtual devices and transform the device operating as service event/control process.

Our work embeds the event/process control into the dynamic physical behaviors (Level 2 in S-PDH). We go further by introducing hybrid system behaviors, which leverages CPS services to more complex environments.

Time-Spatial Extension Methods. Time-spatial constraints are vital ingredients in CPSs. So some researchers focus on how to extend the capacity of time-spatial handling in SOA. For example, [9,10] utilize time-space π-calculus or real-time control middleware to operate the resource, time and space constraints of CPSs.

As we discussed in the motivating example, only time-spatial constraint is not enough to keep the system's efficiency and safety. Our work considers the physical properties as well as behaviors at various levels. So we get a more powerful methods to handle the efficiency and safety requirements.

Hybrid System Extension Methods. Our former work [24,25] proposed a CPS service extension method based on hybrid system, which can model the system physical behavior well. They merely focused on compatibility verification instead of the comprehensive framework here. Our recent work [16] focuses the implementation rather than the framework. They can be considered as the supplement of this article.

7   Conclusion and Future Work

We develop a framework S-PDH that provides a comprehensive model to develop CPS services. First, by casting physical behaviors into service contracts, a service consumer is able to anticipate the physical state of the service provider dynamically based on the physical process pattern, which will contribute a lot to precise control of conflict goals in CPS. Then, we leverage the contract notion to implement CPS service composition, which results in a scalable facility to support large-scale CPS construction.

On the other hand, with the physical behaviors contract extension, SOC is capable of dealing with the interacting dynamic systems with both discrete and continuous behaviors. This might leverage SOA technology to a new frontier.

There are still many research issues around the proposed framework, e.g. service compatibility analysis, model checking, and automatic compositing about CPS services. We will work on them in the future work.

Acknowledgments. The work is partially supported by NSFC (No.60873115), MoE & China Mobile Joint Foundation (No.MCM20123011), Shanghai S & T Funds (No.13dz2260200 & No.13511504300), National Hi-tech Project (No. 2012AA02A602).

References

1. Poovendran, R., et al.: Special issue on cyber - physical systems. Proc. IEEE **100**, 6–12 (2012)
2. Lee, E.A., Seshia, S.A.: Introduction to Embedded Systems: ACyber-Physical Systems Approach. Lee and Seshia (2011). http://LeeSeshia.org
3. Papazoglou, M.P., Traverso, P., Dustdar, S., Leymann, F.: Service-oriented computing: a research roadmap. Int. J. Coop. Inf. Syst. **17**, 223–255 (2008)
4. Jian, H., et al.: Real-time service-oriented distributed governance. In: 6th World Congress on Services, Miami, pp. 479–484 (2010)
5. Wang, T., Niu, C., Cheng, L.: A two-phase context-sensitive service composition method with the workflow model in cyber-physical systems. In: 2014 IEEE 17th International Conference on Computational Science and Engineering (CSE), pp. 1475–1482 (2014)
6. Guinard, D., Trifa, V., Karnouskos, S., Spiess, P., Savio, D.: Interacting with the soa-based internet of things: discovery, query, selection, and on-demand provisioning of web services. IEEE Trans. Serv. Comput. **3**, 223–235 (2010)
7. Theorin, A., Ollinger, L., Johnsson, C.: Service-oriented process control with grafchart and the devices profile for web services. In: Borangiu, T., Thomas, A., Trentesaux, D. (eds.) Service Orientation in Holonic and Multi Agent. SCI, vol. 472, pp. 213–228. Springer, Heidelberg (2013)
8. Haber, A., Ringert, J.O., Rumpe, B.: Montiarc-architectural modeling of interactivedistributed and cyber-physical systems (2014). arXiv preprint arXiv:1409.6578
9. Peng, W., Yang, X., Shao, H.Z.: Cyber-physical system components composition analysis and formal verification based on service-oriented architecture. In: IEEE Ninth International Conference on e-Business Engineering (ICEBE), Hangzhou, pp. 327–332 (2012)

10. Ringert, J.O., Rumpe, B., Wortmann, A.: A requirements modeling language for the componentbehavior of cyber physical robotics systems (2014). arXiv preprint arXiv:1409.0394
11. Dorf, R.C., Bishop, R.H.: Modern Control Systems, 12th edn. Pearson, Boston (2011)
12. Derler, P., Lee, E.A., Vincentelli, A.S.: Modeling cyberphysical systems. Proc. IEEE **100**, 13–28 (2012)
13. Wikipedia. Hybrid system. http://en.wikipedia.org/wiki/Hybrid-system
14. Platzer, A.: Logical Analysis of Hybrid Systems: Proving Theorems for Complex Dynamics. Springer, Heidelberg (2010)
15. Platzer, A., Quesel, J.-D.: KeYmaera: a hybrid theorem prover for hybrid systems (system description). In: Armando, A., Baumgartner, P., Dowek, G. (eds.) IJCAR 2008. LNCS (LNAI), vol. 5195, pp. 171–178. Springer, Heidelberg (2008)
16. Qian, K.Y., Ye, L., Zhang, L.: A collaborative smart car system based on CPS services. In: Proceedings of National Conference on Services Computing 2015, Xianning, China (in Chinese)
17. Meredith, L.G., Bjorg, S.: Contracts and types. Commun. ACM **46**, 41–47 (2003)
18. Castagna, G., Gesbert, N., Padovani, L.: A theory of contracts for web services. In: ACM SIGPLAN Notices, vol. 43, pp. 261–272. ACM (2008)
19. Brogi, A.: On the potential advantages of exploiting behavioural information for contract-based service discovery and composition. J. Logic Algebraic Program. **80**, 3–12 (2011)
20. Uckelmann, D., Harrison, M., Michahelles, F.: Architecting the Internet of Things. Springer, Heidelberg (2011)
21. Hu, X., Chu, T.H., Chan, H.C., Leung, V.C.: Vita: a crowdsensing-oriented mobile cyber-physical system. IEEE Trans. Emerg. Top. Comput. **1**, 148–165 (2013)
22. Garcia Valls, M., Lopez, I.R., Villar, L.F.: iLAND: an enhanced middleware for real-time reconfiguration of service oriented distributed real-time systems. IEEE Trans. Ind. Inform. **9**, 228–236 (2013)
23. Thramboulidis, K.: An open distributed architecture for flexible hybridassembly systems: a model driven engineering approach (2014). arXiv preprint arXiv:411.1307
24. Ye, L., Tang, P., Guo, L.P., Zhang, L.: Modeling and verifying services of internet of things based on hybrid system methodology. J. Chin. Comput. Syst. **34**, 2663–2668 (2013). (in Chinese)
25. Tang, P., Ye, L., Guo, L.P., Zhang, L.: Composition and verifying of internet of things system. Comput. Eng. **39**, 45–48 (2013). (in Chinese)

Towards RAM-Based Variant Generation
of Business Process Models

Ahmed Tealeb$^{(\boxtimes)}$, Ahmed Awad, and Galal Galal-Edeen

Information Systems Department, Faculty of Computers and Information,
Cairo University, Giza, Egypt
ahtealeb@gmail.com, a.gaafar@fci-cu.edu.eg, galal@acm.org

Abstract. Variability management of process models is a major challenge for Process-Aware Information Systems. Process model variants can be attributed to any of the following reasons: new technologies, governmental rules, organizational context or adoption of new standards. Current approaches to manage variants of process models address issues such as reducing the huge effort of modeling from scratch, preventing redundancy, and controlling inconsistency in process models. Although the effort to manage process model variants has been exerted, there are still limitations. Furthermore, existing approaches do not focus on variants that come from change in organizational perspective of process models. Organizational-driven variant management is an important area that still needs more study that we focus on in this paper. Resource Assignment Matrix (RAM) is an important aspect of the organizational perspective that has different variations. This paper introduces an approach inspired by real life scenario to generate consistent process model variants that come from adaptations in the RAM.

Keywords: Organizational-driven variant · Responsibility Assignment Matrix (RAM) · RACI Variants · Business Process Management (BPM) · Process-Aware Information Systems (PAISs)

1 Introduction

In recent years, the increasing adoption of PAISs has resulted in large process model repositories [1]. One of the fundamental challenges of modeling business process is to deal with the multitude of variants that may exist for a particular process [2]. Each process variant constitutes an adjustment of a reference or basic process model to specific requirements. Efficient management of process model variants is a critical issue for organizations with the aim of helping them reduce the huge effort of modeling from scratch, prevent redundancy, and tackle inconsistency in process models.

Despite the efforts done in current approaches e.g., in Provop [3], C-EPCs [4], and PPM [5] to manage process model variants, there are still unaddressed issues. Current approaches focus on dealing with variants coming from change in

A. Norta et al. (Eds.): ICSOC 2015 Workshops, LNCS 9586, pp. 91–102, 2016.
DOI: 10.1007/978-3-662-50539-7_8

the control and the behavioral perspectives of process models. However, variants originating from the organizational perspective still need to be studied.

The organizational perspective is one of the different views integrated in the process model. It identifies the hierarchy of the organization within which the process will be executed. Russell et al. [6] introduced a set of Workflow Resource patterns (WRP) to capture the requirements for resource management such as representation and utilization in workflow environment [6]. Awad et al. [7] proposed an extension metamodel for BPMN to enable representation of resource assignment constraints using Object Constraints Language (OCL) [8] to WRP [6]. We, in a previous work, discussed organizational structures as an aspect of the organizational perspective based on general concepts such as abstraction and polymorphism [9].

Another important aspect of the organizational perspective is the Responsibility Assignment Matrix (RAM). RAM enables organization's stakeholders to understand the responsibilities of each person. RAM provides important information about resource assignments which till now is not supported completely by Business Process Model and Notation (BPMN) 2.0 [10]. The aim of this paper is to propose a context-based approach for generating consistent process model variants focusing on the different variations of RAM. We extract the RAM for a given base model. Then, we enable the user to adapt RAM and validate the different changes. Finally, we generate the variant of the base model in hand.

The rest of this paper is organized as follows: Sect. 2 introduces the basic concepts related to our approach and discusses a motivating scenario. Section 3 presents our RAM-based algorithms for generating consistent process model variants. Section 4 discusses related work. Finally, Sect. 5 concludes our approach and outlines directions for future research.

2   Background

In this section, we introduce in brief the background that is related to our approach. We present RAM in brief and the work of Cabanillas et al. [14] for mixing RAM with BPMN as follows in the Sects. 2.1 and 2.2 respectively. Then, we present our motivating scenario in Sect. 2.3.

2.1   RAM in Brief

RAM is a matrix-based chart represented in a grid in order to identify the roles (people or groups or departments) and their responsibilities for a given task. RAM is also known as RACI (pronounced 'racey') matrix or Linear Responsibility Chart (LRC). Project Management Institute defined RACI in [11] as a common type of RAM that uses responsible, accountable, consult, and inform statuses to define the involvement of stakeholders in project activities. RACI matrix has four association types or patterns as defined in [12]:

– *Responsible (R):* "The Doer" who is actually responsible for the execution of the work. There is typically one person responsible for a task but the responsibility can be shared in some cases. Moreover, the person who is *Responsible (R)* for a task in some cases is also *Accountable (A)*.

- *Accountable (A):* "The Buck Stops Here" who ultimately approves or authorizes the work performed by the person *Responsible (R)* for a task. There must be one and only one role/person accountable for any given task.
- *Consulted (C):* "In the Loop" who are the subject matter experts to be consulted before and during the task performed as a two-way communication.
- *Informed (I):* "Keep in the Picture" who need to be informed about the status of the task performed as a one-way communication.
- *Support (S):* is another association type that is sometimes used in addition to the above four types who provides the resources and hence support for a specific task. This is an optional type and if this category used along with the other four RACI categories, then matrix will be called RASCI matrix.

There are several variants for RACI matrix such as RASI, RASCI, RACI-VS, DACI, CAIRO [13]. We will make use of some of these alternatives as variants for the RACI matrix as will be explained in Sect. 3.

2.2   RASCI-aware BPMN

Cabanillas et al. [14] introduced an approach for mixing RAM information with business process models together in BPMN. The approach is based on *RASCI patterns* in order to make the process models RASCI-aware [14]. The five RASCI patterns are Responsible, Accountable, Support, Consulted, and Informed patterns. Moreover, they proposed an extension of BPMN with a set of RASCI tasks and collapsed subprocesses. They identified some specifications and constraints for these patterns along with process model in BPMN [14]. We use these patterns with some adaptations in our approach as in Sects. 3.1, 3.2 and the Appendix: RAM Patterns. Furthermore, they used Resource Assignment Language (RAL) which is defined with examples in [15,16] instead of XPath to build resource assignment expressions. RAL allows expressing both *direct assignments* extracted from RASCI matrices as well as *binding information*. Cabanillas et al. [17] implemented CRISTAL tool, which composed several tools such as RACI2BPMN, DT RAL Solver, and RT RAL Solver. CRISTAL is used for generating RACI-aware business process model automatically.

The aim of Cabanillas et al.'s [14–17] intensive work is introducing a novel approach to integrate RACI matrix information with process model using BPMN. However, our approach addresses the issue of generating consistent process model variants from adaptations in RACI matrix based on context.

2.3   Motivating Scenario

In this section, we introduce a real life scenario that motivated the development of our approach. We introduce the base model for "Purchase Request" business process enriched by Cabanillas et al. RASCI patterns.

Purchase request (PR) is one of the most frequently executed business processes in organizations. The process of PR starts when an employee creates a PR. Then, the employee may consult his Boss in filling the PR. Once the PR is sent for approval, the Boss of the employee receives the request; the Boss either approves or rejects the PR. If the PR is rejected, the process sends a message with the rejection of PR to the Employee. If the PR is approved, the process sends a message with approval of PR to the Purchasing Department (PD). The PD gets quotations and makes a purchase order. Figure 1 represents a *base model* for the "Purchase Request" process.

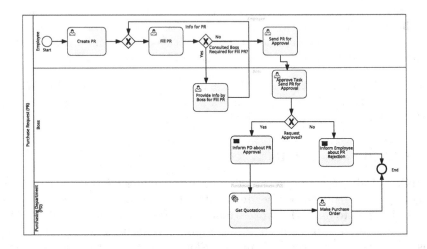

Fig. 1. Purchase request - base process model

The PR process may vary from one department to another as in the Ministry of Interior (MOI) — State of Qatar. We discuss in detail how these variants may be generated in Sect. 3.

3   RAM-Based Variants Generation

In this section, we introduce a solution for generating consistent process model variants based on RAM and RASCI-aware BPMN mentioned in Sect. 2. We present two RAM-based algorithms as follows: *"RAM Extraction"* and *"RAM-Based Variant Generator"* in the Sects. 3.1, and 3.2 respectively. Firstly, the RAM Extraction algorithm generates the corresponding RAM for a given base model. The base model has to be a RASCI-aware model. Secondly, we enable the user to adapt the Extracted RAM as in Sect. 3.1. Thirdly, RAM-Based Variant Generator validates the user's inputs in RAM. Finally, we generate the variant process model for the given base model as in Sect. 3.2.

3.1   RAM Extraction

The "RAM Extraction" algorithm is responsible for generating the RAM for a given base process model as in Fig. 1. RAM Extraction starts with reading the base model either enriched with RASCI-aware BPMN or Not. Then, it extracts the corresponding RAM from the base model. If the base model is not enriched with RASCI patterns then only the 'Responsible' pattern is displayed.

Algorithm 3.1. RAM Extraction.

Inputs: BM is the base model of a process
Outputs: RAM is the responsibility assignment matrix of the base model
Constants:
A represents the Accountable pattern, C represents the Consulted pattern, I represents the Informed pattern, S represents the Support pattern
Variables:
LS is a set of different lanes in base of process model
L represents one lane
T represents a task
RAM initially is "Two Dimensional Table"

```
1   For each L in LS
2     RAM.addRoleToCoulmn(L)
3      For each T in L
4        RAM.addTaskToRow(T)
5        RAM.updateCell(L, T, R)
6      End For
7   End For
8   For each T in BM
9     L = BM.getLaneName(T)
10    If (T.Name Like 'Approve Task%') Then
11      RAM.updateCell(L, T, A)
12    Else
13      RAM.updateCell(L, T, R/A)
14    End If
15    If (T.Name Like 'Provide Info by '+L+'%') Then
16      RAM.updateCell(L, T, C)
17    End If
18    If (T.Name Like 'Inform '+L+' about %') Then
19      RAM.updateCell(L, T, I)
20    End If
21    If (T.Name Like 'Decide if Support from '+L+' Required for%') Then
22      RAM.updateCell(L, T, S)
23    End If
24  End For
```

Lines 1–7 are responsible for constructing a RAM Table with 'Responsible (R)' pattern for the given BM. Line 8 reads each task in the BM. Line 9 get the lane name for the current task. In case 'Accountable' pattern exists; Update intersected cell between 'Task Name' and the Role to 'A' as in Lines 10–11. Otherwise, Update intersected cell between 'Task Name' and its assigned role to 'R/A' as in Lines 12–14. In case 'Consulted' pattern exists; Update intersected cell between 'Task Name' and the Role to 'C' as in Lines 15–17. In case 'Informed' pattern exists; Update intersected cell between 'Task Name' and the Role to 'I' as in Lines 18–20. In case 'Support' pattern exists; Update intersected cell between 'Task Name' and the Role to 'S' as in Lines 21–23. Line 24 exits while reach the end of tasks in the base model. For more details about RAM patterns, see "Appendix - RAM Patterns". Moreover, we will enable the user to configure other "Keywords" or "expressions" than the used in the algorithm for each RAM pattern.

Table 1 shows the corresponding RACI matrix for the base model in Fig. 1 based on RAM Extraction algorithm discussed in Sect. 3.1.

Table 1. RACI matrix of base process model

Tasks—Roles	Employee	Boss	Purchasing Department (PD)
Create PR	R/A		
Fill PR	R/A	C	
Provide Info by Boss for Fill BR		R/A	
Send PR for Approval	R	A	
Approve Task Send PR for Approval		R/A	
Inform PD about PR Approval		R/A	I
Inform Employee about PR Rejection	I	R/A	
Get Quotations			R/A
Make Purchase Order			R/A

We enable the user to configure and adapt the extracted RAM in Table 1 based on context. The users of different departments may apply different RAM patterns for the same task. Table 2 represents RASI as one of RACI's different variants. The assignment of consultation of "Boss" for "Fill PR" is replaced by another assignment. Firstly, we remove the 'C' from intersection cell Boss and "Fill PR"; colored with red. Based on this, the whole row for the task "Provide Info by Boss for Fill BR" will be removed also as this task is part of Consulted pattern; colored with red. Secondly, we add a new role called "Administrative Manager (AM)" with the orange color. Finally, we update the intersection cell between "AM" and "Fill PR" by 'S' for Support responsibility with green color. The new assignment means that the "Employee" delegates the task "Fill PR" to the "AM".

3.2   RAM-Based Process Variant Generator

The "RAM-Based Process Variant Generator" algorithm manages the issue of generating consistent process model variants caused by adaptations in RAM generated by "RAM Extraction" algorithm. RAM-Based Process Variant Generator validates the "Adapted RAM" as in Table 2. Then, it manipulates the base model using the "Adapted RAM" to generate consistent process model variant.

Table 2. RASI matrix of base model

Tasks—Roles	Employee	Boss	Purchasing Department (PD)	Administrative Manager (AM)
Create PR	R/A			
Fill PR	R/A			S
Provide Info by Boss for Fill BR		R/A		
Send PR for Approval	R	A		
Approve Task Send PR for Approval		R/A		
Inform PD about PR Approval		R/A	I	
Inform Employee about PR Rejection	I	R/A		
Get Quotations			R/A	
Make Purchase Order			R/A	

General Validations for RAM:

- For each task, there is one and only one role with Accountable (A).
- For each task, there is at least one role with Responsible (R); we assume also one and only one role with Responsible (R) for simplicity as configurable validation that may or may not validated based on user's selection.

Algorithm 3.2. RAM-Based Process Variant Generator.

Inputs: BM is the base model of a process; Validated Adapted RAM the output of RAM Extraction
Outputs: VPM variant process model
Variables:
RAMChanges[] is an array of changes to RAM
OPR represents the operation done for each changed cell in RAM Changes[]
CCV represents the value of each changed cell in RAM Changes[]
VPM initially is the base model

```
1    i = 0; VPM = BM
2    For each i in RAMChanges[]
3        OPR = i.getCellOperation()
4        CCV = i.getCellValue()
5        // OPR and CCV recognize the RAM patterns tasks relationships.
6        If OPR = Insert in Empty Cell Then
7            VPM.insertPattern(CCV)
8        Else If OPR = Delete from Existing Cell Then
9            VPM.deletePattern(CCV)
10       Else If OPR = Update Existing Cell Then
11           VPM.updatePattern(CCV)
12       Else If OPR = Insert New Role Then
13           VPM.insertNewLane(CCV)
14       Else If OPR = Insert New Task Then
15           VPM.insertNewTask(CCV)
16       End If
17       i = i + 1
18   End For
19   return VPM
```

Line 1 defines and initializes a counter for the array of RAM changes and set VPM initially to BM. Line 2 reads each change in the array of RAM changes. Line 3 retrieves the operation performed on the changed cell in RAM. Line 4 retrieves the value of the changed cell in RAM. Then, the algorithm checks the type of OPR. Lines 6–7 if correct, algorithm performs an insert operation for the desired pattern based on value in Line 4. Lines 8–9 if correct, it performs a delete operation for the desired pattern based on value in Line 4. Lines 10–11 if correct, it performs an update operation for the desired pattern based on value in Line 4. Lines 12–13 if correct, it performs an insert operation for a new lane based on value in Line 4. Lines 14–15 if correct, it performs an insert operation for a new task based on value in Line 4. Line 19 returns the generated VPM. These operations applied to the process base model using the RAM patterns as in "Appendix - RAM Patterns".

Figure 2 shows the generated variant of the base model in Fig. 1. Figure 3 shows the detailed subprocess of "Fill PR" with 'Support (S)' pattern and the added role "Administrative Manager".

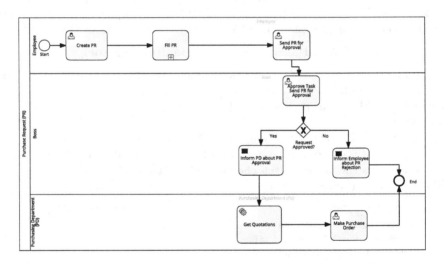

Fig. 2. Purchase request - RASI variant

So, we can conclude that the common source for *the variant* introduced for the process of "Purchase Request" before is the changes in RAM.

4   Related Work

Several approaches have been developed in recent years to manage the different variants of process models, Such as PROcess Variants by OPtions (Provop),

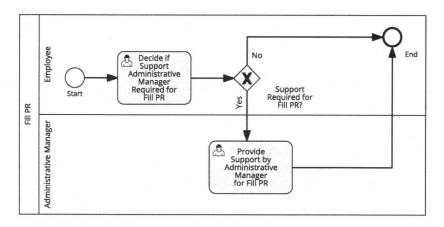

Fig. 3. Fill PR subprocess

Configurable Event-driven Process Chains (C-EPCs), and Partial Process Models (PPM). In this section, we state the pros and cons for each approach.

Provop is an approach for managing a set of related process variants throughout the entire Business Process Life Cycle (BPLC) [3]. In Provop, a specific variant is derived by adjusting the basic process model using a set of well-defined change operations [3]. Change Operations represent the difference between basic model and variant such as INSERT, DELETE, and MOVE process fragments, and MODIFY process elements attributes. Furthermore, Provop supports the context-aware process configuration either statically or dynamically [18]. The Provop lifecycle [19] consists of three major phases: the modeling phase, the configuration phase and the execution phase. Provop has been extended with a procedure to guarantee the correctness and soundness for a *family of configurable process variants* [20]. An extension has been developed for ARIS Business Architect to cope with variability in process models based on Provop [2]. Provop uses a bottom-up technique from process variants to the basic process model. Each variant is maintained through the base model only. So, the changes in any variant may not be consistent with other variants of the same process.

The concept of configurable process model has been defined by [4]. It merges variants of process models into a single configurable model. Configurable process models are integrated representations for variants of a process model in a specific domain. A framework to manage the configuration of business process models consists of three parts: *a conceptual foundation for process model configuration, a questionnaire-based approach for validating modeling, and a meta-model for holistic process configuration* [21]. C-EPCs are configurable version of EPCs, which provides a means to capture variability in EPC process models.

C-EPCs identify a set of variation points which are called *configurable nodes* in the model and constraints, which are called *configuration requirements* to restrict the different combinations of allowed variants in order to be assigned for variants called *alternatives* [21]. La Rosa et al. [22] proposed C-iEPC, that extends C-EPC notation with the notions of roles and objects associated to functions. C-iEPC supports variants from organizational perspective. C-EPCs uses a top-down technique from holistic or reference process model to process variants. Specifying all variants in a holistic reference model for a particular process is difficult to maintain.

PPM is a query-based approach that depends on defining process model views to maintain consistency among process variants [5]. These views are defined using a visual query language for business process models called BPMN-Q [23]. Based on BPMN-Q, a framework for querying and reusing business process models has been developed by [24]. PPM is using inheritance mechanisms from software engineering to make best use of the reusability as a concept of Object-Oriented Modeling of object orientation [5]. PPM approach provides support for consistency of process model variants, and allows handling issues for multiple inheritance levels. PPM uses both top-down and bottom-up techniques in handling process variants. Context issues related to variants of business process are not covered in the PPM approach.

Despite the significant effort that has gone into the current approaches to manage process models variants, the organizational perspective has many aspects still need to be studied. So, Our approach focus on RAM as one important aspect of organizational perspective to manage generating the process model variants consistently.

5   Conclusions and Future Work

This paper introduces an approach to manage the generation of consistent process model variants that come from adaptations in RAM. The approach helps practitioners, such as process owners and/or designers in generating consistent variants of their process models depending on the case in hand. The most significant finding behind the approach is the importance of the organizational perspective's aspects such as RAM. In this paper, we presented two context-based algorithms to derive variants of process models based on RAM. We applied the approach to real life process models to further illustrate our ideas.

In future work, we seek to apply the approach for more real world cases in different domains. Furthermore, we look for other aspects from the organizational perspective to complete our approach. Finally, a proof-of-concept prototype that validates the concept behind approach will be implemented.

Appendix: RAM Patterns

No.	Pattern Name	Pattern Representation
1	Responsible Pattern (R)	
2	Accountable Pattern (A)	
3	Consulted Pattern (C)	
4	Informed Pattern (I)	
5	Support Pattern (S)	

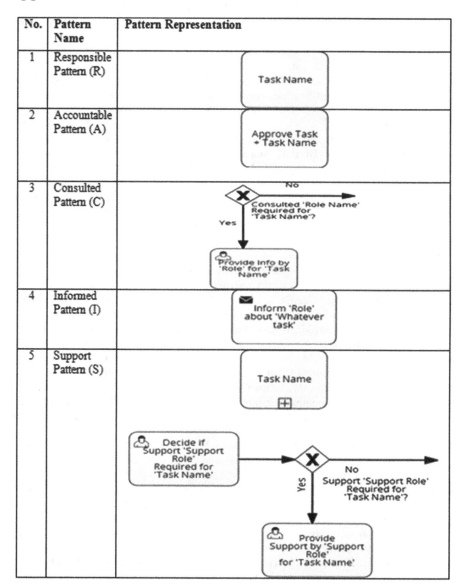

References

1. Dijkman, R., La Rosa, M., Reijers, H.A.: Managing large collections of business process models - current techniques and challenges. Comput. Ind. **63**(2), 91–97 (2012)
2. Reichert, M., Rechtenbach, S., Hallerbach, A., Bauer, T.: Extending a business process modeling tool with process configuration facilities: the provop demonstrator. In: BPMDemos, CEUR-WS, Ulm, Germany, vol. 489 (2009)

3. Hallerbach, A., Bauer, T., Reichert, M.: Managing process variants in the process life-cycle. In: ICEIS 2008, ISAS-2, Barcelona, Spain, pp. 154–161 (2008)

4. Rosemann, M., van der Aalst, W.M.P.: A configurable reference modelling language. J. Inf. Syst. **32**(1), 1–23 (2007)

5. Pascalau, E., Awad, A., Sakr, S., Weske, M.: Partial process models to manage business process variants. Int. J. Bus. Process Integr. Manage. **5**(3), 240–256 (2011)

6. Russell, N., van der Aalst, W.M.P., ter Hofstede, A.H.M., Edmond, D.: Workflow resource patterns: identification, representation and tool support. In: Pastor, Ó., Falcão e Cunha, J. (eds.) CAiSE 2005. LNCS, vol. 3520, pp. 216–232. Springer, Heidelberg (2005)

7. Awad, A., Grosskopf, A., Meyer, A., Weske, M.: Enabling Resource Assignment Constraints in BPMN. BPT Technical report 04–2009 (2009)

8. Object Constraint Language OCL 2.4 Specification. OMG (2014)

9. Tealeb, A., Awad, A., Galal-Edeen, G.: Context-based variant generation of business process models. In: Bider, I., Gaaloul, K., Krogstie, J., Nurcan, S., Proper, H.A., Schmidt, R., Soffer, P. (eds.) Enterprise, Business-Process and Information Systems Modeling. LNBIP, vol. 175, pp. 363–377. Springer, Heidelberg.(2014)

10. OMG: BPMN 2.0 Specification, Technical report (2011)

11. PMI.: A Guide to the Project Management Body of Knowledge: PMBOK® Guide — 5th (edn.), Project Management Institute Inc., Pennsylvania, USA (2013)

12. Smith, M.: Role & Responsibility Charting (RACI). In: PM Forum (2005)

13. Responsibility Matrix —RACI, RASCI, and More, May-2015. http://www.bawiki.com/wiki/techniques/responsibility-matrix-raci-rasci-and-more

14. Cabanillas, C., Resinas, M., Ruiz-Cortés, A.: Mixing RASCI matrices and BPMN together for responsibility management. In: JCIS 2011, vol. 1, pp. 167–180 (2011)

15. Cabanillas, C., Resinas, M., Ruiz-Cortés, A.: Towards the Definition and Analysis of Resource Assignments in BPMN 2.0. ISA-11-TR-01, University of Seville (2011)

16. Cabanillas, C., Resinas, M., Ruiz-Cortés, A.: RAL: a high-level user-oriented resource assignment language for business processes. In: Daniel, F., Barkaoui, K., Dustdar, S. (eds.) Business Process Management Workshops. BPD 2011, vol. 99, pp. 50–61. Springer, Heidelberg (2011)

17. Cabanillas, C., del-Río-Ortega, A., Resinas, M., Ruiz-Cortés, A.: CRISTAL: collection of resource-centrIc supporting tools and languages. In: BPMDemos, CEUR-WS, vol. 940, pp. 51–56 (2012)

18. Hallerbach, A., Bauer, T., Reichert, M.: Context-based configuration of process variants. In: TCoB 2008, Barcelona, Spain, pp. 31–40 (2008)

19. Hallerbach, A., Bauer, T., Reichert, M.: Capturing variability in business process models: the provop approach. J. Softw. Maintenance Evol. Res. Pract. **22**(6–7), 519–546 (2010). Wiley InterScience

20. Hallerbach, A., Bauer, T., Reichert, M.: Guaranteeing soundness of configurable process variants in provop. In: IEEE Computer Society, CEC09, pp. 98–105 (2009)

21. La Rosa, M.: Managing Variability in Process-Aware Information Systems. PhD thesis, Queensland University of Technology, Brisbane, Australia (2009)

22. La Rosa, M., Dumas, M., ter Hofstede, A.H.M., Mendling, M.: Configurable multi-perspective business process models. J. Inf. Syst. **36**(2), 313–340 (2011)

23. Awad, A.: BPMN-Q: a language to query business processes. In: EMISA. LNI, Germany, vol. P-119, pp. 115–128 (2007)

24. Sakr, S., Awad, A.: A framework for querying graph-based business process models. In: WWW, pp. 1297–1300. ACM (2010)

Extending Generic BPM with Computer Vision Capabilities

Adrian Mos[(⊠)], Adrien Gaidon, and Eleonora Vig

Xerox Research, 6 Chemin de Maupertuis, Meylan 38240, France
{adrian.mos, adrien.gaidon,
eleonora.vig}@xrce.xerox.com

Abstract. Leveraging Business Process Management (BPM) is key to enabling business agility in organizations. Video analysis is a nascent technology that allows for innovative sensing and understanding of a large family of tasks across many diverse application domains. This includes interactions between persons, objects, and the environment in domains such as Healthcare and Retail, as well as more general activities (e.g., in video-surveillance or Transportation). It can, therefore, enable better BPM by giving the opportunity to augment, complement, and improve the observation, description, monitoring, triggering, and execution of a broad array of tasks, including new ones that can only be described visually. This may be of particular interests in cyber-physical systems where interactions between human agents and artificial agents can be tracked and managed in the context of various business processes. This paper proposes a way to integrate video data and analysis into the control flow of business processes, in a way that enables the seamless augmentation of business process execution with information from the observable environment.

Keywords: BPM · Modelling · Computer vision · BPMN

1 Introduction and Overview

Cameras are now ubiquitous in public spaces, industrial sites, and workspaces (*e.g.,* warehouses). However, their capabilities are currently exploited through human vision only. This results in an underuse of the information provided by cameras, as they cannot be easily integrated into existing BPM suites. We propose to leverage **Computer Vision (CV)** techniques in order to *automatically transform visual data into actionable data for BPM.*

Our approach allows modelling the vocabulary (visual concepts) and grammar (interactions) needed to **represent complex processes by composition**. This allows the re-use of component models (*e.g.,* pedestrian detectors), composition rules (*e.g.,* spatio-temporal relations), and training data across domains. This also enables business agility, as new business processes (BPs) can be easily modelled by reusing visual components of other processes.

We also propose a specific model management approach to bridge the gap between the yet unconnected worlds of video analysis and BPM. This allows business experts to leverage CV technology for BPM, without the need for a CV expert or laborious

© Springer-Verlag Berlin Heidelberg 2016
A. Norta et al. (Eds.): ICSOC 2015 Workshops, LNCS 9586, pp. 103–114, 2016.
DOI: 10.1007/978-3-662-50539-7_9

manual description. We also investigate the impact of the **uncertainty associated to video-based observations** in BPM.

To the best of our knowledge, integrating automatic video analysis in BPM platforms is a novel concept with a broad interest. In today's state-of-the-art BPM environments, if one wanted to add computer vision capabilities, one would need to manually create all the connecting glue to integrate with some computer vision software and most importantly manually collect CV training sets for the *specific events* of interest in a *specific context*. For instance, a parking management business process that includes visual occupancy monitoring would require: (i) the collection of video data from each camera in each specific parking lot, (ii) a manual video labelling stage in order to build a per-camera (and per-parking lot) training dataset, (iii) a per-dataset learning phase to get per-camera individual visual models (*e.g.*, by relying on scene-specific background subtraction). This type of effort would then be repeated each time new computer vision support is needed (for instance to monitor different visual events), and in each context (*e.g.*, on-street vs. off-street parking). This approach is not scalable, neither in terms of cost (acquiring and labelling data is expensive and infeasible for each additional modelled event), nor in terms of usability (due to the re-designing from scratch of every new event model).

Our approach is different in that it entails a modular CV engine where various patterns are individually described and can be composed *on-the-fly for any (BP)*. To do so, we propose composition mechanisms accessible through APIs that are automatically employed by specific BPM elements. While some off-line pre-training still needs to be performed in order to enable the detection of *generic patterns*, the modularity of our method allows for the reuse and combination of any number of patterns to model arbitrary events. Furthermore, our approach significantly simplifies the usage in BPM, by reducing it to selecting CV elements and making simple parameter choices in their properties. In the previous example, our approach would rely on generic pre-trained car detectors (e.g., on the KITTI dataset [1]), reusing them across cameras and parking lots (or other contexts), in order to meet different business process needs (*e.g.*, occupancy measurement, entry-exit monitoring, or even different applications such as lane enforcement). Similarly, this generic pattern detection approach could be applied to a healthcare cyber-physical system where we might have human agents such as patients, nurses and doctors in explicit and implicit interactions with artificial agents such as video cameras, personnel and patient badges or medical monitoring equipment. Computer vision elements could then be used to detect and track such agents and interaction patterns. Their detection could be based on pre-trained atomic elements such as person detectors and then parameterised as part of their usage with information such as uniform colour, badge detection and others. Such CV elements could make first class citizens in processes such as reactive optimization of patient treatment depending on personnel and equipment availability, patient arrivals and other observable properties of the environment. Other types of processes that could benefit from such elements include room preparation and allocation, equipment management (to ensure availability at each floor for instance) or tool preparation and regulatory compliance in operating rooms.

2   Architectural Details

We propose a practical system composed of several components and interface mechanisms for bridging BPM and CV listed below and illustrated in Fig. 1.

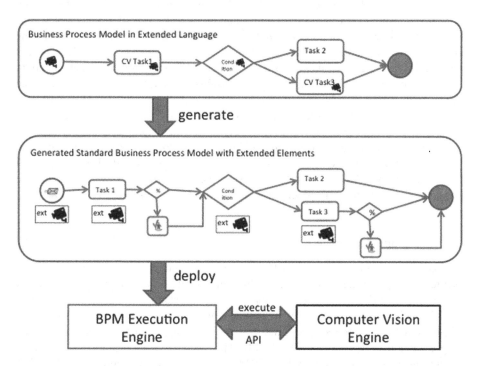

Fig. 1. Overall architecture

- A modelling environment for designing business processes that natively interface with CV capabilities (**VEPE: Vision Enabled Process Environment**). This comprises specific language extensions and BPM-type modelling support for bringing CV capabilities into business process design.
- A **generation component (GEM)** that takes process designs created in the VEPE and creates plain executable business process design models in a language understood by commercial off the shelf (COTS) BPM Suites. We target BPMN 2.0 here, as it is the most common standard BP design language. These generated models may include extensions added to the plain language elements using extensibility mechanisms of the standard process languages (BPMN 2 provides extension points for its elements).
- An enhanced **BPM engine (BPME)** for interfacing with CV capabilities at runtime when BPs execute. This engine will be an extension of COTS BPM engines that supports any extensions to the plain BP design models generated by the GEM.

- A **CV Engine (CVE)** using a modular approach that employs the expressivity and modularity required for interfacing with BPM elements. The CVE provides an API that the BPME uses to leverage the CV capabilities.

The process designer would create a BP diagram in the VEPE, which will have palettes of standard BP elements as well as CV-enabled elements. In Fig. 1 the starting element is a vision-event-based start, with some of the tasks as well as the gateway also vision-based. Task 2 is the only one not vision-based in this example, to illustrate the mix of plain BP elements with CV elements. The system would use the GEM to first translate this language into standard BPMN that is enriched with extensions that pertain to the appropriate CV extensions. These extensions are markers for API usage in the engine, with properties attached that correspond to API parameters. This generated model would also contain specific patterns automatically added in order to accommodate the uncertainty of the various CV events (in this example, a simple gateway checking for the confidence level and deciding whether to involve a human validation step or not). Lastly the generated process is deployed onto the BPME engine, which would employ the CVE for all tasks that require CV functionality by interpreting the markers and thus translating process semantics into CV operations.

2.1 VEPE and Language Extensions

In typical BPM solutions, once BPs are designed and configured with enterprise resources (people, roles, services etc.) they are executed and monitored by a BPM engine. The VEPE modelling environment could be a stand-alone process editor or it could be built on top of existing modelling environments such as the open source Eclipse BPMN 2.0 Modeller [2] or indeed any other graphical process editor based on Eclipse Modelling Framework (EMF) [3]. This includes a large variety of industry leading business process studios from IBM, Tibco, SAP, Oracle and others. If VEPE were designed as a stand-alone editor, it would have just enough basic process design functionality to cover the structural elements of normal process design and the needs of CV-based processes. The assumption with this approach would be that most of the business functionality that is not CV centric would then be enriched in a standard BPM editor at a later stage, after the GEM generation of the BPMN.

If VEPE is designed as an extra layer on top of existing process environments, it can add specific support for designing the CV processes in the form of additional dedicated tool palettes containing the vision elements, property sheets and configuration panels for the specification of the various parameters required by the CV elements, as well as any other graphical support necessary to highlight and differentiate such elements from standard BPM elements. Additionally, a specific decorator for CV could be enabled which, when applied to any supported BP elements would transform it into a CV element (e.g. by dragging and dropping a camera icon onto a BP task). In this case, the GEM would either run in the background, constantly translating the vision elements into BPM elements or would run when the model is saved for instance or any other chosen moments (similar to how a spell-checker could either be used as you type or when you specifically choose to execute it).

Language extensions are required in order to support the definition of BPs that use CV capabilities. The GEM would use them in the generation phase. Creating such language extensions may imply definition of new elements or extending and customizing existing elements. We consider BPMN 2.0 our main target in terms of extensions, as it is by far the most widely used BP design language, supported by most industry-leading solutions. It has basic extension capabilities that allow the enrichment of standard elements with a variety of options. Where such extension capabilities do not suffice, new elements can be introduced. The additional elements and the extensions to the existing elements need to be supported by the BPME.

2.2   BPME

The contribution presented in this paper does not aim to replace existing BPM engines but rather to leverage them through strategic extensions. For open source engines such as Stardust [4], Bonita [5] and others, extensions are relatively straightforward to implement as the code is readily available. For proprietary solutions, extensions can be added through special agreements with the vendors or indeed through specific APIs. In fact it is possible that any extensions required for CV be implemented as specific types of BPMN Service Tasks prefilled with appropriate data.

Adding the extensions would involve adding connectivity to the CV Engine using its APIs in one of two ways: The first option involves natively supporting them, meaning they would be first class elements of the engine (this would only be necessary for extensions that the GEM cannot map to standard BPMN). A simple option for most of the extensions would involve the intermediate transformation operation in which the BPs expressed with language extensions would first be converted by the GEM to a more classical form of BP descriptions before being executed by the engine. For instance in this case the CV Task would first be converted into a normal BPMN Task with prefilled specific parameters and the engine would execute it as a normal Task, by simply calling a web service that would be provided by the CV Engine. This can be achieved through a BPMN Service Task prefilled with web service information that points to a specific web service that acts as a façade to the CVE. More likely, a combination of the two options would be used, where a GEM transformation will generate an almost-classical BP process and the BPM engine will have minimal extensions to support very specific CV operations.

2.3   CVE and Uncertainty

The Computer Vision Engine provides the execution support for CV-enabled BPs. Its functionality can be divided in three main parts: native support for a video domain-specific language (VDSL) by allowing the specification of composite actions, patterns and associated queries using the elements specified in the VDSL definition; call-back functionality for triggering actions in a BP when certain events are detected; allowing the specification of rules in the observed scenes (to be then used for detecting conformance, compliance, and raising alerts).

A specific challenge of integrating CV capabilities in BPM relates to the inherent uncertainty that CV algorithms entail. Detecting an event in a video stream comes with an associated confidence level so the BPs need to account for that. For instance if the system if 99 % certain that a certain event was detected, we can consider that the risks that this is wrong are minimal and therefore the process can assume it's true. For a lower value (e.g. 80 %), the BP might need to have additional logic in order to deal with the lack of certainty, for instance by executing additional tasks by a human supervisor to double-check the data. Such handling may even depend on the nature of the task (for instance critical tasks may need a higher degree of certainty than others and in some cases a human may need to be briefly involved all the time for targeted double-checking of certain visual sequences). For the purpose of this contribution we take a simplified approach and provide a threshold-based pattern where humans only need to be involved in cases of lower confidence of video detection operations. Other more complex patterns can be used and added to the system as plugins to the GEM that will drive the specific generation of the confidence-handling elements.

3   Language Extensions

As described in Sect. 2.1, a number of new elements specific to CV need to be made available to process designers using the VEPE.

These elements are either available in a palette or they can be generated by adding the CV decorator (camera icon) onto existing standard BPMN elements. Regardless of how they are created, these elements have embedded CV semantics that will ensure their correct execution by the BPME using the CVE. Figure 2 lists a number of such elements showing the CV element, its icon, the BPMN counterpart and API usage indicator, pointing to the possible API that could be leveraged to achieve the required functionality. More elements could naturally be made available however in this contribution we do not aim to provide an exhaustive list of all possible implementations, rather to show that this approach can be achieved using existing technologies and standards. For most of the elements, the BPMN counterpart is an element as well, however the CV Task mapping to a complex pattern illustrates the variety of mappings that can be used. Once the mappings are decided, they need to be stored in a way that can be leveraged by the GEM, as the GEM will ultimately use this information when generating BPMN from CV process designs.

It is important to note that the GEM functionality can be achieved using existing technologies such as EMF approaches for model to model transformations. Even elements that are not specifically created as extensions for CV process design can still benefit from CV input. For instance, role assignment to a process or a task could benefit from compliance checking if the CVE has the capability to discern between various subjects in a scene.

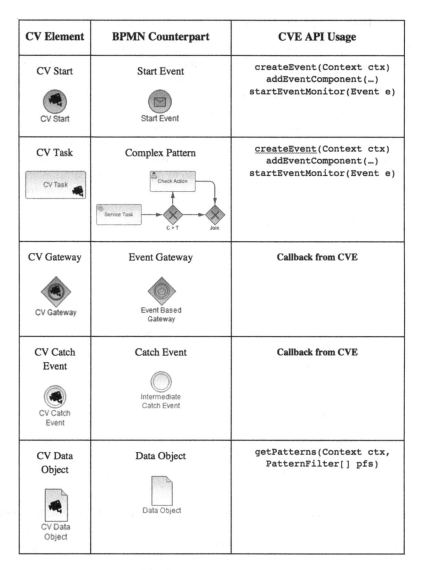

Fig. 2. Language extensions

4   Computer Vision Engine (CVE)

After generating a vision-extended business process model, a BPM execution engine can leverage the visual information available from cameras by querying a Computer Vision Engine (CVE). We first describe the internal components of the CVE, based on a Video Domain-Specific Language. Consequently, we provide the external API of the CVE used to formulate queries from the BPM execution engine.

4.1   Video Domain-Specific Language (VDSL) Elements

The diagram in Fig. 3 illustrates the different elements of our proposed VDSL. It organizes visual concepts in different entity (the *vocabulary*) and relation categories (the *grammar*) depending on their functional roles, their semantic, and their dependency on data. The first category pertains to **relations** applicable to visual concepts. *Geometrical transforms* (such as translation, scaling, rotation…) can be measured via image matching and optical flow estimation techniques. They are needed to describe the motion of objects and to reason about the dynamics of a scene. *Pairwise spatio-temporal relations* describe spatio-temporal arrangements between visual entities. They are required to reason about interactions, but also to represent the relative evolution of the different components of a process. Note that these generic rules (geometrical and spatio-temporal) are formalized *a priori*. Finally, *similarities* are measures of visual relatedness according to different predefined visual features (*e.g.*, colours).

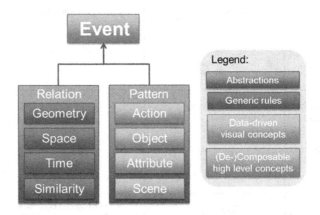

Fig. 3. Video domain specific language elements

The second set of VDSL elements we define are **patterns**. This abstraction unifies low-level visual concepts such as actions, objects, attributes, and scenes, which are *visually detectable*. *Actions* are the verbs in our VDSL, and are modelled using motion features. *Objects* are nouns modelled by appearance (*e.g.,* via edges, shape, parts…). Note that although this includes "persons", this important category of objects requires separate treatment in the internals of the CVE. *Attributes* are adjectives corresponding to visual properties (such as colour or texture). *Scenes* are semantic location units (*e.g.,* sky, road…). Patterns are data-driven concepts: their underlying visual detectors need to be trained on visual examples. Note that some patterns are generic (*e.g.*, persons, vehicles, colours, atomic motions…), and can therefore be pre-trained in a generic fashion in order to allow for immediate re-use across a variety of domains. Domain-specific patterns need, however, to be defined *by user-provided examples*. The number of such examples can be fairly low in practice, depending on the specificity of the pattern (*e.g.*, as low as one for near-duplicate detection via template matching) and on the availability of weakly or unlabelled data (*e.g.*, when using semi-supervised learning approaches). The third element in our VDSL is **events**. They formalize the high-level visual phenomena that the CVE is asked to observe and report about according to a query from the BPME. In contrast to patterns, models of events cannot be cost-effectively learned from user-provided examples. Events are indeed defined *at runtime* by particular *query* from the BPME. Therefore, we propose to *handle both the specificity and complexity of queried events by composition*. We detail in the following our approach to *modelling at query time an event* from the aforementioned elements of our VDSL.

4.2   CVE API

The BPME formulates queries to the CVE using the API summarised below.

A **Context** object holds a specific configuration of a set of cameras and their related information. It also incorporates constraints via a set of constraints from the BPME (*e.g.*, to interact with signals from other parts of the BP). The API allows filtering of the video streams processed (for instance to limit cameras to certain locations).

```
Context = {CameraInfo[] cis, BPConstraints[] bpls}
Context getContext(CameraFilter[] cfs, BPConstraints[] bpcs)
```

Pattern objects are *detectable* visual entities. They are accessible via:

```
PatternType = Enum{Action, Object, Attribute, Scene}
Pattern = {PatternType pt, SpatioTemporalExtent ste, Confidence c}
Pattern[] getPatterns(Context ctx, PatternFilter[] pfs)
```

The available patterns (actions, objects, attributes, and scenes) are the ones for which the CVE has a pre-trained detector. Note that these detectors might be coupled in practice (multi-label detectors) in order to mutualize the cost of search for related patterns (*e.g.*, objects that rely on the same underlying visual features). The pattern filter and context arguments allow searches for patterns verifying certain conditions.

Relations describe the interactions between two patterns:

```
RelationType = Enum{Geometry, Space, Time, Similarity}
Relation = {RelationType rt, RelationParameter[] rps, Confidence c}
Relation[] getRelations(Pattern p1, Pattern p2)
```

The Geometry, Space, Time, and Similarity relation types correspond respectively to a list of predetermined geometrical transformations (e.g., translation, rotation, affine, homography), spatial relations (above, below, next to, left to...), temporal relations (as defined in Allen's temporal logic), and visual similarities (*e.g.*, according to different pre-determined features) [6]. Note that these relations are defined a priori with fixed parametric forms. Their parameters can be estimated directly from the information of two patterns.

Events allow to hierarchically compose patterns and relations in order to create arbitrarily complex models of visual phenomena, *e.g.*, groups of patterns with complex time evolving structures. Events are internally represented as directed multi-graphs where nodes are patterns and directed edges are relations. Two nodes can have multiple edges, for instance both a temporal and a spatial relation. Events are initialized from a context, and built incrementally by adding relations between patterns.

```
Event createEvent (Context ctx)
Event addEventComponent (
Event e, Pattern p1, int id1, Pattern p2, int id2, Relation[]
rs)
   (add two pattern nodes with specified IDs and relations to the
event)
   CallbackStatus startEventMonitor(Event e)
   (instruct the CVE to send notifications each time an event
happens)
   stopEventMonitor(Event e)
```

5   Related Work

To the best of our knowledge, while there is a plethora of work around data-centric BPM [7] and context-aware processes (e.g. [8]), there has been no systematic approach to integrating BPM with CV. This is very likely due to the major challenges in BPM itself that have steadily been tackled by the community over the past few years and the typical approach taken in CV by tackling each new problem with one application.

In CV, event detection has been investigated extensively and multiple research directions to event modelling emerged [9]. Traditionally, events have been represented and recognized **holistically**. This involved the global classification of (pre-segmented) video clips [10]. However, understanding events that involve complex activities (*e.g.*, human interactions, sports, street scenes, etc.) requires reasoning about the spatio-temporal "structure" of the event, including interaction between agents and objects. To enable such reasoning, **part-based methods** were proposed. These methods typically define an event in terms of *event primitives* and their space-time *relations*. Two different mechanisms to discover these primitives are common in the literature. On the one hand, primitives are often pre-defined by hand and their space-time relationships are either learned or manually configured [11, 12]. Other approaches go further and learn the event primitives from data [13, 14]. The third and most recent line of research represents events using **attributes** by making use of libraries of reusable high-level semantic concepts [15]. Continuing this line of research, current trends are towards leveraging knowledge bases for high-level reasoning [16]. Existing methods to event detection learn *event-specific representations* from a vast pool of training data. Hence, the availability of training data is critical for these approaches and is often the major bottleneck to their generalization capability. In contrast, here we *reuse generic visual elements* from our VDSL across events by interfacing with a BPM execution engine.

6 Summary and Conclusion

This paper presents an approach to integrate computer vision capabilities in BPM in a modular, composable and generic way. It proposes a Vision Enabled Process Environment that allows new CV elements to be added to the BPM standard languages as well as graphical modelling tools for designing with CV elements. The approach also entails a model generation system for attaching these CV entities into BPMN 2 or other process description and execution languages. Importantly, the user *does not need to program the connection between the BPMS and CV*, instead, they simply select to use CV-enabled elements in their BPs, the connections being generated. The execution support is provided by an extended BPM engine that executes the generated processes. This support can be readily applied to any BPMS that uses an extensible standard such as BPMN, or to any engine that has extension points. It can also be added to BPM engines through partnerships with the respective vendors. Lastly, the CV engine supports the VDSL and provides the API used by the engine to leverage the visual information available from cameras *in a modular way*.

We have started the implementation of this approach using a mix of domain-specific modelling environments, open source BPMS and computer vision libraries developed in house. We believe that this work has great potential to bring added value to enterprise business processes in a cost-effective way by bridging process design and execution with visual information through modular computer vision capabilities.

References

1. Geiger, A., Lenz, P., Urtasun, R.: Are we ready for autonomous driving? KITTI Vision Benchmark Suite. In: Conference on Computer Vision and Pattern Recognition (CVPR) (2012)
2. BPMN2 Modeler. https://www.eclipse.org/bpmn2-modeler/
3. Budinsky, F., Brodsky, S.A., Merks, E.: Eclipse Modeling Framework. Pearson, London (2003)
4. Stardust BPMS. http://www.eclipse.org/stardust/
5. Bonita BPM. http://www.bonitasoft.com/
6. Szeliski, S.: Computer Vision: Algorithms and Applications. Pearson, New Jersey (2010)
7. Cohn, D., Hull, R.: Business artifacts: a data-centric approach to modeling business operations and processes. Bull. IEEE CS TC Data Eng. **32**(3), 3–9 (2009)
8. Moon, J., Kim, D.: Context-aware business process management for personalized healthcare services. In: IEEE SCC (2013)
9. Weinland, D., Ronfard, R., Boyer, E.: A survey of vision-based methods for action representation, segmentation and recognition. CVIU **115**, 224–241 (2011)
10. Wang, H., Kläser, A., Schmid, C., Liu, C.: Dense trajectories and motion boundary descriptors for action recognition. IJCV **103**, 60–79 (2013)
11. Gaidon, A., Harchaoui, Z., Schmid, C.: Activity representation with motion hierarchies. IJCV **107**, 219–238 (2014)
12. Sadanand, S., Corso, J.: A high-level representation of activity in video. In: CVPR (2012)
13. Pirsiavash, H., et al.: Parsing videos of actions with segmental grammars. In: CVPR (2014)

14. Tang, K., Fei-Fei, L., Koller, D.: Learning latent temporal structure for complex event detection. In: CVPR (2012)
15. Liu, J., Kuipers, B., Savarese, S.: Recognizing human actions by attributes. In: CVPR (2011)
16. Deng, J., et al.: Large-scale object classification using label relation graphs. In: Fleet, D., Pajdla, T., Schiele, B., Tuytelaars, T. (eds.) ECCV 2014, Part I. LNCS, vol. 8689, pp. 48–64. Springer, Heidelberg (2014)

Engineering for Service-Oriented Enterprise

Extraction of Topic Map Ontology for Web Service-Oriented Enterprises

Suman Roy[1]([⊠]), Kiran Prakash Sawant[2], Aditya Kale[3],
and Olivier Maurice Charvin[4]

[1] Infosys Ltd., # 44 Electronics City, Hosur Road, Bangalore, India
Suman_Roy@infosys.com
[2] Department of CSE, IIT Bombay, Mumbai, India
krnswnt@cse.iitb.ac.in
[3] Visa Inc Technology Center, Bagmane Tech Park, Bangalore, India
kaleaditya92@gmail.com
[4] Technical University of Munich, Munich, Germany
Olivier.Charvin@tum.de

Abstract. A Service Oriented Enterprise (SOE) is a new model of
organization linking business processes and IT infrastructure across the
enterprise. It can be enabled through the deployment of Service Oriented Architectures (SOA). At the heart of SOA are the services that
are orchestrated using message passing, action coordination etc., web
services being an example. However, there is almost no standard business semantics of web services which makes them isolated and opaque. In
order to provide a common understanding of business of each other organizations are using trading exchange languages like Universal Business
Languages (UBL). Although, these standards provide syntactic interoperability, they do not support efficient sharing of conceptualizations.
Ontology can play an important part here, by providing a formal approach to specify shared conceptualization, and thus enabling semantic
interoperability. This paper presents an approach for ontology modeling
for business process standards used in B2B transactions in web services
in terms of a semantic web formalism, *viz*. Topic Map.

Keywords: Service oriented enterprise (SOE) · Web services · Business
process · UBL · XML · Topic Map · Ontology · Tolog

1 Introduction

A Service Oriented Enterprise (SOE) is a model of organization whose business processes and IT infrastructure are integrated across the enterprise to

---

Olivier Charvin, then a student of École Polytechnique, PALAISEAU Cedex, France,
was an InStep intern with Infosys Labs during July-Aug'12 and Aditya Kale, then
a student of dept of CSE at IIT Kharagpur, did his internship with Infosys Labs
during May-June'13.

© Springer-Verlag Berlin Heidelberg 2016
A. Norta et al. (Eds.): ICSOC 2015 Workshops, LNCS 9586, pp. 117–129, 2016.
DOI: 10.1007/978-3-662-50539-7_10

deliver on-demand services to customers, partners and suppliers. It can benefit the organization by showing its agility to respond quickly to constantly changing business scenario. SOE combines internet technologies and business process management in a three layer model: Enterprise Performance Layer, Business Process Management Layer and the underlying Service Oriented Architecture (SOA). SOA consists of a collection of services communicating with each other through transferring simple data or coordinating on the same action. Web services provide the connection technology of SOA in the sense that it is designed to support interoperable machine-to-machine interaction over a network. However, there are commonly known inhibitors of web services adoption, which includes a lack of semantic consistency in business processes such as ordering and billing, and absence of work-flow mechanisms to orchestrate a group of specialized web services in support of a single web service.

In a global business environment of changing business values these days, organizations are finding it beneficial to interact with other trading partners for which they need to agree on a common business semantics in a web services environment. They should understand the business processes of each other and align the processes to the common need of organizations using a common language. Example of trading exchange languages are UBL and ebXML, - they define how enterprises can conduct business across the globe, removing barriers associated with distance and language with e-commerce facilitated by Web services. Universal Business Language (UBL) [15], an OASIS initiative, is designed to standardize common business documents as well as processes, which can facilitate B2B integration. It is sponsored by governments and tested in large-scale deployments supporting cheap, painless e-commerce transactions between enterprises of all sizes. It has a library of reusable components such as Address and Price, and a set of document schema such as Order and Invoice to be used in E-business, using XML. Although UBL acts as a medium of common language between their users, the XML documents reflect only syntax and not the semantics of transactions. Effectively managing the data stored in these artifacts is of utmost importance to any company for not only business accountability, but for information retrieval, discovery and auditing. Therefore, it is necessary to add structure and semantics to provide a mechanism for precisely describing data in UBL business documents. Such semantic information can be defined effectively through ontology languages like, semantic web initiatives [1], OWL, Topic Map [7] etc.

Ontologies are usually rooted in a logic-based formalisms which can capture precise and consistent descriptions of classes, instances, properties and associations, and reason about them. These ontologies include a wide range of models of varying degree of semantic richness and complexity. Topic Map, a form of semantic web technology is a standard for the representation and interchange of knowledge with a suitable query mechanism [7,12]. While DL-based languages like OWL-DL [1] reside on the upper level of the ontology spectrum, formalisms like RDF and Topic Map (TM) are at the middle level of the spectrum offering weaker semantic models. TM is simple to use, requires less storage space, renders easy visualization and facilitates faster query processing. Hence, for most of the business standards used in B2B exchange through Internet, we believe that Topic Map would be the appropriate formalism for ontology extraction.

We use a top-down approach for ontology design which starts with identifying the most general concepts, organizing them into a high-level taxonomy and system of axioms and proceed to more specific concepts and axioms. We first define a Topic Map model of entities in UBL processes, - the basic set of topics and associations of the ontology are defined, which is followed by constructing a Topic Map ontology for capturing flow diagram of UBL processes. In the next step, we ensure all the concepts in the UBL document schema are captured in the ontology. Finally all the Topic Maps are merged using common concepts/topics.

The paper is organized as follows. We shall quickly dispense with preliminaries in Sect. 2. While we provide a mapping of UBL processes to Topic Map in Sect. 3 we briefly discuss the translation of UBL schema to Topic Map ontology in Sect. 4. We undertake a performance evaluation of our approach in Sect. 5. A case study on Freight Billing process is described in Sect. 6. Finally we conclude in Sect. 7.

Related work. Semantic interoperability in business processes is one of the major themes in B2B integration in web services literature. Lenders and Wende [10] have suggested that inter-organizational business process design should be driven more by semantics. Gong *et al.* [3] identify semantic web technologies as important vehicle for integration and collaboration of business processes. Moreover, a semantic agent-based approach is proposed by them for achieving cross-organizational interoperability. Wu and Yang [16] mention the importance of ontology in business process design and provide a modeling framework for E-business in terms of building blocks that aid process automation.

There are works related to ontology development for business processes. Examples include ontology for WS-BPEL [11], OWL-DL ontology for business processes [4], OntologyUBL [13] to design an ontology for UBL, to name a few. In [6], Heravi, Bell and Lycett propose an ontology for ebBP schema with a view to capture semantics embedded within B2B processes, thus enabling reasoning over the shared concepts. However, none of the works provides a comprehensive ontology for B2B process interactions.

In [17] Yarimagan et al. discuss a method to enrich UBL with semantics-based translations for maintaining interoperability between schema documents. They propose a component ontology for UBL using OWL for representing the semantics of individual components and their relationship within schema. However, their ontology scheme is not easy to understand and not amenable to visualization. In this work, we try to alleviate these problems by using Topic Map for ontology modeling of UBL, which offers advantages like reduced storage space, less conversion time, easy visualization and simple querying. Topic Map has been earlier used for extracting knowledge out of UBL documents which has been later used for information retrieval purposes [8]. This work aims to sharpen and generalize the conversion technique defined in that work.

2   Preliminaries

Universal Business Language (UBL). In this paper, we are using one particular business specification language called Universal Business Language (UBL), which is an OASIS standard providing a library of reusable component schema defined using XML Schema. UBL comprises of business processes (activity diagrams with swim-lanes/roles) and embedded schema documents, containing a set of information components that are exchanged as part of a business transaction such as placing an order etc.

UBL is being used by several communities around the globe [17]. As UBL is being adapted in different industries, across geopolitical and regulatory contexts, it will be useful to customize UBL schema as per the need of user community. However, these customizations may be a hindrance to interoperability as communities may prefer using non-standard schema. With a view to providing a solution to this problem we propose a method to extract ontology out of UBL that can provide efficient semantic interoperability. This ontology extraction works in two parts, UBL processes are first converted to Topic Map ontology and then UBL schema are translated to Topic Map ontology. Finally these Topic Maps are merged to generate the final ontology. When two parties from different communities want to make a business transaction by using the artifacts tailored for their purposes they can still use them, and still maintain the interoperability by using the generated ontologies from these artifacts.

Topic Map. Topic Map (TM) is an ISO standard for knowledge representation and interchange with an emphasis on navigation and retrieval of information. As defined by the standard, Topic Map can be used to represent information as topics. It links topics together in a meaningful way to facilitate navigation and filtering of information [7]. In general, a Topic Map portrays groupings of addressable information objects around topics ("occurrences"), and relationships between topics ("associations"). A topic has three characteristics; names, occurrences and roles in associations. A topic can possess one or more names. A topic is linked to related information resources through occurrences. Moreover, a topic can be associated with other topics through roles in associations. While a topic can be an instance of zero, one, or, more classes, these classes themselves correspond to topics. An occurrence can be captured as an instance of one class, but not necessarily. Similarly, for an association. Some topics play a role in an association, they are called role playing topics or short role players.

3   Translation of UBL Process to Topic Map

UBL processes are captured using mostly the constructs of standard UML Activity Diagrams. With this one can associate a Business Process Diagram (BPD) which is based on flowchart related ideas, and provides a graphical notation for business process modeling. In a flow graph the control flow relation linking two nodes is represented by a *directed edge* capturing the execution order between tasks of a BPD. A *node* can be a task (also called an activity), an event or a split/join gateway. In a BPD, there is a *start event* denoting the beginning of a process, and *end events* denoting the end of a process. A sequence is made of a collection of nodes each of which has an incoming and an outgoing arc. The gateway (control node) is represented by a diamond with a '+' sign inside for an AND-gateway, and a '×' sign inside for an XOR-gateway. A *fork* (AND-split) and a *synchronizer* (AND-join) portray their usual meaning. Similarly for, *choice* (XOR-split) and a *merge* (XOR-join). One can define swim-lanes/partitions for these processes just like partitions for activity diagrams; swim-lanes depict those actors/agents that are responsible for execution of particular tasks.

We shall now impose a few syntactic restrictions on process models to reduce ambiguity and lack of well-formedness. A UBL process (or a process) is *well-formed* (like a well-formed business process in [5]) if and only if there is only one outgoing edge from a start event, and only one incoming edge to an end event, there is only one incoming edge to a task and exactly one outgoing edge out of a task, every fork and choice has exactly one incoming edge and at least two outgoing edges, every synchronizer and merge has at least two incoming edges and exactly one outgoing edge, and every node is on a path from a start node to some end node.

A pattern-oriented method of process modeling and retrieval was proposed in [4] using OWL-DL representation. We adopt a similar approach for ontology creation using Topic Map, wherein we decompose the process in several patterns and generate Topic Map descriptions for each of them. Then using the connectivity information of the processes we tie the Topic Map for the patterns together and generate the whole Topic Map. We also maintain a Topic Map model which describes activities, events, gateways and their hierarchies. In the end we merge these two Topic Maps to get the overall Topic Map for an individual process. We admit that the presented mapping is a syntactic one, however the semantics of control flow of business process can be captured rigorous formalisms (with higher querying time) [4] which is beyond the scope of this work.

We consider basic control flow patterns (as suggested in [14]) of business processes and translate them to corresponding Topic Map preserving control flow of the process diagram. We create some basic topics corresponding to events, actors, artifacts, activities and gateways which are connected to a main topic called "processName" through *contains* association. There are only two kinds of events: a unique Start event and End events. A gateway will contain Split and Merge gateways. Also a Split gateway will contain XOR-split and AND-split gateways. Same holds for Merge gateways too. In cases of process having swimlanes, Actors are modeled as topics contained in the Topic Map model. Moreover, an Activity (Task) can be connected to an Actor through *assignedTo* association. A Topic Map Model for basic process elements is shown in Fig. 1(a).

A sequence of two nodes is modeled as an association class called *sequence* which connects association roles *from* and *to*. Depending on the direction of the connectivity of two nodes, they are suitably connected to association roles 'from' and 'to', see Fig. 1(d). A Start event and an End event with succeeding and preceding nodes respectively are modeled in a similar fashion, see Fig. 1(b) and 1(c). An AND-split is modeled as an association class *AND-split* linked to

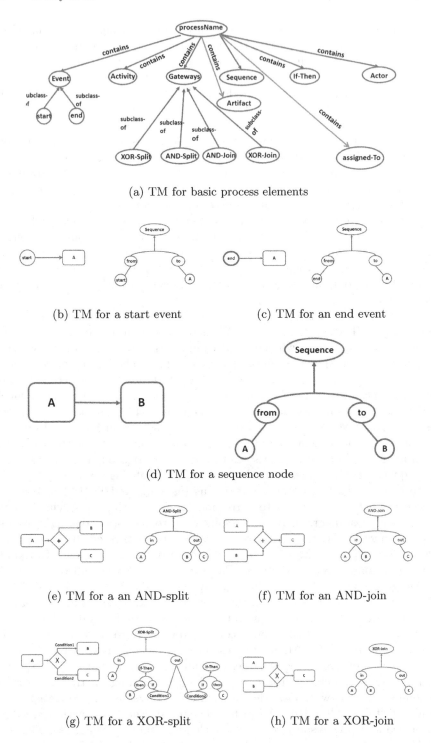

(a) TM for basic process elements

(b) TM for a start event   (c) TM for an end event

(d) TM for a sequence node

(e) TM for a an AND-split   (f) TM for an AND-join

(g) TM for a XOR-split   (h) TM for a XOR-join

Fig. 1. Mapping of process patterns to Topic Map

two association roles *in* and *out*, see Fig. 1(e). Similarly, an AND-join is modeled as an association class *AND-join* linked to two association roles *in* and *out*. The role 'in' will be connected to incoming node topics and the 'out' will be connected to one outgoing topic node, see Fig. 1(f). An XOR-split is captured like an AND-split, however the association role 'out' is connected to Condition topics. One association class *if-then* is connected to roles *if* and *then*. The role 'if' is connected to condition topic coming out of the split association role and 'then' association role is connected to the appropriate topic node arising out of the occurrence of this condition, see Fig. 1(g). A XOR-join is modeled similar to an AND-join, see Fig. 1(h).

4   Translation of UBL Schema to Topic Map Ontology

UBL makes use of a set of XML Schema documents to define various types of XML files that are used for B2B purposes. All allowed B2B communications take place via exchange of XML files adhering to these schema files.

Translation of XML to Topic Map. XML resembles a tree model, where in nodes are labeled and outgoing edges are ordered. However, Topic Map is based on graph model, where almost everything is modeled as a topic (node) which are linked with association, with other topics playing association roles. Our mapping exploits the relational structure of the XML schema and turns a link between nodes into an association. We assume that an XML schema (XSD) is always available with each XML document. The conversion can be divided into two tasks, TM model extraction from XML Schema and instance generation from one or more XML instances (see Fig. 2).

In many cases XML schema contains "import" or "include" constructs. UBL documents [15] have multi-layered transitive imports. Also, internal references are given by the construct ref in XSD files. These references are common features in XSDs and handling them could be problematic for any XSD to ontology converter. Our converter is able to handle internal references in XML Schemas, both in element and type. As a pre-processing step we remove import constructs and internal references using *schema consolidation* described in detail in [9].

(a) Topic Map model generation

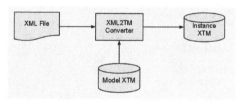

(b) Topic Map instance generation

Fig. 2. Architecture of XML to Topic Map converter

XSD to Topic Map Model. Each XML schema complexType is mapped to an association topic. For example, compositors like, sequence, choice and all are mapped to the respective association classes like sequence, choice and all.

The root member of this compositor is mapped to the association role 'has' which is linked with the corresponding role playing topic. For "sequence" type, other members are mapped to association roles member(1), member(2), ... in the proper order. In the case of type "all" each member is mapped to the association role member, while for type "choice" all the members are mapped to the association role altmember. Again all the association roles are properly connected to role playing topics. A role playing topic corresponding to has role will be linked with a topic via an association instanceof later. The other role playing topics are connected to occurrence topics suitably. For a simpleType compositor, the main element is connected to occurrence types which takes a particular occurrence value. An attribute or element declaration is mapped to suitable occurrences. Some of these occurrences may be an instance of a class. Model group definitions and attribute group definitions are specializations of complex types and hence, they are handled in a similar fashion. It may be noted that a type in a XSD can be suitably mapped to a topic type.

Cardinalities are handled in a special way. An element having minOccurs or maxOccurs with integer type can be mapped to an occurrence of interval type. These occurrences can be seen as a subclass of a topic of the set of all intervals of integers. In case of an element having only maxOccurs the mapped interval is bounded below with 0 as the left boundary point. Similarly, for element having only minOccurs the mapped interval is bounded above with ∞ as the right boundary point. Table 1 highlights the key aspects of the mapping.

Table 1. Mapping between elements of XSD and Topic Map

XSD	Topic Map
xsd:elements, containing other elements or having at least one attribute	tm:Topic Types coupled with tm:Association Types
xsd:elements, with neither sub-elements nor attributes	tm:Occurrence Types
xsd:minOccurs, xsd:maxOccurs	tm:Occurrence Types
xsd:sequence	tm:Association "seq" with member1,...,membern
xsd:all	tm:Association "all" with member association role
xsd:choice	tm:Association "choice" with altmember association role

XML to Topic Map Instance. There may exist several XML instances for a XSD file. All such XML instances need to be added to the Topic Map ontology. We only gather information related to actual values from XML files, as all other information regarding the Topic Map model ontology will already be picked from its corresponding XSD file. In order to uniquely identify each XML instance added to the TM ontology, we assume that the name of the XML instance file will be unique with regards to other such XML instance file names. Based upon this assumption we assign this file name, without the '.*xml*' extension, as the name of the instance which is to be added to the ontology. Further, this name will be used as a prefix for creation of instances of the topic types contained within the Topic Map model ontology. So if we have "*note1.xml*" as the XML instance file name, then we create "*note1*" as the instance to be added to the TM ontology. Also, if there exists a topic type "*person*", then we create "*note1_person*" as its instance gathered from the corresponding XML file *note1.xml*. This way we make sure that each and every instance file can be uniquely identified in the TM ontology.

The root element of XML file will become the top element of both the Topic Map model and the Topic Map instance, which are connected to XML elements through *contains* association. This will help in merging the model and instance Topic Map to get the final Topic Map Ontology.

Gaps in the Translation: Future Work. Currently we are not handling some language components like, abstract, final, block, default, form, wildcard identity constraints definitions and complexTypes derived by restriction from simpleTypes. Some of these are not commonly used, and others can not be handled using the current feature of Topic Map, which will not be detrimental for further development.

5   Performance Measures

In this section we consider performance issues for our translation. We used a laptop with Windows 7 (64-bit) on Intel Core i3-2310M processor with 2.10 GHz speed, 4 GB RAM and 320 GB of hard disk capacity for the evaluation.

We consider the dataset UBL-1.0[1]. The size of Topic Map generated for UBL processes are small in size, and hence we do not consider their performance. In this dataset we have 8 XML schema files, out of which only 7 contain the corresponding XML files. We consider these 7 XSD/XML file combinations for conversion. These schema files contain a very high level of recursive imports and are first subjected to Schema Consolidation and then the consolidated schema is given as input to the converter. The performance measures for the UBL dataset are given in Table 2.

Figure 3(a) shows a graph which compares the time taken for the conversion to XTM (Serialization of Topic Map) Model ontology with the Consolidated Schema size. This graph shows that as the size of the Consolidated Schema increases, the time taken for the Model Generation increases linearly. The size of the generated XTM Model Ontology also increases linearly when compared to the Consolidated Schema size. In Fig. 3(b), we can see that the performance is similarly linear for Topic Map instance ontology generation. We could not compare our result with that of [17] as we could not find an online implementation of that work.

---

[1] Available at http://www.w3.org/XML/Binary/2005/03/test-data/UBL-1.0/.

Table 2. Performance Measures for UBL Dataset

Dataset	Schema Size (KB)	Model XTM Generation (ms)	XML Size (KB)	Instance XTM Generation (ms)	XTM Size (KB)
DespatchAdvice	3846.74	3509	6.16	21.54	5629.18
Invoice	1393.73	1228	8.8	28.03	2439.86
Order	5182.27	4481	6.61	22.53	8238.43
OrderCancellation	147	183	1.23	5.15	239.46
OrderChange	5186.51	4509	7.25	24.7	8190.23
OrderResponseSimple	147	185	1.26	5.14	240.82
ReceiptAdvice	2974.95	2987	4.07	14.55	4398.74

6   Case Study: Freight Billing Process

Let us now describe a case study of a simple UBL process for illustration purposes, - Freight Billing process given in Fig. 4 which is bereft of any gateways. In this process diagram, while Send Freight Invoice and Receive Freight Invoice are Activities, Freight Invoice is a document interchanged between actors, Accounting Supplier and Accounting Customer.

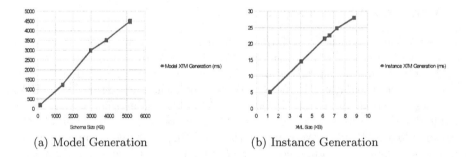

(a) Model Generation   (b) Instance Generation

Fig. 3. Graph of performance measures from UBL Dataset

For this Topic Map model; Event, Activity, Sequence and Gateways are modeled as follows. There is a main topic Freight Billing Process which is connected to topics; Actor, Event, Artifact and Activity through 'contains' association. Consider an example, where activity 'Send Freight Invoice' is performed by 'Accounting Supplier'. In the Topic Map we represent it by drawing an arrow from activity 'Send Freight Invoice' to the actor 'Accounting Supplier' through an association 'assigned-To'. Next we introduce association class named 'docTransfer' with 'producingActivity', 'consumingActivity' and 'doc' as association roles. In this process, activity 'Send Freight Invoice' plays the role of 'producingActivity', 'Receive Freight Invoice' the role of 'consumingActivity' and 'Freight

Invoice' the role of 'doc' in 'docTransfer' association. Moreover, the topic 'Freight Invoice' becomes the root element of the schema ontology through *contains* association. The resulting Topic Map is shown in Fig. 5.

For querying Topic Map, a query language called Tolog is used which is similar to Datalog (Horn-clause fragment of Logic Programs) and SQL. For example we pose the following queries on the Topic Map for Freight Billing Process.

Q1. List all activities in the process: instance-of($TOPIC, activity)?

Q2. Is activity Receive Freight Invoice followed by Send Freight Invoice: docTransfer(Receive Freight Invoice:producing Activity, Send Freight Invoice: consuming Activity)?

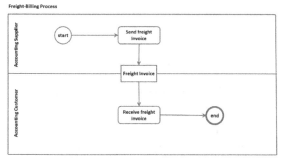

Fig. 4. Freight Billing Process

For each process in UBL we can extract an ontology out of it and create a repository of ontology for all of them by using a root topic element *UBLProcess* which would connect all processes. For generating transitive relationships, inheritance relationship and the like, among processes we can design some inference rules using Tolog, a sample of rules is presented below.

progeny-Of($El1, $El2) :- subclass-Of($E11,$E12).
progeny-Of($El1, $El2) :- subclass-Of($E11,$E13),progeny-Of($El3, $El2).

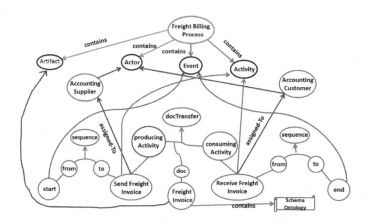

Fig. 5. Topic Map of Freight Billing Process

7   Conclusion

Our work can be seen as model-based ontology development [2] of SOE which will of be interest to KBE community as it is trying to embrace a methodological approach on the lines of software engineering with knowledge as its main focus. This approach advocates methods and techniques for knowledge acquisition, modeling and representation, and proposes method of extracting ontology automatically from models commonly used in software engineering such as business processes. Such kind of ontology creation will be useful for development and maintenance of complex KBE-based applications of SOE.

References

1. Berners-Lee, T., Hendler, J., Lassila, O.: The semantic web. Scientific American (2004)
2. Gasevic, D., Djuric, D., Devedzic, V.: MDA-based automatic OWL ontology development. STTT **9**(2), 103–117 (2007)
3. Gong, R., Li, Q., Ning, K., Chen, Y., O'Sullivan, D.: Business process collaboration using semantic interoperability: review and framework. In: Mizoguchi, R., Shi, Z.-Z., Giunchiglia, F. (eds.) ASWC 2006. LNCS, vol. 4185, pp. 191–204. Springer, Heidelberg (2006)
4. Groener, G., Staab, S.: Modeling and query patterns for process retrieval in OWL. In: Bernstein, A., Karger, D.R., Heath, T., Feigenbaum, L., Maynard, D., Motta, E., Thirunarayan, K. (eds.) ISWC 2009. LNCS, vol. 5823, pp. 243–259. Springer, Heidelberg (2009)
5. Hauser, R., Friess, M., Küster, J.M., Vanhatalo, J.: Combining analysis of unstructured workflows with transformation to structured workflows. In: 10th IEEE International Enterprise Distributed Object Computing Conference (EDOC 2006) (2006)
6. Heravi, B.R., Bell, D., Lycett, M., Green, S.D.: Towards an ontology for automating collaborative business processes. In: Proceedings of the 2010 14th IEEE International Enterprise Distributed Object Computing Conference Workshops, EDOCW 2010, pp. 311–319. IEEE Computer Society (2010)
7. ISO/IEC 13250. Topic Maps (2002). http://www1.y12.doe.gov/capabilities/sgml/sc34/document/0322_files/iso13250-2nd-ed-v2.pdf
8. Karjikar, F., Roy, S., Padmanabhuni, S.: Intelligent business knowledge management using topic maps. In: Proceedings of the 2nd Bangalore Annual Compute Conference. ACM (2009)
9. Lacoste, D., Sawant, K.P., Roy, S.: An efficient XML to OWL converter. In: Proceedings of the 4th Indian Software Engineering Conference (ISEC), pp. 145–154. ACM, New York (2011)
10. Legner, C., Wende, K.: The challenges of inter-organizational business process design - a research agenda. In: ECIS, pp. 106–118 (2007)
11. Nitzsche, J., Wutke, D., Lessen, T.V.: An ontology for executable business processes. In: Proceedings of Workshop on Semantic Business Process and Product Lifecycle Management (SBPM 2007), vol. 251. CEUR Workshop (2007)
12. Rath, H.H.: Topic Maps Handbook. Empolis, Gütersloh (2003)
13. The Ontology Forum: UBL Ontology (2003)

14. Van Der Aalst, W.M.P., Ter Hofstede, A.H.M., Kiepuszewski, B., Barros, A.P.: Workflow patterns. Distrib. Parallel Databases **14**(1), 5–51 (2003)
15. W3C Recommendation: Universal Business Language v2.0 (2006). http://docs. oasis-open.org/ubl/cs-UBL-2.0/UBL-2.0.html
16. Wu, B., Li, L., Yang,Y.: Ontological approach towards e-business process automation. In: Proceedings of the IEEE International Conference on e-Business Engineering, ICEBE 2006, pp. 154–161. IEEE Computer Society (2006)
17. Yarimagan, Y., Dogac, A.: A semantic-based solution for UBL schema interoperability. IEEE Internet Comput. **13**(3), 64–71 (2009)

Case Study Method and Research Design for the Dynamic Multilevel Component Selection Problem

Andreea Vescan[(✉)]

Computer Science Department 1, Babes-Bolyai University,
M. Kogalniceanu, Cluj-Napoca, Romania
avescan@cs.ubbcluj.ro

Abstract. The architecture of a system changes after the deployment phase due to new requirements of the stakeholders. The software architect must make decisions about the selection of the right software components out of a range of choices to satisfy a set of requirements. This work deals with the component selection problem with a multilevel system view in a dynamic environment.

To validate our approach we have used the case study method. Three different case studies were performed but only one is presented in the current paper. The research design was conducted using a research question, propositions and for interpreting the study's findings we have use the Wilcoxon signed ranks statistical test. The tests performed show the potential of evolutionary algorithms for the dynamic multilevel component selection problem.

Keywords: Case study · Research design · Component selection · Dynamic · Multilevel · Multiobjective optimization

1 Introduction

The problems of identification and selection the right software components out of a range of choices to satisfy a set of requirements have received considerable attention in the field of component-based software engineering during the last two decades [2,8].

Identification of a software architecture for a given system may be achieved in two ways: (1) Component Identification and (2) Component Selection. Component Identification has the scope to partition functionalities of a given system into non-intersecting logical components to provide the starting points for designing the architecture. The aim of Component Selection methods is to find suitable components from repository to satisfy a set of requirements under various constraints/criteria (i.e. cost, number of used components, etc.). This paper has focused on the component selection process, the goal being to provide the suitable existing components matching software requirements.

© Springer-Verlag Berlin Heidelberg 2016
A. Norta et al. (Eds.): ICSOC 2015 Workshops, LNCS 9586, pp. 130–141, 2016.
DOI: 10.1007/978-3-662-50539-7_11

After the deployment phase, the maintenance phase requires more attention and the software architects need assistance in the decisions of the frequent
changes of the software system. Thus, software maintenance phase is dedicated
not only to the removal of possible remaining bugs and/or release of new software
versions but also needs to consider adding new requirements (i.e., the stakeholder
need some new requirements to be added) or removing some of the requirements
(i.e., the development team found out that some requirements were not correctly
specified first or even not needed). So, the other perspective concerning *component configurations* refers to updating, adding, removing one or many requirements from an already constructed system. This represents the *reconfiguration
problem* [13], transforming the structural view of a component system, changing
the system's functionality. Our previous research regarding this perspective was
proposed in [11].

The **contribution** to this paper is **the use of the case study method and
the research design** from the book of Yin [14] to validate our research proposal
for the **Dynamic Multilevel Component Selection Problem**. A research
question and propositions are used to conduct research design. For interpreting
the study's findings we used the Wilcoxon signed ranks statistical test.

Our approach combines the multilevel configuration [10] of the component
selection problem with the dynamical changing requirements, i.e. updating,
adding, removing requirements (or components) from an already constructed
system [11].

Our previous studies analyzed the current state of art regarding the component selection problem and also analyzed the difference compared with our
approach. For more details see [9]. A similar approach considering evolution of
software architecture was proposed by [3].

The paper is organized as follows: Sect. 2 contains configuration and reconfiguration description problems, the description of the optimization process, and
the proposed evolutionary-based algorithm approach. Section 3 presents the reasons for using case study method and the research design, the criteria used to
interpret the findings of the results, i.e. the evaluation are presented in Sect. 4.
In Sect. 5 we apply the approach to one example to validate the proposed approach. Some experiments are performed considering two dynamics: requirements
changes over time and component repository varies over time. We conclude our
paper in Sect. 6.

2   Dynamic Multilevel Component Selection Problem

2.1   Component Systems, Configurations and Reconfigurations

A component [4] is an independent software package that provides functionality
via defined interfaces. The interface may be an export interface through which
a component provides functionality to other components or an import interface
through which a component gains services from other components.

A configuration [13] of a component system is described as the structural
relationship between components, indicated by the layout of components and

connectors. A reconfiguration is to modify the structure of a component system in terms of additions, deletion, and replacement of components and/or connectors. While the reconfiguration transforms the structural view of a component system, it changes the system's functionality and service specifications. From another aspect, a reconfiguration may consist of several individual updates or changes to components and/or connectors.

There are two type of components: *simple component* - is specified by the inports (the set of input variables/parameters), outports (the set of output variables/parameters) and a function (the computation function of the component) and *compound component* - is a group of connected components in which the output of a component is used as input by another component from the group. For details about the component model please refer to [10].

2.2   Dynamic Multilevel Component Selection Problem Formulation

An informal specification of the *configuration problem* is described in the following. It is needed to construct a final system specified by input data and output data. We can see the final system as a compound component and thus the input data becomes the required interfaces of the component and the output data becomes the provided interfaces, and in this context we have the required interfaces as provided and we need to provide the internal structure of the final compound component by offering the provided interfaces.

A formal definition of the *configuration problem* [10] (seen as a compound component) is as follows. Consider SR the set of final system requirements (the provided functionalities of the final compound component) as $SR = \{r_1, r_2, ..., r_n\}$ and SC the set of components (repository) available for selection as $SC = \{c_1, c_2, ..., c_m\}$. Each component c_i can satisfy a subset of the requirements from SR (the provided functionalities) denoted $SP_{c_i} = \{p_{i_1}, p_{i_2}, ..., p_{i_k}\}$ and has a set of requirements denoted $SR_{c_i} = \{r_{i_1}, r_{i_2}, ..., r_{i_h}\}$. The goal is to find a set of components Sol in such a way that every requirement r_j $(j = \overline{1, n})$ from the set SR can be assigned a component c_i from Sol where r_j is in SP_{c_i} $(i = \overline{1, m})$, while minimizing the number of used components and the total cost of assembly. All the requirements of the selected components must be satisfied by the components in the solution. If a selected component is a compound component, the internal structure is also provided. All the levels of the system are constructed.

The *reconfiguration problem* [13] is define similar to the *configuration problem* but considering the dynamical changes of either requirements or component. Regarding the *reconfiguration problem* [11], the dynamics of the component selection problem can be viewed in two ways: the system requirements or the repository containing the components varies over time.

2.3   Dynamic Multilevel Component Selection Optimisation Process

Our approach starts by considering a set of components (repository) available for selection and the specification of a final system (input and output).

The optimisation process begins with the *Dynamic Multilevel Component Selection Problem Formulation* (see Fig. 1 for details). The result of this step is the transformation of the final system specification as the set of required interfaces (and the set of provided interfaces). In the second step, the construction of the multilevel configurations is done by applying the evolutionary optimisation algorithm (from the fourth step, see Fig. 1) for each time steps (from the Dynamic Changing Requirements or Dynamic Changing Components step). The evolutionary optimisation algorithm is applied for each time steps (i.e. if there are still changing requirements or components) and for each compound component from each level. The solution with best fitness value is selected at each level. The fifth step presents the results.

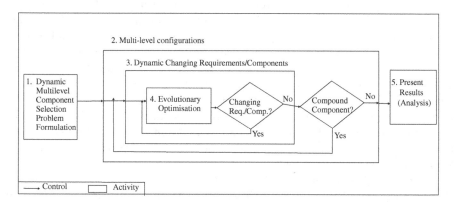

Fig. 1. Dynamic multilevel component selection optimisation process.

2.4   Evolutionary Optimisation

The approach presented in this paper uses principles of evolutionary computation and multiobjective optimization [6]. First, the problem is formulated as a multiple objective optimization problem having 5 objectives: the number of used components, the number of new requirements, the number of provided interfaces, the number of the initial requirements that are not in solution, and the cost of a component (group of components). All objectives are to be minimized. The percentage importance of each objective to the fitness functions are: 30 % number of distinct used components, 30 % number of new requirements, 5 % number of provided interfaces, 5 % number of initial requirements that are not in solution, and 30 % cost value. We have selected these percentages because of their impact in finding the final solution (number of new requirements will finally be 0 for final solutions (but is needed to be 30 % during the population "improvement" process). The number of provided interfaces does not play an important role in finding the final solution but the number of distinct components does. Also, the cost value plays an important role in selecting the final cheapest solution among many obtained.

There are several ways to deal with a multiobjective optimization problem. In this paper the Pareto dominance [6] principle is used.

Definition 1. *Pareto dominance. Consider a maximization problem. Let x, y be two decision vectors (solutions) from the definition domain. Solution x dominate y (also written as $x \succ y$) if and only if the following conditions are fulfilled: $f_i(x) = f_i(y), \forall i = 1, n; \exists j \in \{1, 2, ...n\} : f_j(x) > f_j(y)$. That is, a feasible vector x is Pareto optimal if no feasible vector y can increase some criterion without causing a simultaneous decrease in at least one other criterion.*

Solution Representation. The current solution representation was used in [11].

A solution (chromosome) is represented as a 5-tuple ($lstProv$, $lstComp$, $lstInitReq$, $lstNewReq$, $cost$) with the following information: list of provided interfaces ($lstProv$); list of components ($lstComp$); list of initial requirements ($lstInitReq$); list of new requirements ($lstNewReq$); cost (sum of the cost of each component in the chromosome). The value of $i - th$ component represents the component satisfying the $i - th$ provided interface from the list of provided interfaces. A chromosome is initialized with the list of provided interfaces by the list of requirements of the final required system and with the list of initial requirements with the list of the requirements of the final required system (these will be provided as implicit, being input data of the problem/system). An example is given in what follows.

A valid chromosome may be structured as follows: $Crom_0 = ((3, 4), (12, 24), (1, 2), (5, 7, 8, 11, 33, 30), (67))$. This chromosome does not represent a solution, it is only an initialized chromosome without any applied genetic operator. The provided interfaces (3, 4) are offered by the components (12, 24). The set of initial requirements are: (1, 2). By using a component we need to provide it's requirements: component 12 requires the (5, 7, 8, 11) new requirements and component 24 requires the (33, 30) new requirements.

Genetic Operator. Because the current paper uses the same genetic algorithm as in [11] paper, the mutation operator keeps the computation method. There are two types of mutations that ca be applied to a chromosome, depending of the chromosome "status".

If the chromosome still has new requirements to satisfy then the following steps will be applied:

- randomly select a requirement from the list of new requirements;
- add the associated provided interface of the new requirement in the list of provided interfaces;
- add the component that satisfies the added provided interface (a component is randomly selected from the set of components that offer it);
- remove the selected requirement from the list of new requirements, and add to the list of new requirements the requirements of the added component (if there exist).

If the chromosome representations does not have any other new requirements to be satisfied then the following steps will be applied:

- randomly select a provided from the list of providers;
- search if exists another component in the chromosome that could satisfy this provided interface.
  - If exist then add this component. No new requirements are needed to be added.;
  - If it does not exist another component to satisfy the provided interface then choose another component. All the dependencies of the previous used component are deleted and new requirements (of the new added component) are added (if exists).

The above chromosome after applying mutation operator has the internal structure:
$Crom_0 = ((3, 4, 8), (12, 24, 2), (1, 2), (5, 7, 11, 33, 30, 9, 10), (122))$.

In order to provide the 8th new requirement we have selected component 2. New requirements are added for the component 8. Each time the mutation operator is applied to this new chromosome a new requirement is satisfied by a randomly selected component (that can provide the selected requirement) and new requirements may be added due to component selection and dependencies. A final chromosome may be as the following:
$Crom_0 = ((3, 4, 8, 9, 5, 11, 7, 10, 6), (12, 12, 2, 21, 6, 21, 2, 21, 6), (1, 2),$
$(), (153))$. All the above mutation cases were applied to the chromosome described above. The selection of the component 2 for satisfying the provided interface 8 corresponds to the first type of mutation but the modification of the 24 component (to satisfy the 4 provided) into the component 12 corresponds to the second type of mutation. The dependencies of the 24 component were deleted from the chromosome (33 and 30).

3   Case Study Method and Research Design

The book of Yin [14] provided us with a strategy of identifying the method for our research project, showing when to choose the case study method and how to do research design. Defining the *Research Questions* is the most important step to be taken in a research study. In general, case studies are the preferred strategy when "how" or "why" questions are being posed.

Our Research Question: How and Why do Search-based Algorithms (in our case a Genetic Algorithm and a Random Search Algorithm) provide different results for the Dynamic Multilevel Component Selection Problem?

Another component of the research design are the *Propositions* that direct attention to something that should be examined within the scope of study. These propositions begin to tell you where to look for relevant evidence.

Our Proposition: The Search-based Algorithms (in our case a Genetic Algorithm and a Random Search Algorithm) provide different results for the Dynamic Multilevel Component Selection Problem because in the case of Genetic Algorithm the fitness of a solution is reevaluated.

Criteria for interpreting a study's findings represents the third component of the research design of a case study according to [14]. Statistical analysis offer some explicit criteria for such interpretation.

Our Criteria for interpreting the study is based on the Wilcoxon signed ranks statistical test that aims to detect significant differences between two sample means, that is, the behavior of the two algorithms. For more information regarding the Wilcoxon statistical test see Sect. 4.

After covering these components of research designs, the construction of a theory related to our topic of study will follow. *Our Theory development*: The case study will show why the Genetic Algorithm performs better than the Random Search Algorithm.

An issue related to case studies is referring to the generalization from a case study to theory. According to [14] statistical generalization is the common way when doing surveys, but in doing case studies the analytic generalization should be used. Multiple cases resemble multiple experiments and under these circumstances the mode of generalization is analytic. If two or more cases are shown to support the same theory, replication [14] may be claimed. The replication logic is analogous to that used in multiple experiments. Some of the replications might attempt to duplicate the exact conditions of the original experiment. Other replications might alter one or two experimental conditions considered unimportant to the original findings, to see whether the findings could still be duplicated. Only with such replications would the original finding be considered robust.

Our Replication strategy: The time steps for the dynamic changing requirements (Level 1) and for the dynamic changing components (Level 1, 2, and 3) were modified for Case study 2 and for Case Study 3.

Thus, we have selected the case study method and conducted three case studies, the first one is a real case study for constructing a *Reservation System* (reported in [9]) and the last two of them are constructed using artificial data (the current paper reports the second experiment and the third experiment is going to be published). For each case study we specify the component selection problem. After that, the experimental studies are followed for each considered case study: the two perspectives, changing requirements and changing component repository. Following the replication approach to multiple-case studies [14], each individual case study will be finalized by an individual case report that will be next considered to be part of a summary report, i.e. a cross-case conclusions. Thus, in our case the results obtained are reported and conclusions about the potential of evolutionary algorithms for the dynamic multiobjective multilevel component selection problem are drawn.

4   Interpreting the Study

When comparing [7] two algorithms, the best fitness values obtained by the searches concerned are an obvious indicator to how well the optimisation process performed. Inferential statistics may be applied to discern whether one set of experiments are significantly different in some aspect from another. Usually we wish to be in a position to make a claim that we have evidence that suggests that Algorithm A (Genetic Algorithm) is better than Algorithm B (Random Search). The Wilcoxon signed ranks test [5] is used for answering the following question: do two samples represent two different populations? It is a nonparametric procedure employed in hypothesis testing situations, involving a design with two samples. It is a pairwise test that aims to detect significant differences between two sample means, that is, the behavior of two algorithms. The best fitness value (from the entire population) was used for comparing the two algorithms.

The Wilcoxon signed ranks test has two hypothesis:

1. Null hypothesis H_0: The median difference is zero versus.
2. Research hypothesis H_1: The median difference is not zero, $\alpha = 0.05$.

Steps of the Wilcoxon signed ranks test: Compute W_- and W_+, Check if $W_- + W_+ = n(n+1)/2$, Select the test statistic (for the two tailed test the test statistic is the smaller of W_- and W_+), We must determine whether the observed test statistic W_t supports the H_0 or H_1, i.e. we determine a critical value of W_c such that if the observed value of W_t is less or equal to critical value W_c, we reject H_0 in favor to H_1.

Due to stochastic nature of optimisation algorithms, searches must be repeated several times in order to mitigate against the effect of random variation. How many runs do we need when we analyze and compare algorithms? In many fields of science (i.e. medicine and behaviour science) a common rule of thumb [1] is to use at least $n = 30$ observations. We have also used in our evaluation 30 executions for each algorithm.

5   Experimental Results

In this section, the proposed approach is evaluated and the results are reported. According to the book of Yin [14] and as stated in Sect. 3 we have conducted three different experiments. The first one was reported in [9]. The current paper reports the second experiment. The third experiment is going to be published.

5.1   Component Selection Problem Formulation

Having specified two input data (customerData, calendarData) and two output data (doneReservation, requestConfirmation) needed to be computed, and having a set of 150 available components, the goal is to find a subset of the given components such that all the requirements are satisfied considering the optimisation criteria specified above. The set of requirements $SR = \{r_6, r_8\}$ (view as provided interfaces $\{p_6, p_8\}$) and the set of components $SC = \{c_0, c_1, c_2, c_3, c_4, c_5, c_6, ..., c_{150}\}$ are given. The final system has as input data (transformed in required interfaces) the set $\{r_3, r_4\}$.

Remark. Due to lack of space the component repository is not described in this paper but may be found at [12].

Experimental Studies - Case 1: Dynamic Changing Requirements. As in the case of the first case study, we consider two types of dynamics and, consequently two experiments corresponding to each of them: the requirements of the problem change over time, and the components available at a certain time step change.

Five different time steps are built using artificially generated data and the dynamics at each of these steps are: T = 1 - The initial requirements, T = 2- Add one new requirement, T = 3- Add one new requirement, T = 4 - Remove one requirement, and T = 5 - Add one new requirement.

Performed tests. The role of the performed test was to see if the number of iterations and the population size play a role in finding the Pareto solutions. The conclusions about the findings of this type of experiments are given in Sect. 5.2.

Multilevel configurations. The compound components are next constructed by applying the same algorithm but with different requirements and input data. For the Second Level of the system the set of required interfaces is $\{r_1, r_2\}$ and the set of provided interfaces is $\{p_{18}, p_{19}\}$. For the Third Level of the system the set of required interfaces is $\{r_{27}, r_{31}\}$ and the set of provided interfaces is $\{p_{28}, p_{34}\}$. The conclusions about the findings of this type of experiments are given in Sect. 5.2.

Remark. We have not presented the charts regarding the influence of population size or iteration number in finding the Pareto solutions, because we have concentrated our findings in comparing the algorithm using the Wilcoxon statistical test.

Wilcoxon statistical test. In Sect. 4 we have described in details the Wilcoxon statistical test that we have use to compare our Genetic Algorithm with the Random Search Algorithm. In Table 1 we have the test results for the Case Study 1 - Dynamic Changing Requirements.

The Wilcoxon statistical test (see Table 1) shows that we have statistically significant evidence at $\alpha = 0.05$ to show that the median is positive, i.e. the H_0 Null-Hypothesis is rejected in favor of H_1 for all levels and for all time steps.

Table 1. Wilcoxon statistical test for Case Study 1 - *changing requirements* experiment.

L-T	W_-	W_+	W_{test}	N	W_{critic}	H_0	H_1
L1-T0	46.5	278.5	46.5	25	89	×	✓
L1-T1	93	342	93	29	126	×	✓
L1-T2	0	465	0	30	137	×	✓
L1-T3	0	78	0	12	13	×	✓
L1-T4	0	105	0	14	21	×	✓
L2-T0	38	152	38	19	46	×	✓
L3-T0	0	276	0	23	73	×	✓

Experimental Studies - Case 2: Dynamic Changing Components. As in the first and second case study, the repository containing components changes over time. This modification of the available components may be seen as an update of the COTS market, new components being available or other being withdrawn from the market.

Four different time steps are built using artificially generated data and the dynamics at each of these steps are: T = 1 - The initial components, and T = 2 - Add two new components.

Performed tests. The aim of the performed tests is the same as in the first and second case study: to see if the number of iterations and the population size play a role in finding the Pareto solutions. The conclusions about the findings of this type of experiments are given in Sect. 5.2.

Multilevel configurations. The compound components are next constructed by applying the same algorithm but with different requirements and input data. For the second level of the system the set of required interfaces is $\{r_1, r_2\}$ and the set of provided interfaces is $\{p_{18}, p_{19}\}$. For the second level we have four time steps: T = 1 - No modifications of the component repository, T = 2 - Adding three new components and removing three old components, T = 3 - Adding two new components, and T = 4 - Adding one new component and removing one old component.

For the third Level of the system the set of required interfaces is $\{r_{27}, r_{31}\}$ and the set of provided interfaces is $\{p_{28}, p_{34}\}$. The conclusions about the findings of this type of experiments are given in Sect. 5.2. For the third level we have five time steps: T = 1 - No modifications of the component repository, T = 2 - Adding two new components and removing two old components, T = 3 - Adding one new component and removing one old component, T = 4 - Adding one new component and removing one old component, and T = 5 - Adding one new component and removing two old components.

Remark. We have not presented the charts regarding the influence of population size or iteration number in finding the Pareto solutions, because we have concentrated our findings in comparing the algorithm using the Wilcoxon statistical test.

Wilcoxon statistical test. In Sect. 4 we have described in details the Wilcoxon statistical test that we have use to compare our Genetic Algorithm with the Random Search Algorithm. In Table 2 we have the test results for the Case Study 3 - Dynamic Changing Components.

The Wilcoxon statistical test (see Table 2) shows that we have statistically significant evidence at $\alpha = 0.05$ to show that the median is positive, i.e. the H_0 Null-Hypothesis is rejected in favor of H_1 for all levels and for all time steps.

5.2   Summary Report

For each individual case (also for those in [9]), the report indicated that the proposition from Sect. 5 was demonstrated, i.e. "The Search-based Algorithms

Table 2. Wilcoxon statistical test for Case Study 3 - *changing components* experiment.

L-T	W_-	W_+	W_{test}	N	W_{critic}	H_0	H_1
L1-T0	-8	47	8	10	8	×	✓
L1-T1	-7	48	7	10	8	×	✓
L2-T0	-52.5	200.5	52.5	22	65	×	✓
L2-T1	-75	303	75	27	107	×	✓
L2-T2	-36	315	36	26	98	×	✓
L2-T3	-85	325	85	28	116	×	✓
L3-T0	0	171	0	18	40	×	✓
L3-T1	-30	180	30	20	52	×	✓
L3-T2	-65	235	65	24	81	×	✓
L3-T3	-133	38	38	18	40	×	✓
L3-T4	-64	287	64	26	98	×	✓

(in our case a Genetic Algorithm and a Random Search Algorithm) provided different results for the Dynamic Multilevel Component Selection Problem because in the case of Genetic Algorithm the fitness of a solution is reevaluated."

Regarding the research question from Sect. 5, i.e. "How and Why do Search-based Algorithms (in our case a Genetic Algorithm and a Random Search Algorithm) provide different results for the Dynamic Multilevel Component Selection Problem?", the conclusions sustained by the conducted case studies is that the Genetic Algorithm provides better results than the Random Search Algorithm for the Dynamic Multilevel Component Selection Problem and that we have statistically significant evidence at $\alpha = 0.05$.

6   Conclusion

The current work investigated the potential of evolutionary algorithms in a particular case of multiobjective dynamic system: multilevel component selection problem. The case study method was used to validate our approach and the research design was conducted. Referring to the generalization from a case study to theory, three different case studies were performed but only one is presented in the current paper.

Our Criteria for interpreting the study is based on the Wilcoxon signed ranks statistical test that was used to compare our Genetic Algorithm approach with a Random Search Algorithm. The tests performed show the potential of evolutionary algorithms for this particular problem and for other similar ones.

References

1. Arcuri, A., Briand, L.: A practical guide for using statistical tests to assess randomized algorithms in software engineering. In: The 33rd International Conference on Software Engineering, pp. 1–10 (2011)

2. Becker, C., Rauber, A.: Improving component selection and monitoring with controlled experimentation and automated measurements. Inf. Softw. Technol. **52**(6), 641–655 (2010)
3. Cortellessa, V., Mirandola, R., Potena, P.: Managing the evolution of a software architecture at minimal cost under performance and reliability constraints. Sci. Comput. Program. **98**, 439–463 (2015)
4. Crnkovic, I.: Building Reliable Component-Based Software Systems. Artech House Inc., Norwood (2002)
5. Derrac, J., Garcia, S., Molina, D., Herrera, F.: A practical tutorial on the use of nonparametric statistical tests as a methodology for comparing evolutionary and swarm intelligence algorithms. Swarm Evol. Comput. **1**, 3–18 (2011)
6. Grosan, C.: A comparison of several evolutionary models and representations for multiobjective optimisation. In: ISE Book Series on Real Word Multi-Objective System Engineering, Nova Science (2005)
7. Harman, M., McMinn, P., de Souza, J.T., Yoo, S.: Search based software engineering: techniques, taxonomy, tutorial. In: Meyer, B., Nordio, M. (eds.) Empirical Software Engineering and Verification. LNCS, vol. 7007, pp. 1–59. Springer, Heidelberg (2012)
8. Iribarne, L., Troya, J., Vallecillo, A.: Selecting software components with multiple interfaces. In: The 28th EUROMICRO Conference Component-Based Software Engineering, pp. 26–32 (2002)
9. Vescan, A.: An evolutionary multiobjective approach for the dynamic multilevel component selection problem. In: The First International Workshop on Big Data Services and Computational Intelligence, in Conjunction with ICSOC (BSCI accepted) (2015)
10. Vescan, A., Grosan, C.: Evolutionary multiobjective approach for multilevel component composition. Studia Univ. Babes-Bolyai, Informatica **LV**(4), 18–32 (2010)
11. Vescan, A., Grosan, C., Yang, S.: A hybrid evolutionary multiobjective approach for the dynamic component selection problem. In: The 11th International Conference on Hybrid Intelligent Systems (HIS), pp. 714–721 (2011)
12. Vescan, A., Serban, C.: Details on case study for the dynamic multilevel component selection optimisation approach (2015). http://www.cs.ubbcluj.ro/~avescan/?q=node/178
13. Wei, L.: QoS assurance for dynamic reconfiguration of component-based software systems. IEEE Trans. Softw. Eng. **38**(3), 658–676 (2012)
14. Yin, R.K.: Case Study Research: Design and Methods. SAGE Publications, Thousand Oaks (2009)

Formal Modeling and Verification
of Service-Based Systems

Expressive Equivalence and Succinctness of Parametrized Automata with Respect to Finite Memory Automata

Tushant Jha[1($\boxtimes$)], Walid Belkhir[1], Yannick Chevalier[2],
and Michael Rusinowitch[1]

[1] INRIA Nancy–Grand Est & LORIA, Villers-lès-Nancy, France
particle.mania@gmail.com, walid.belkhir@inria.fr, rusi@loria.fr
[2] Université Paul Sabatier & IRIT Toulouse, Toulouse, France
ychevali@irit.fr

Abstract. We compare parametrized automata, a class of automata recently introduced by the authors, against finite memory automata with non-deterministic assignment, an existing class of automata used to model services. We prove that both classes have the same expressive power, while parametrized automata can be exponentially succinct in some cases. We then prove that deciding simulation preorder for parametrized automata is EXPTIME-complete, extending an earlier result showing it in EXPTIME.

1 Introduction

The simple and powerful formalism of finite automata (FAs in short) is widely used for service specification and verification. Considerable efforts have been devoted to extend finite automata to infinite alphabets: data automata [6], finite memory automata [11], usage automata [7], fresh-variable automata [2] and parametrized automata (PAs in short) [3,4], only to cite a few (see [12] for a survey). They have been applied recently to formal verification, see e.g. [8]. When developing formalisms over infinite alphabets, the main challenge is to preserve as much as possible useful properties such as compositionality (i.e. closure under basic operations) and decidability of basic problems such as nonemptiness, membership, universality, language containment, simulation, etc.

Our interest for simulation preorders is motivated by the composition synthesis problem for web services in which the agents (i.e. client and the available services) exchange data ranging over an infinite domain. One of the most successful approaches to composition amounts to abstract services as finite-state automata and synthesize a new service satisfying the given client requests from an existing community of services (e.g. [5,13]). This amounts to computing a simulation relation of the client by the community of the available services, e.g. [5]. Simulation preorder can also be employed to efficiently underapproximate the language containment relation (e.g. [9]), which has applications in verification.

Akroun et al. have used such classes of automata over infinite alphabet to model verification and synthesis problems for Web Services, and give a

© Springer-Verlag Berlin Heidelberg 2016
A. Norta et al. (Eds.): ICSOC 2015 Workshops, LNCS 9586, pp. 145–156, 2016.
DOI: 10.1007/978-3-662-50539-7_12

detailed study in [1]. Parametrized automata, a class of automata introduced by the authors, is shown to be equivalent to finite memory automata with non-deterministic reassignment (NFMAs) [11] in terms of the class of languages they can represent. We have shown in our previous works [2,3] how to extend the automata-based service composition approach to the case of infinite alphabets, also showing an EXPTIME solution for solving simulation preorder. Akroun et al. [1] further demonstrate that it is EXPTIME-complete. However, we also provide a simpler proof of the EXPTIME-completeness claim in this paper.

Contributions. In this paper, we first compare the expressiveness of PAs and NFMAs, in Sect. 3, proving their expressive equivalence. However, we claim and prove, that for many languages, PAs provide a succinct representation against NFMAs. We prove this by showing a class of languages for which the smallest NFMA that recognize them are exponentially large as compared to smallest PA that recognize the same.

We then prove, in Sect. 4, the EXPTIME-completeness of deciding whether one PA can be simulated by other, extending the result from [3], where its membership in EXPTIME was shown. We do this by providing a proof for the EXPTIME-hardness in this paper using reduction from Countdown Games, which were introduced and shown to be EXPTIME-complete by Jurdzinski et al. in [10].

2   Preliminaries

Before introducing formally the class of PAs, let us first explain the main ideas behind them. The transitions of a PA are labeled with letters or variables ranging over an infinite set of letters. Transitions can also be labeled with a guard, a conjunction of equalities and disequalities that permits to fire the transition only when the guard is true. We emphasize that while reading a guarded transition some variables of the guard might be free and we need to *guess* their value. Finally, some variables are refreshed in some states, that is, variables can be *freed* in these states so that new letters can be assigned to them. In other words, once a letter is assigned to a variable, this variable can not get another letter unless it is refreshed.

2.1   Technical Preliminaries

Let $\mathcal{X}$ be a finite set of variables, Σ an infinite alphabet of letters. A substitution σ is an idempotent mapping $\{x_1 \mapsto \alpha_1, \ldots, x_n \mapsto \alpha_n\} \cup \bigcup_{a \in \Sigma}\{a \mapsto a\}$ with variables $x_1, \ldots, x_n$ in $\mathcal{X}$ and $\alpha_1, \ldots, \alpha_n$ in $\mathcal{X} \cup \Sigma$, for some $n \in \mathbb{N}$. We call $\{x_1, \ldots, x_n\}$ its *proper domain*, and denote it by $dom(\sigma)$. We denote by $Dom(\sigma)$ the set $dom(\sigma) \cup \Sigma$, and by $codom(\sigma)$ the set $\{a \in \Sigma \mid \exists x \in dom(\sigma) \text{ s.t. } \sigma(x) = a\}$. If all the $\alpha_i, i = 1 \ldots n$ are letters then we say that σ is ground. The empty substitution (*i.e.*, with an empty proper domain) is denoted by $\emptyset$. The set of substitutions from $\mathcal{X} \cup \Sigma$ to a set A is denoted by $\zeta_{\mathcal{X},A}$, or by $\zeta_{\mathcal{X}}$, or simply by ζ if there is no ambiguity. If σ_1 and σ_2 are substitutions that coincide on the domain $dom(\sigma_1) \cap dom(\sigma_2)$, then

$\sigma_1 \cup \sigma_2$ denotes their union in the usual sense. If $dom(\sigma_1) \cap dom(\sigma_2) = \emptyset$ then we denote by $\sigma_1 \uplus \sigma_2$ their *disjoint* union. We define the function $\mathcal{V} : \Sigma \cup \mathcal{X} \longrightarrow \mathcal{P}(\mathcal{X})$ by $\mathcal{V}(\alpha) = \{\alpha\}$ if $\alpha \in \mathcal{X}$, and $\mathcal{V}(\alpha) = \emptyset$, otherwise. For a function $F : A \to B$, and $A' \subseteq A$, the restriction of F on A' is denoted by $F_{|A'}$. For $n \in \mathbb{N}^+$, we denote by $[n]$ the set $\{1, \ldots, n\}$.

2.2   Parametrized Automata

Firstly, we introduce the syntax and semantics of guards.

Definition 1. *The set $\mathbb{G}$ of guards over $\Sigma \cup \mathcal{X}$, where Σ is an infinite set of letters and $\mathcal{X}$ is a finite set of variables, is inductively defined as follows:*

$$G := \texttt{true} \mid \alpha = \beta \mid \alpha \neq \beta \mid \mathsf{G} \wedge \mathsf{G},$$

where $\alpha, \beta \in \Sigma \cup \mathcal{X}$. We write $\sigma \models g$ if a substitution σ satisfies a guard g.

Note that a disjunction of guard expressions here is equivalent to multiple parallel edges, with those guards, as a result of Non-determinism.

For a guard g, we denote the set of variables used in g with $\mathcal{V}(g)$ and the set of constants used in g with Σ_g, which can be defined inductively over guard expressions. Substitutions can be applied similarly, inductively, and we write $\sigma \vdash g$ if there exists a substitution γ s.t. $\sigma \uplus \gamma \models g$.

The formal definition of PAs follows.

Definition 2. *A PA is a tuple $\mathcal{A} = \langle \Sigma, \mathcal{X}, Q, Q_0, \delta, F, \kappa \rangle$ where*

- *Σ is an infinite set of letters,*
- *$\mathcal{X}$ is a finite set of variables,*
- *Q is a finite set of states,*
- *$Q_0 \subseteq Q$ is a set of initial states,*
- *$\delta : Q \times (\Sigma_\mathcal{A} \cup \mathcal{X} \cup \{\varepsilon\}) \times \mathbb{G} \to 2^Q$ is a transition function where $\Sigma_\mathcal{A}$ is a finite subset of Σ,*
- *$F \subseteq Q$ is a set of accepting states, and*
- *$\kappa : \mathcal{X} \to 2^Q$ is called the refreshing function.*

The run of a PA is defined over *configurations*. A *configuration* is defined as a pair (γ, q) where γ is a substitution such that for all variables x in $dom(\gamma)$, $\gamma(x)$ can be interpreted as the current value of x, and $q \in Q$ is a state of the PA.

Intuitively, when a PA $\mathcal{A}$ is in state q, and (γ, q) is the current configuration, and there is a transition $q \xrightarrow{\alpha, g} q'$ in $\mathcal{A}$ then:

(i) if α is a free variable (i.e. $\alpha \in \mathcal{X} \setminus dom(\gamma)$) then α stores the input letter and some values for all the other free variables of $\gamma(g)$ are *guessed* such that $\gamma(g)$ holds, and $\mathcal{A}$ enters the state $q' \in \delta(q, \alpha, g)$,

(ii) if α is a bound variable or a letter (i.e. $\alpha \in Dom(\gamma)$) and $\gamma(\alpha)$ is equal to the input letter l then some values for all the free variables of $\gamma(g)$ are *guessed* such that $\gamma(g)$ holds, and $\mathcal{A}$ enters the state $q' \in \delta(q, \alpha, g)$.

Fig. 1. Two PAs $\mathcal{A}_1$ and $\mathcal{A}_2$ where the variable y_1 is refreshed in the state p, and the variables x_2, y_2 are refreshed in the state q.

Example 1. Let $\mathcal{A}_1$ and $\mathcal{A}_2$ be the PAs depicted above in Fig. 1 where the variable y_1 is refreshed in the state p, and the variables x_2, y_2 are refreshed in the state q. That is, $\mathcal{A}_1 = \langle \Sigma, \{x_1, y_1\}, \{p, p'\}, \{p\}, \delta_1, \{p'\}, \kappa_1 \rangle$ with

$$\begin{cases} \delta_1(p, y_1, (y_1 \neq x_1)) = \{p\} \text{ and } \delta_1(p, x_1, \texttt{true}) = \{p'\}, \text{ and} \\ \kappa_1(y_1) = \{p\} \end{cases}$$

And $\mathcal{A}_2 = \langle \Sigma, \{x_2, y_2\}, \{q, q'\}, \{q\}, \delta_2, \{q'\}, \kappa_2 \rangle$ with

$$\begin{cases} \delta_2(q, x_2, \texttt{true}) = \{q'\} \text{ and } \delta_2(q', y_2, (y_2 \neq x_2)) = \{q\}, \text{ and} \\ \kappa_2(x_2) = \kappa_2(y_2) = \{q\}. \end{cases}$$

We notice that while making the first loop over the state p of $\mathcal{A}_1$, the variable x_1 of the guard $(y_1 \neq x_1)$ is free and its value is guessed. Then the variable y_1 is refreshed in p, and at each loop the input letter should be different from the value of the variable x_1 already guessed. More precisely, the behaviour of $\mathcal{A}_1$ on an input word is as follows. Being in the initial state p, either

– the automaton makes the transition $p \xrightarrow{x_1} p'$ by reading the input symbol and binding the variable x_1 to this input symbol, then enters the state p'. Or,
– the automaton makes the transition $p \xrightarrow{y_1, y_1 \neq x_1} p$ by:
  1. reading the input symbol and binding the variable y_1 to it,
  2. guessing a symbol in Σ that is different from the input symbol (i.e. the value of x_1) and binds the variable y_1 to the guessed symbol, then enters the state p,
  3. in the state p the variable y_1 is refreshed, that is, it is no longer bound to the input symbol. Then, start again.

We illustrate the run of $\mathcal{A}_1$ on the word $w = abbc$, starting from the initial configuration $(\emptyset, p)$ as follows:

$$(\emptyset, p) \xrightarrow{a} (\{x_1 \mapsto c\}, p) \xrightarrow{b} (\{x_1 \mapsto c\}, p) \xrightarrow{b} (\{x_1 \mapsto c\}, p) \xrightarrow{c} (\{x_1 \mapsto c\}, p')$$

Notice that the variable y_1 does not appear in any of the configurations of this run since it is refreshed in the state p. Hence, the language $\mathcal{L}(\mathcal{A}_1)$ consists of all the words in Σ^* in which the last letter is different from all the other letters. By following similar reasoning, we get $\mathcal{L}(\mathcal{A}_2) = \{w_1 w_1' \cdots w_n w_n' \mid w_i, w_i' \in \Sigma, n \geq 1$, and $w_i \neq w_i', \forall i \in [n]\}$. This language can be recognized by an NFMA [11] but not by a fresh-variable automaton [2].

3   Comparison Between PAs and NFMAs

In this section, we show that parametrized automata (PAs) and finite-memory automata with non-deterministic reassignment (NFMAs), which are discussed in [11], have the same expressive power (i.e. for any language over infinite alphabet, there exists an NFMA recognizing it iff there exists a PA that recognizes it), but there are languages for which PAs can be exponentially more succinct than NFMAs.

3.1   Expressiveness

We recall that an NFMA (as defined in [11]) is a 8-tuple $\mathcal{F} = \langle \Sigma, k, Q, q_0, \boldsymbol{u}, \rho, \delta, F \rangle$ where $k \in \mathbb{N}^+$ is the number of registers, Q is a finite set of states, $q_0 \in Q$ is the initial state, $\boldsymbol{u} : [k] \rightharpoonup \Sigma$ is a partial function called the *initial assignment* of the k registers, $\rho : \{(p,q) : (p, \varepsilon, q) \in \delta\} \rightharpoonup [k]$ is a function called the *non-deterministic reassignment*, $\delta : Q \times ([k] \cup \{\varepsilon\}) \times Q$ is the *transition relation*, and $F \subseteq Q$ is the set of final states. Intuitively, if $\mathcal{F}$ is in state p, and there is an ε-transition from p to q and $\rho(p,q) = l$, then $\mathcal{F}$ can non-deterministically replace the content of the lth register with an element of Σ not occurring in any other register and enter state q. However, if $\mathcal{F}$ is in state p, and the input symbol is equal to the content of the lth register and $(p, l, q) \in \delta$ then $\mathcal{F}$ may enter state q and pass to the next input symbol. An ε-transition $(p, \varepsilon, q) \in \delta$ with $\rho(p,q) = l$, for a register $l \in [k]$, is denoted by $(p, \varepsilon/l, q)$.

Interpreting registers of the NFMAs as variables, the semantics of NFMAs can be given as a relation over configurations of the form (q, σ) where q is a state of the NFMA and σ is a substitution of registers with letters.

It is easy to see, as illustrated in Fig. 2, that any NFMA (with k registers) can be translated into a PA (with k variables) of linear size, that recognizes the

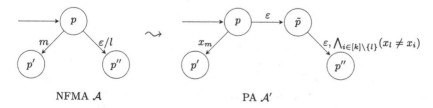

NFMA $\mathcal{A}$ PA $\mathcal{A}'$

Fig. 2. A translation schema of NFMA to PA. The registers of the NFMA $\mathcal{A}$ are $\{1, \ldots, k\}$, they correspond to the variables $\{x_1, \ldots, x_k\}$ of the PA $\mathcal{A}'$. The variable x_l is refreshed in the state $\tilde{p}$ of $\mathcal{A}'$.

same language. More precisely, as shown in Fig. 2: (i) a transition (p, m, p') of the NFMA is translated as such, i.e. to (p, x_m, p'); and, (ii) a transition $(p, \varepsilon/l, p'')$ of the NFMA is translated to two transitions $(p, \varepsilon, \tilde{p})$ and $(\tilde{p}, (x_l, g), p'')$ where $g = \bigwedge_{i \in [k] \setminus \{l\}} (x_l \neq x_i)$ and x_l is refreshed in state $\tilde{p}$.

Lemma 1. *For any NFMA over Σ with k registers and q states, there exists a corresponding PA with k variables and number of states linear in q, that recognizes the same language.*

We show next that a PA can be translated into an NFMA recognizing the same language, by introducing an intermediary class of PAs, called $\overline{PA}$s, in which the variables should have distinct values. The idea is that the ε-transitions of the NFMA are used to encode the refreshing of the variables of the $\overline{PA}$s, which are translated into NFMA.

Definition 3. *Let $\overline{PA}$s be the subclass of PAs such that every $\mathcal{A}$ in $\overline{PA}$s, verifies i) $\mathcal{A}$ has no constants, i.e. $\Sigma_{\mathcal{A}} = \emptyset$, and ii) for every reachable configuration (σ, q) of $\mathcal{A}$ and for all $x, y \in dom(\sigma)$, $\sigma(x) \neq \sigma(y)$.*

It can be shown that PAs and $\overline{PA}$s recognize the same language, more precisely we have:

Lemma 2. *For every PA $\mathcal{A}$ with k variables and n states there is a $\overline{PA}$ with $k + m$ variables and $O(n \cdot (k + m)!)$ states recognizing the same languages, where $m = |\Sigma_{\mathcal{A}}|$.*

For the proof and construction of the same, let $\mathcal{X}$ and $\mathcal{X}'$ be two disjoint sets of variables, and let ψ be a total function from $\mathcal{X}$ to $\mathcal{X}'$, and let g be a conjunction of equalities between variables in $\mathcal{X}$. Then define $g \sqsubset \psi$ iff there exists $x' \in \mathcal{X}'$ s.t. $\psi(x) = x'$ for all x in $\mathcal{V}(g)$. And let $\mathcal{A} = \langle \Sigma, \mathcal{X}, Q, Q_0, \delta, F, \kappa \rangle$ be a PA with $\mathcal{X} = \{x_1, \ldots, x_k\}$.

Firstly, we transform the PA $\mathcal{A}$ into a PA $\boldsymbol{\mathcal{A}}$ recognizing the same language and in which each state is labeled with the set of variables being free in this state. We define $\boldsymbol{\mathcal{A}} = \langle \Sigma, \mathcal{X}, \boldsymbol{Q}, \boldsymbol{Q_0}, \boldsymbol{F}, \boldsymbol{\delta}, \boldsymbol{\kappa} \rangle$ by:

$$\begin{cases} \boldsymbol{Q} & = \{(q, X) \mid q \in Q \text{ and } X \subseteq \mathcal{X}\}, \\ \boldsymbol{Q_0} & = \{(q, \mathcal{X}) \mid q \in Q_0\}, \\ \boldsymbol{F} & = \{(q, X) \mid q \in F \text{ and } X \subseteq \mathcal{X}\}. \end{cases}$$

The transition function $\boldsymbol{\delta}$ is defined by $(q', X') \in \boldsymbol{\delta}((q, X), \alpha, g)$, where $\alpha \in \Sigma \cup \mathcal{X}$ and g is a guard, if and only if, $X' = (X \setminus (\{\alpha\} \cup \mathcal{V}(g))) \cup \kappa^{-1}(q')$. Finally, the refreshing function κ' is defined by $\boldsymbol{\kappa}(x) = \{(q, X) \mid q \in \kappa(x)\}$.

Secondly, we can assume w.l.o.g. that $\boldsymbol{\mathcal{A}}$ has no constants and the variables are refreshed only in the states preceded by ε-transitions. The constants can be replaced by additional variables that have to be initialized with the related constants using an ε-transition outgoing from the initial state. And, if some variables, say $X \subseteq \mathcal{X}$, are refreshed in a state, say $\boldsymbol{q}$, then we add an ε-transition

$q \xrightarrow{\varepsilon} \tilde{q}$ where the variables X are refreshed in $\tilde{q}$ instead of q and the outgoing transitions of q become the outgoing transitions of $\tilde{q}$. Thus, the guards of $\mathcal{A}$ are of the form $\phi \wedge \phi'$ where ϕ (resp. ϕ') is a conjunction of equalities (resp. inequalities) between *variables*.

Thirdly, we let $\mathcal{A}'$ to be the $\overline{\mathrm{PA}}$ $\mathcal{A}' = \langle \Sigma, \mathcal{X}', Q', Q'_0, \delta', F', \kappa' \rangle$ defined by

$$\begin{cases} \mathcal{X}' &= \{x'_1, \ldots, x'_k\} \\ Q' &= Q \times \mathcal{X}^{\mathcal{X}'} \\ Q'_0 &= Q_0 \times \mathcal{X}^{\mathcal{X}'} \\ \kappa' &= \kappa \times \mathcal{X}^{\mathcal{X}'} \end{cases}$$

and δ' is defined by [where g (resp. g') is a conjunction of equalities (resp. inequalities)] :

$$((q_1, X_1, \psi_1), (\alpha, \psi_1(g \wedge g')), (q_2, X_2, \psi_1)) \in \delta' \text{ iff } \begin{cases} ((q_1, X_1), (\alpha, g \wedge g'), (q_2, X_2)) \in \delta \text{ and} \\ \alpha \neq \varepsilon \text{ and} \\ g \sqsubseteq \psi_1 \text{ and} \\ \mathcal{V}(g') = codom(\psi_1) \text{ and} \\ \mathcal{V}(g \wedge g') \cap X_1 = \emptyset \end{cases}$$

And,

$$((q_1, X_1, \psi_1), (\varepsilon, \psi_1(g \wedge g')), (q_2, X_2, \psi_2)) \in \delta' \text{ iff } \begin{cases} ((q_1, X_1), (\varepsilon, g \wedge g'), (q_2, X_2)) \in \delta \text{ and} \\ \mathcal{V}(g') = codom(\psi_1) \text{ and} \\ \mathcal{V}(g \wedge g') \subseteq X_1 \text{ and} \\ \psi_2 = \psi_1 \cup \{x \mapsto x_0 \mid x \in \mathcal{V}(g)\} \cup \\ \qquad \{x \mapsto y_0 \mid x \in \mathcal{V}(g')\} \\ x_0 = get(X' \setminus codom(\psi_1)) \\ y_0 = get(X' \setminus (codom(\psi_1) \cup \{x_0\})) \end{cases}$$

Therefore having proved the expressive equivalence of $\overline{\mathrm{PA}}$ and PA, we now show every $\overline{\mathrm{PA}}$ can be turned into an NFMA recognizing the same languages by encoding the refreshing of the variables of the $\overline{\mathrm{PA}}$s with ε-transitions. Hence,

Lemma 3. *For every PA with k variables and n states there exists an NFMA with $n \cdot k!$ states recognizing the same languages.*

Theorem 1. *For every language L over Σ, there exists an NFMA $\mathcal{F}$ such that $\mathcal{L}(\mathcal{F}) = L$, if and only if there exists a PA $\mathcal{A}$ such that $\mathcal{L}(\mathcal{A}) = L$.*

3.2   Succinctness of PAs over NFMAs

We next show that while PAs and NFMAs have the same expressive power, PAs can be exponentially succinct than NFMAs. That is, we prove that there exists a class of PAs such that any NFMA that recognizes the same language must be exponentially larger.

Theorem 2. *There exists a countably infinite class of languages $\{L_1, L_2, ...\}$, such that for every n, there exists a PA $\mathcal{A}_n$, of size $\mathcal{O}(\log n)$, such that $\mathcal{L}(\mathcal{A}_n) = L_n$, but there does not exist any NFMA $\mathcal{F}$, of size $o(n)$, such that $\mathcal{L}(\mathcal{F}) = L_n$.*

We prove the existence by taking the class of languages $L_n = \{a^n\}$. We first argue in Lemma 4 the existence of a PA with $\mathcal{O}(\log n)$ states and $\mathcal{O}(\log n)$ variables, that recognizes L_n. Then we prove in Lemma 6 that any NFMA that accepts the language L_n must have at least $\Omega(n)$ states.

Lemma 4. *For every $n \geq 1$, there exists a PA $\mathcal{A}_n$ with $\mathcal{O}(\log n)$ states and $\mathcal{O}(\log n)$ variables, such that $\mathcal{L}(\mathcal{A}_n) = L_n = \{a^n\}$.*

It has already been shown in [3] that addition and comparison for bounded integers can be implemented in PAs, with constants to denote 0 and 1, in $\mathcal{O}(\log n)$ states and $\mathcal{O}(\log n)$ variables that encode bit representation of an integer. To construct a PA for the language $L_n = \{a^n\}$, we construct a PA that acts as a Counter, i.e. the value encoded by variables is incremented every time a is read, until $\bigwedge_{i=1,...,m}(x_i = c_i)$, which allows transition from the seed state to an accepting state, where $c_1 c_2 \ldots c_m$ is the binary representation of n.

Such a PA, acting as a Counter, recognizes only $L_n = \{a^n\}$, by counting till n using the variables for bit representation.

We now show that any NFMA that recognizes the $L_n = \{a^n\}$ must require at least $\mathcal{O}(n)$ states. Let us take an NFMA $\mathcal{F}$, with $\mathcal{L}(\mathcal{F}) = L_n$.

Since $\mathcal{F}$ accepts a^n, we know that there exists a configuration path

$$\wp = c_1 \rightarrow c_2 \ldots \rightarrow c_m = (q_1, \sigma_1) \rightarrow (q_2, \sigma_2) \ldots \rightarrow (q_m, \sigma_m) \tag{1}$$

such that

$$trace(\wp) = a^n \tag{2}$$

where $\wp$ is a path over the set of configurations of $\mathcal{F}$, and $m \geq n$.

Since a is a constant, and L_n includes only a^n, we argue that a must be stored in some NFMA register initially, which we can call without loss of generality l_0.

Lemma 5. *$\wp$ (from Eq. (1), a path in $\mathcal{F}$ that accepts a^n) contains only ε-transitions and l_0-transitions.*

Proof. It can be easily seen that l_0-transitions are the only non-ε-transitions in $\wp$. Since the trace contains only a's, if on the contrary there was some l_k-transition for any $k \neq 0$, it would require $\sigma(l_k) = a$ at that transition. However, due to implicit dis-equality, since $\sigma_1(l_k) \neq a$, there must be some i such that $c_i \xrightarrow{\varepsilon/l_k} c_{i+1}$, and $\sigma_i(l_{k'}) \neq a$ for all $k' \neq k$, at which stage l_k stored a.

But if this holds, then it is also possible for l_k to get assigned to some completely different letter b, such that $b \neq \sigma_i(l_{k'})$ for any k', from the infinite alphabet Σ, at the ith transition. Since this would imply that $\mathcal{F}$ also accepts another string with some a's in $trace(\wp)$ replaced with b's, hence by contradiction, we know that $\wp$ only contains ε-transitions and l_0-transitions.

We observe $\forall i : \sigma_i(l_0) = a$, and therefore the sub-NFMA $\mathcal{F}'$, with only the ε-transitions and l_0 labelled transitions of $\mathcal{F}$ is sufficient for recognizing the singleton language. In fact, all accepting paths in $\mathcal{F}$ are accepting paths in $\mathcal{F}'$.

We now define the notion of strong bisimilarity for NFMAs to argue for an important assertion for our proof.

Definition 4 (NFMA Bisimulation). *Two NFMA configurations (q_1, σ_1) and (q_2, σ_2) are said to be strongly bisimilar, i.e. $(q_1, \sigma_1) \sim (q_2, \sigma_2) \leftrightarrow (q_2, \sigma_2) \sim (q_1, \sigma_1)$, if*

1. *for all $\alpha \in \Sigma$, if there exists (q_1', σ_1') with $(q_1, \sigma_1) \xrightarrow{\alpha} (q_1', \sigma_1')$, then there must exist (q_2', σ_2'), such that $(q_2, \sigma_2) \xrightarrow{\alpha} (q_2', \sigma_2')$ and $(q_2', \sigma_2') \sim (q_1', \sigma_1')$. And vice versa.*
2. *if there exists (q_1', σ_1') such that $(q_1, \sigma_1) \xrightarrow{\varepsilon} (q_1', \sigma_1')$, then there must exist (q_2', σ_2') with $(q_2, \sigma_2) \xrightarrow{\varepsilon} (q_2', \sigma_2')$, such that $(q_2', \sigma_2') \sim (q_1', \sigma_1')$. And vice versa.*

Lemma 6. *For an NFMA with all non-ε-transitions restricted to registers in a subset $\mathbb{L}$ of the set of registers, if σ_1 agrees with σ_2 over $\mathbb{L}$ then (q, σ_1) is bisimilar to (q, σ_2), for all states q.*

This follows by observing that:

- for all transitions $(q, l_j, q') \in \delta$, with $l_j \in \mathbb{L}$ and $\sigma_1(l_j) = \sigma_2(l_j)$, $(q, \sigma_1) \xrightarrow{\alpha} (q', \sigma_1')$ if and only if $(q, \sigma_2) \xrightarrow{\alpha} (q', \sigma_2')$, for any $\alpha \in \Sigma$.
- for all transitions $(q, \varepsilon/l_j, q')$, if $(q, \sigma_1) \xrightarrow{\varepsilon} (q', \sigma_1')$, with $\sigma_1'(l_j) = \beta$, for some $\beta \in \Sigma$ without loss of generality, then there exists σ_2', where $\sigma_2'(l_j) = \beta$ and $\sigma_2'(l_k) = \sigma_2(l_k)$ for all $k \neq j$, such that $(q, \sigma_2) \xrightarrow{\varepsilon} (q', \sigma_2')$. And vice versa.

Now applying Lemma 6 to the $\mathcal{F}'$ for which $\mathcal{L}(\mathcal{F}') = L_n$ and contains only ε-transitions and l_0 labelled transitions, as argued above, we claim that $\mathcal{F}'$ must contain $\Omega(n)$ states.

Lemma 7. *An NFMA $\mathcal{F}'$ that recognizes $\{a^n\}$ has at least $n + 1$ states.*

Proof. Towards a contradiction, let us assume that there are less than $n + 1$ states in $\wp$ (from Eq. (1)). Then we can argue that $\exists i \neq j : q_i = q_j$ and the trace from configuration c_i to c_j is a^{n_1} for $n_1 > 0$. Since, otherwise, if there are no such i and j then there must be at least $n + 1$ states.

Now, let the trace from c_1 to c_i be a^{n_0}, from c_i to c_j be a^{n_1}, and c_j to c_m be a^{n_2}, with $n_0, n_1, n_2 > 0$. And thus $n_0 + n_1 + n_2 = n$.

But since $q_i = q_j$, thus the path from c_j to c_m can also be simulated from c_i, by Lemma 6, since the substitutions already agree on l_0. Hence the automata $\mathcal{F}$ also accepts $a^{(n_0 + n_2)}$, which is in contradiction to the language.

Hence by contradiction there are at least $n + 1$ states in $\mathcal{F}$, which is exponential in the size of comparable PA, proving Theorem 2.

4   Complexity of Simulation Preorder over PAs

Theorem 3. *Deciding the simulation preorder over PA is EXPTIME-complete.*

An EXPTIME algorithm for deciding if a PA simulates another PA was given in [3], and we show that this problem is indeed EXPTIME-complete, by reduction from Countdown Games(CG) [10].

In [10], Jurdzinski et al. introduce Countdown Games (CG), and prove that the problem of deciding the winner for these games is EXPTIME-complete. We reduce the problem of deciding winner to deciding simulation of PA by giving a construction for PAs $\mathcal{A}_\forall$ and $\mathcal{A}_\exists$, for any CG, such that Eloise wins the game iff $\mathcal{A}_\forall$ is simulated by $\mathcal{A}_\exists$.

The *countdown game* is defined as a tuple $(Q, \rightarrowtail, q^0, k^*)$ where Q is a finite set of states, $\rightarrowtail \ \subseteq Q \times \mathbb{N} \setminus \{0\} \times Q$ is a transition relation, $q^0 \in Q$ is the initial state, and k^* is the final value. We write $q \overset{\ell}{\rightarrowtail} r$ if $(q, \ell, r) \in \rightarrowtail$. A configuration of the game is an element $(q, k) \in Q \times \mathbb{N}$. The game starts in configuration $(q^0, 0)$ and proceeds in moves: if the current configuration is $(q, k) \in Q \times \mathbb{N}$, first Player 0 chooses a number ℓ with $0 < \ell \leq k^* - k$ and $q \overset{\ell}{\rightarrowtail} r$ for at least one $r \in Q$; then Player 1 chooses a state $r \in Q$, with $q \overset{\ell}{\rightarrowtail} r$. The resulting new configuration is $(r, k + \ell)$. Player 0 wins if she hits a configuration from $Q \times \{k^*\}$, and she loses if she cannot move (and has not yet won).

We proceed by reducing this game to a Simulation game, played between a Duplicator (Eloise) and a Spoiler (Abelard). Thus, Abelard wins if he is able to make a transition on $\mathcal{A}_\forall$ which cannot be simulated on $\mathcal{A}_\exists$, and Eloise otherwise.

To explicitly describe the construction, we first define a function $\lambda : Q \rightarrow 2^{\mathbb{Z}^+}$, where for each state q, $\lambda(q) = \{\ell \mid \exists q' : q \overset{\ell}{\rightarrowtail} q'\}$ We also note that the number of positive integers that occur in a CG will be less than the number of edges, and thus cannot be superpolynomial in the size of the description of the game. Let us denote these integers that occur as labels by the set $\Lambda = \{\ell_1, \ell_2, ...\} = \bigcup_{q \in Q} \lambda(q)$

Now let us define $\mathcal{A}_\forall$, as a PA, with the set of states, $Q_\forall = \{p_0, p_\perp, p_{\ell_1}, p_{\ell_2}, ...\}$, with a state for each label in Λ, in addition to an initial state and a dump state. We associate a letter α_i from the infinite alphabet Σ, to every integer $\ell_i \in \Lambda$, and define the transitions as:

- For each $\ell_i \in \Lambda$, there is $p_0 \overset{\alpha_i}{\longrightarrow} p_{\ell_i}$ and $p_{\ell_i} \overset{+\ell_i}{\longrightarrow} p_0$,
- And finally, we have $p_0 \overset{\beta, k = k^*}{\longrightarrow} p_\perp$, where $\beta \in \Sigma$ and is not equal to any α_i

We now define $\mathcal{A}_\exists$ as a PA, given a corresponding CG with states Q. The states of $\mathcal{A}_\exists$ are $Q_\exists = Q \uplus \{q_\top\} \uplus (\rightarrowtail)$, with the following transitions:

- For each $q \overset{\ell_j}{\rightarrowtail} q'$ in the CG, we have $q \overset{\alpha_j}{\longrightarrow} (q, \ell_j, q')$ and $(q, \ell_j, q') \overset{+\ell_j}{\longrightarrow} q'$
- For each $q_i \in Q$, we have $q_i \overset{x, x \in \Lambda \setminus \lambda(q_i)}{\longrightarrow} q_\top$
- For each $q_i \in Q$, we have $q_i \overset{x, k > k^*}{\longrightarrow} q_\top$

- And we ensure that $q_\top$ is a universal simulator, i.e. $q_\top$ can simulate any PA transition, by allowing $q_\top \xrightarrow{y} q_\top$ and making it a refresh state for y.

Notice that the "macro" transitions $p_{\ell_i} \xrightarrow{+\alpha_i} p_0$ and $q_i \xrightarrow{x,k>k^*} q_\top$ can be translated into a series of transitions of a PA of linear size, by implementing corresponding adders and comparators, using $log(k^*)$ variables, as shown earlier in [3].

We now show that Player 0 wins the CG iff Abelard wins the corresponding simulation game. In fact, we prove that a configuration (q, k) of CG is a winning configuration for Player 0 iff $[\mathcal{A}_\forall : (p_0, k), \mathcal{A}_\exists : (q, k)]$ is a winning configuration for Abelard in the simulation game.

We know that for any configuration of simulation game where $\mathcal{A}_\exists$ is at $q_\top$ will be a losing state for Abelard, by definition, since $q_\top$ can simulate all transitions. Similarly, any configuration of simulation game, where $\mathcal{A}_\forall$ is at $p_\bot$ and $\mathcal{A}_\exists$ is not at $q_\top$, will be a winning state for Abelard since Eloise cannot otherwise duplicate a β-transition.

Abelard wins in $[\mathcal{A}_\forall : (p_0, k), \mathcal{A}_\exists : (q, k)]$ iff either $k = k^*$, since $p_\bot$ is then reachable with a β-transition, or $k < k^*$ and there exists an α_i-transition to a winning state. However, for $\ell_i \notin \lambda(q)$, Eloise can move to $q_\top$, therefore if there exists an α_i-transition to a winning state, then $\ell_i \in \lambda(q)$. Such a transition can be duplicated only by $q \xrightarrow{\alpha_i} (q, \ell_i, q')$, by Eloise for some q', resulting in subsequent duplication of $p_{\ell_i} \xrightarrow{+\ell_i} p_0$ with $(q, \ell_i, q') \xrightarrow{+\ell_i} q'$. Thus, if $k < k^*$ then there exists an α_i-transition to a winning state iff there is an $\ell_i \in \lambda(q)$ such that for all q' such that $q \xrightarrow{\alpha_i} (q, \ell_i, q')$ (which iff $q \xrightarrow{\ell_j} q'$ in CG), $[\mathcal{A}_\forall : (p_0, k + \ell_i), \mathcal{A}_\exists : (q', k + \ell_i)]$ are all winning states.

Since Player 0 wins in configuration (q, k) iff $k = k^*$ or if $k < k^*$ and $\exists \ell_i \in \lambda(q) : \forall q' : q \xrightarrow{\ell_j} q' \implies (q', k + \ell_i)$ is a winning state, therefore we coinductively prove that Abelard wins in $[\mathcal{A}_\forall : (p_0, k), \mathcal{A}_\exists : (q, k)]$ iff Player 0 wins in (q, k).

Therefore the problem of deciding a winner for any CG can be polynomially reduced to the problem of deciding the winner for the simulation game over PAs. This proves that deciding simulation preorder over PAs is EXPTIME-hard, which coupled with previous results, implies that simulation is EXPTIME-complete.

5   Conclusion

We have shown that PAs can be exponentially smaller than NFMAs for some languages and that simulation preorder over PAs is EXPTIME-complete. Finding a good lower bound for deciding simulation preorder over NFMAs, which has an upper bound of EXPTIME, will also reveal more about the relationship between the two models. It is easy to see that it is NP-hard, which also means that for languages where PAs are succinct with respect to NFMAs, while deciding simulation in NFMAs cannot possibly be done in polynomial time in n, checking the same over PAs would require time exponential in $log(n)$, i.e. polynomial in n.

Further, it will be interesting to see if there are interesting subclasses of PAs, for which language containment is decidable or simulation preorder is efficiently decidable.

References

1. Akroun, L., Benatallah, B., Nourine, L., Toumani, F.: Decidability and complexity of simulation preorder for data-centric web services. In: Franch, X., Ghose, A.K., Lewis, G.A., Bhiri, S. (eds.) ICSOC 2014. LNCS, vol. 8831, pp. 535–542. Springer, Heidelberg (2014)
2. Belkhir, W., Chevalier, Y., Rusinowitch, M.: Fresh-variable automata: application to service composition. In: 15th International Symposium on Symbolic and Numeric Algorithms for Scientific Computing, SYNASC, pp. 153–160. IEEE Computer Science (2013)
3. Belkhir, W., Chevalier, Y., Rusinowitch, M.: Parametrized automata simulation and application to service composition. J. Symb. Comput. (2014). http://www.sciencedirect.com/science/article/pii/S0747717114000972
4. Belkhir, W., Rossi, G., Rusinowitch, M.: A parametrized propositional dynamic logic with application to service synthesis. In: Tenth conference on "Advances in Modal Logic," 5–8 August 2014, Groningen, The Netherlands, pp. 34–53 (2014)
5. Berardi, D., Cheikh, F., Giacomo, G.D., Patrizi, F.: Automatic service composition via simulation. Int. J. Found. Comput. Sci. **19**(2), 429–451 (2008)
6. Bojanczyk, M., Muscholl, A., Schwentick, T., Segoufin, L., David, C.: Two-variable logic on words with data. In: LICS, pp. 7–16. IEEE (2006)
7. Degano, P., Ferrari, G.-L., Mezzetti, G.: Nominal automata for resource usage control. In: Moreira, N., Reis, R. (eds.) CIAA 2012. LNCS, vol. 7381, pp. 125–137. Springer, Heidelberg (2012)
8. Delzanno, G., Sangnier, A., Traverso, R.: Parameterized verification of broadcast networks of register automata. In: Abdulla, P.A., Potapov, I. (eds.) RP 2013. LNCS, vol. 8169, pp. 109–121. Springer, Heidelberg (2013)
9. Dill, D.L., Hu, A.J., Wong-Toi, H.: Checking for language inclusion using simulation preorders. In: Larsen, K.G., Skou, A. (eds.) CAV 1991. LNCS, vol. 575, pp. 255–265. Springer, Heidelberg (1992)
10. Jurdziński, M., Laroussinie, F., Sproston, J.: Model checking probabilistic timed automata with one or two clocks. Logical Methods Comput. Sci. **4**(312), 1–28 (2008)
11. Kaminski, M., Zeitlin, D.: Finite-memory automata with non-deterministic reassignment. Int. J. Found. Comput. Sci. **21**(5), 741–760 (2010)
12. Manuel, A., Ramanujam, R.: Automata over infinite alphabets. World Sci. Rev. **9**, 329–363 (2011)
13. Muscholl, A., Walukiewicz, I.: A lower bound on web services composition. Logical Methods Comput. Sci. **4**(2), 1–14 (2008)

Toward the Formalization of BPEL

Laila Boumlik and Mohamed Mejri$^{(\boxtimes)}$

Department of Computer Science, Laval University, Quebec, Canada
laila.boumlik.1@ulaval.ca, Mohamed.Mejri@ift.ulaval.ca

Abstract. During the recent years, the composition, the orchestration and the interaction of web services have generated a great deal of interest for the Internet community. BPEL is the most important standard language for web services orchestration. It provides a variety of constructors allowing to build complex services from simple ones. However, many of its features are complex and source of a large misunderstanding due to the absence of formalization. For instance, understanding the Event Handler, the Fault Handler, the Compensation Handler and the Termination Handler (EFCT) of BPEL is a big challenge even for an experienced programmer.

This paper aims to formalize the EFCT fragment of BPEL using a process algebra called AV-BPEL specially defined to fit with the BPEL language and endowed with a small steps operational semantics.

Keywords: Web services · BPEL · Formal methods · Process algebra

1 Introduction

With the great success of Service Oriented Computing (SOC) [1], web services are becoming the main model for automated interaction between distributed systems on the Web. SOC is based on the composition of several services that are typically designed to interact with other web services through the Internet to form larger applications. Standard web service framework are essentially based on three technologies: SOAP [2], WSDL [3] and UDDI [4]. The WSDL (Web Service Description Language) provides an abstract language to describe messages to be exchanged between services. The SOAP (Simple Object Access Protocol) is a protocol for exchanging structured information between the involved parties and the UDDI (Universal Description Discovery and Integration) is used to publish and discover web services.

Having the possibility of constructing new web services by composing existing ones has opened a new interesting prospective and has significantly influenced the way industrial applications are developed. BPEL (Business Process Execution Language) [6] is the standard of web services composition and orchestration. Among the interesting features of this expressive language, we found the fault and the compensation handling mechanism. In fact, sometime it is useful to give the end-users the possibility to cancel some services if other fails. For example, if Alice wants to book a plane ticket and a hotel for a given period of time but

© Springer-Verlag Berlin Heidelberg 2016
A. Norta et al. (Eds.): ICSOC 2015 Workshops, LNCS 9586, pp. 157–167, 2016.
DOI: 10.1007/978-3-662-50539-7_13

after booking the hotel she does not find an appropriate plane ticket, then it is
desirable to allow her to cancel the hotel reservation. Compensation are introduced in BPEL to give the possibility to remedy a situation where an activity
of a group fails whereas others terminated with success.

Even if the global ideas of the fault handler and the compensation handler are
clear, it remains that there are a large number of particular cases that need to be
handled: Which fault handler catches which error? Which compensation handler
needs to be called after a given error? Which activities need to be stopped when
an error occurs? What happens if an error occurs during a compensation? What
happens if an error occurs in a fault handler itself? These are only a part of the
particular situations that need to be clarified. Combined with other features, like
event handler and termination handler, the number of these kind of questions
explode justifying the urgent need of a suitable formalization for BPEL.

Contribution: The main contribution of this paper is a detailed formalization
of the EFCT of BPEL, that address the above questions, based on a dedicated
process algebra endowed with a small step operational semantics.

The remainder of this paper is organized as follows. Section 2 presents a
simplified language that abstracts BPEL for XML syntax and formalizes it.
Section 3 gives some related work. Finally, some concluding remarks are given
in Sect. 4.

2   BPEL Formalisation

2.1   Syntax of AV-BPEL: Abstracted Version BPEL

Let b be a metavariable that ranges over Boolean expressions and Exp ranges
over classical expressions like arithmetic and string expressions. The syntax of
AV-BPEL, a fragment of $BPEL$ that is abstracted from XML syntax, is given
by the BNF grammar given in Table 1.

A basic activity A contains an empty process (NOP action) 1, an exit process
0, a Boolean expression b, an assignment expression $x := Exp$, a throw action
$\ulcorner_e$, a send action $a!\vec{v}$ and a receive action $a?\vec{x}$.

A composed activity S can be any basic activity in A, a different composition
of two activities or or a scope $< \mathcal{E}, F, C, T, E, S >_n$.

A process Pr (either $< \mathcal{E}, F, E, S >_n$ or $< \mathcal{E}, F, E, I >_n$) has a name n,
a running environment $\mathcal{E}$, a fault handler F an event handler E and either a
normal activity S or an instantiation bloc I.

An instantiation bloc I allows a service to fork an activity when a request of
an operation is received $(a?\vec{x})$.

An event handler E always starts by waiting for some event (receiving a
message or an alarm based on a "timing out").

A compensation handler (respectively a termination handler) can be a basic
activity, an indication to compensate a particular scope $\$_n$ or $\$$, an indication
to compensate all the reached scopes that terminated with success. It can also

Table 1. Syntax of BPEL.

A	::=	1	(Empty)
		0	(Exit)
		b	Condition
		$x := Exp$	(Assignement)
		$\uparrow_e$	(Throw)
		$a!\overrightarrow{v}$	(Send action)
		$a?\overrightarrow{x}$	(Receive action)
F	::=		Fault Handler
		A	Activity
		$\uparrow_e \mid \uparrow$	(catch e), (catch all)
		$\$_n \mid \$$	(compensate n), (compensate all)
		RS	(Root Scop)
		$F.F \mid F+F \mid F^*F \mid F\|_\gamma F$	
C,T	::=		Compensation and Termination Handler
		A	Activity
		$\$_n \mid \$$	(compensate n), (compensate all)
		RS	(Root Scop)
		$T.T \mid T+T \mid T^*T \mid T\|_\gamma T$	
E	::=		Event Handler
		$a?x.S$	OnEvent
		$\delta^n.S$	(OnAlarm)
		$E+E$	(Choice)
S	::=	A	
		$S_1.S_2$	(Sequential composition)
		$S_1 + S_2$	(choice)
		$S_1\|_\gamma S_2$	(Merge, parallel composition)
		$S_1^* S_2$	(Iteration operator)
		$< \mathcal{E},F,C,T,E,S >_n$	(Scope)
I	::=		(Insntantiation Bloc)
		$(a?\overrightarrow{x})^+.S$	(Receive with create Instance)
		$(\sum_{i\in\Theta} a_i?\overrightarrow{x_i}.S_i)^+$	(Pick Activity)
		$I_1 + I_2$	(choice)
		$I_1\|_\gamma I_2$	(Merge, parallel composition)
		$< \mathcal{E},F,C,T,E,I >_n$	(Scope)
RS	::=	$< \mathcal{E},F,T,E,S >_n$	(Root Scop)
Pr	::=	$< \mathcal{E},F,E,S >_n \mid < \mathcal{E},F,E,I >_n$	(Process)
D	::=		(Deployment)
		P^m	(Processess)
		S^m	(Sequence)
		I^m	(Instantiation)
		$a\uparrow\overrightarrow{v} \parallel D$	(Message Transit)
		$D\|D$	(Process Parallel composition)

be a root scope RS (similar to a normal scope except that it cannot contains a compensation handler itself.).

A fault handler can be a basic activity, a catch for a named error ($\urcorner_e$), a catch all $\urcorner$, an indication to compensate a particular scope $\$_n$ or $\$$, an indication to compensate all the reached scopes that terminated with success. It can also be a root scope RS.

Besides the above constructors, we introduce a deployment D that does not belongs to the syntax of BPEL, it is useful to formalize asynchronous communications where the sent action is not blocking whereas the receiving is blocking.

2.2 Semantics

Let $\mathcal{D}$ be set of all possible deployments, and let P , Q and R range over $\mathcal{D}$. The operational semantics of AV-BPEL is defined by the transition relation $\longrightarrow \in \mathcal{D} \times \mathcal{A} \times \mathcal{D}$. Table 3 gives some standard rules that are true for all deployments P, P_1, Q and Q_1. Also, it uses the equivalent relation $\equiv \in \mathcal{D} \times \mathcal{D}$ defined by Table 2.

Table 2. Axiom of BPEL.

$P + Q \equiv Q + P$	(A_1)	$P\|_\gamma Q \equiv Q\|_\gamma P$	(A_2)
$(P + Q) + R \equiv P + (Q + R)$	(A_3)	$(P\|_\gamma Q)\|_\gamma R \equiv P\|_\gamma (Q\|_\gamma R)$	(A_4)
$0 + P \equiv P$	(A_5)	$1.P \equiv P$	(A_6)
$0\|_\gamma P \equiv P$	(A_7)	$1\|_\gamma P \equiv P$	(A_8)

We denote by $< \mathcal{E}, F, C^?, T^?, E, P >_n$ a root scope or a process, i.e., the termination handler and the compensation handler are optional.

● *Communication:* Sending values $\overrightarrow{v}$ on a channel a, denoted by $a!\overrightarrow{v}$, is not a blocking action and its produces a floating message, denoted by $a \uparrow \overrightarrow{v}$, meaning that the message has not been received yet. Receiving messages on a channel a, denoted by $a?\overrightarrow{x}$ is however always blocking until seeing a floating message $a \uparrow \overrightarrow{v}$ such that the correlation values in $\overrightarrow{x}$ match with the correlation values in $\overrightarrow{v}$. This matching is denoted by $\overrightarrow{v} \sqsubseteq \overrightarrow{x}$, where $(x_1, \ldots, x_n) \sqsubseteq (v_1, \ldots, v_n)$ if $x_i = v_i$ or x_i is a variable (i.e., there exists a substitution σ from variables to values such that $\sigma(\overrightarrow{x}) = \overrightarrow{v}$.).

To formalize this asynchronous communication, we introduce the relation $\longrightarrow \in \mathcal{D} \times \mathcal{A} \times \mathcal{D}$ that aims to show whether a process is ready to perform an action. This relation is not blocking even for the reception as shown in Table 4. Now, the communication rules are formalized as shown hereafter.

$$(R_{Exp}^1) \frac{P \xrightarrow{x := Exp} Q}{< \mathcal{E}, F, C^?, T^?, E, P >_n^m \xrightarrow{\tau} < \mathcal{E} \dagger [x \mapsto v], F, C^?, T^?, E, Q >_n^m} [\![\mathcal{E}(Exp)]\!] = v$$

$$(R_b^1) \frac{P \xrightarrow{b} Q}{< \mathcal{E}, F, C^?, T^?, E, P >_n^m \xrightarrow{\tau} < \mathcal{E}, F, C^?, T^?, E, Q >_n^m} [\![\mathcal{E}(b)]\!] = 1$$

Table 3. Classical Rules for $\longrightarrow$.

$$(R_\equiv) \frac{P \equiv P_1 \quad P_1 \xrightarrow{a} P_2 \quad P_2 \equiv Q}{P \xrightarrow{a} Q}$$

$$(R_{\uparrow_e}) \frac{\square}{\Gamma_e \xrightarrow{\Gamma_e} 1} \quad (R_!) \frac{\square}{a!\overrightarrow{v} \xrightarrow{a!\overrightarrow{v}} a\uparrow\overrightarrow{v}}$$

$$(R_+) \frac{P \xrightarrow{a} P'}{P + Q \xrightarrow{a} P'} \qquad (R_.) \frac{P \xrightarrow{a} P'}{P.Q \xrightarrow{a} P'.Q}$$

$$(R_*^d) \frac{Q \xrightarrow{a} Q'}{P^*Q \xrightarrow{a} Q'} \qquad (R_*) \frac{P \xrightarrow{a} P'}{P^*Q \xrightarrow{a} P'.(P^*Q)}$$

$$(R_{\|_\gamma}) \frac{P \xrightarrow{a} P'}{P\|_\gamma Q \xrightarrow{a} P'\|_\gamma Q} a \notin \gamma \quad (R_{\|_\gamma}^S) \frac{P \xrightarrow{a!} P' \quad Q \xrightarrow{a?} Q'}{P\|_\gamma Q \xrightarrow{a} P'\|_\gamma Q'} a \in \gamma$$

Table 4. Definition of $\longrightarrow\!\!\!\rightarrow$.

$$(R_\equiv^{\rightarrow}) \frac{P \equiv P_1 \quad P_1 \xrightarrow{a} P_2 \quad P_2 \equiv Q}{P \xrightarrow{a} Q}$$

$$(R_{Exp}) \frac{\square}{x := Exp \xrightarrow{x:=Exp} 1} \quad (R_b) \frac{\square}{b \xrightarrow{b} 1} \quad (R_?) \frac{\square}{a?\overrightarrow{x} \xrightarrow{a?v} 1}$$

$$(R_\uparrow) \frac{\square}{a\uparrow\overrightarrow{v} \xrightarrow{a\uparrow\overrightarrow{v}} 1} \quad (R_{\uparrow_e}^{\rightarrow}) \frac{\square}{\Gamma_e \xrightarrow{\Gamma_e} 1} \quad (R_!^{\rightarrow}) \frac{\square}{a!\overrightarrow{v} \xrightarrow{a!\overrightarrow{v}} a\uparrow\overrightarrow{v}}$$

$$(R_+^1) \frac{\square}{(a?\overrightarrow{x})^+ P \xrightarrow{(a?\overrightarrow{x})^+} P} \quad (R_+^2) \frac{\square}{(\sum_{i\in\Theta} a_i?\overrightarrow{x_i}.S_i)^+ \xrightarrow{(a_i?\overrightarrow{x_i})^+} S_i}$$

$$(R_+^{\rightarrow}) \frac{P \xrightarrow{a} P'}{P + Q \xrightarrow{a} P'} \qquad (R_.^{\rightarrow}) \frac{P \xrightarrow{a} P'}{P.Q \xrightarrow{a} P'.Q}$$

$$(R_*^{d\rightarrow}) \frac{Q \xrightarrow{a} Q'}{P^*Q \xrightarrow{a} Q'} \qquad (R_*^{\rightarrow}) \frac{P \xrightarrow{a} P'}{P^*Q \xrightarrow{a} P'.(P^*Q)}$$

$$(R_{\|_\gamma}^{\rightarrow}) \frac{P \xrightarrow{a} P'}{P\|_\gamma Q \xrightarrow{a} P'\|_\gamma Q} a \notin \gamma \quad (R_{\|_\gamma}^{S\rightarrow}) \frac{P \xrightarrow{a!} P' \quad Q \xrightarrow{a?} Q'}{P\|_\gamma Q \xrightarrow{a} P'\|_\gamma Q'} a \in \gamma$$

$$(R_!^!)\frac{P \xrightarrow{a\uparrow\vec{v}} Q}{< \mathcal{E},F,C^?,T^?,E,P >_n^m \quad \xrightarrow{\mathcal{E}(a)\uparrow\overline{\mathcal{E}(v)}} \quad < \mathcal{E}',F',C'^?,T'^?,E',Q >_n^{m'} \parallel \mathcal{E}(a)\uparrow\overline{\mathcal{E}(v)}}$$

$$(R_!^?)\frac{P \xrightarrow{a?\vec{x}} Q \quad D \xrightarrow{a\uparrow\vec{v}} D'}{< \mathcal{E},F,C^?,T^?,E,P >_n^m \parallel D \quad \xrightarrow{a?\vec{v}} \quad < \mathcal{E}\dagger(\vec{x} \mapsto \vec{v}),F,C^?,T^?,E,Q >_n^{m'} \parallel D'} \vec{v} \sqsubseteq \vec{x}$$

where $m,m' \in \{F,C,FT0,FT1,TC,\}$, and $[\![-]\!]$ is a function that evaluates an expression (Boolean expression, arithmetic expression, string expression, etc.). For the moment, we are not interested by having more details about it. The operator $\dagger$ is defined as follows:

$$\mathcal{E}\dagger(x \mapsto v)(y) = \begin{cases} \mathcal{E}(y) & \text{if } y \neq x \\ v & \text{if } y = x \end{cases}$$

• *Creating an Instance of a Process:* The sysntax of BPEL gives two possibilities to explicitly specify the fact that we want to create an instance of a process when a message is received: first with the parameter `createInstance=YES` used within the definition of a "Receive" action. This case is transformed to $(a?\vec{x})^+$ in our syntax. Or by using a "Pickup" activity that contains only "OnMessage" (same as Receive, but it does not have the `createInstance` option). This case is specified by $(\sum_{i\in\Theta} a_i?x_i.S_i)^+$ in our abstracted syntax.

The operational rule showing the creation of an instance are as shown here after.

$$(R_+^4)\frac{I \xrightarrow{(a?\vec{x})^+} I' \quad D \xrightarrow{a\uparrow\vec{v}} D'}{< \mathcal{E},F,E,I >_n^m \parallel D \quad \xrightarrow{a?\vec{v}} \quad < \mathcal{E},F,E,I >_n^m \parallel < \mathcal{E}'\dagger(\vec{x} \mapsto \vec{v}),F',E',I' >_n^{m'} \parallel D'} \vec{v} \sqsubseteq \vec{x}$$

• *Principal Activity:* Some basic rules showing the evolution of an activity are shown by Table 3. Further behaviors are dictated by specific rules described hereafter.

– Each error thrown by the principal activity should be caught by the fault handler of the same scope.

$$(R_A^2)\frac{P \xrightarrow{\uparrow_e} Q \quad F \xrightarrow{\uparrow_e} F'}{< \mathcal{E},F,C^?,T^?,E,P >_n^{FT} \xrightarrow{\tau} < \mathcal{E},F',C^?,T^?,E,Q >_n^{FT0}}$$

– If a throw $\uparrow_e$ doesn't have a dedicated catch in the fault handler, then it should be handled by the "catch all" activity.

$$(R_A^3)\frac{P \xrightarrow{\uparrow_e} Q \quad F \xrightarrow{\uparrow_e}\!\!\!\!/ \quad F \xrightarrow{\uparrow} F'}{< \mathcal{E},F,C^?,T^?,E,P >_n \xrightarrow{\tau} < \mathcal{E},F',C^?,T^?,E,Q >_n^{FT0}}$$

– If there is neither a specific catch nor a "catch all" activity for a specific error, the fault handler execute the "Compensate all" activity ($\$$).

$$(R_A^4)\frac{P \xrightarrow{\uparrow_e} Q \quad F \xrightarrow{\uparrow_e}\!\!\!\!/ \quad F \xrightarrow{\uparrow}\!\!\!\!/}{< \mathcal{E},F,C^?,T^?,E,P >_n \xrightarrow{\tau} < \mathcal{E},\$,C^?,T^?,E,Q >)n^{FT0}}$$

- When the principal activity of a scope terminates with success, the scope is stored, in a compensation mode, for an eventual future compensation.

$$(R_A^5) \frac{< \mathcal{E}, F, C, T^?, E, P >_n \xrightarrow{a} < \mathcal{E}', F', C, T'^?, E', 1 >_n}{< \mathcal{E}, F, C, T^?, E, P >_n .S \xrightarrow{a} S. < \mathcal{E}', F', 1, T'^?, E', C >_n^C}$$

$$(R_A^6) \frac{< \mathcal{E}, F, C, T^?, E, P >_n \xrightarrow{a} < \mathcal{E}', F', C, T'^?, E', 1 >_n}{< \mathcal{E}, F, C, T^?, E, P >_n \xrightarrow{a} < \mathcal{E}', F', 1, T'^?, E', C >_n^C}$$

- In a compensation mode, a scope is executed like in a normal mode, except that we do not need to store it anymore when it terminates with success. More precisely:

  - If the activity didn't finished yet, the compensation mode behaves like normal mode.

$$(R_C^1) \frac{< \mathcal{E}, F, C, T^?, E, P >_n \xrightarrow{a} < \mathcal{E}', F', C', T'^?, E', Q >_n}{< \mathcal{E}, F, C, T^?, E, P >_n^C \xrightarrow{a} < \mathcal{E}', F', C', T'^?, E', Q >_n^C} Q \neq 1$$

  - If the activity of the compensation mode terminates, the scope is uninstalled.

$$(R_C^2) \frac{< \mathcal{E}, F, C, T^?, E, P >_n \xrightarrow{a} < \mathcal{E}', F', C', T'^?, E', 1 >}{< \mathcal{E}, F, C, T^?, E, P >_n^C \xrightarrow{a} 1}$$

•*Fault Handler, Termination Handler and Compensation Handler:* When an error occurs during the execution of the main activity of a scope, the control is passed to the fault handler which executes a list of treatments in the following order:

1. It stops all the running activities of the scope by the help of the relation $\longrightarrow_t$. The termination produces always a silent action τ.

$$(R_{FT}^1) \frac{P \xrightarrow{\tau}_t Q}{< \mathcal{E}, F, C^?, T^?, E, P >_n^{FT0} \xrightarrow{\tau} < \mathcal{E}, F, C^?, T^?, E, Q >_n^{FT0}}$$

  - Stopping a scope consists on terminating its principal activity.

$$(R_T^1) \frac{P \xrightarrow{\tau}_t Q}{< \mathcal{E}, F, C^?, T^?, E, P >_n \xrightarrow{\tau}_t < \mathcal{E}, F, C^?, T^?, E, Q >_n}$$

  - Terminating two parallel activities turns to terminate each one of them.

$$(R_T^2) \frac{P_1 \xrightarrow{\tau}_t Q_1}{P_1 \| P_2 \xrightarrow{\tau}_t Q_1 \| P_2}$$

  - Terminating an iterative activity consists in removing its code.

$$(R_T^3) \frac{\square}{P_1^* P_2 \xrightarrow{\tau}_t 1}$$

– Stopping a sequence turns to remove all it code except those related to a compensation.

$$(R_T^4)\frac{}{P_1.P_2 \xrightarrow{\tau}_t P_2}P_1 \neq <\mathcal{E}, F, C^?, T^?, E, 1>$$

2. Once an activity is stopped, the termination handler of the scope is executed.

$$(R_T^6)\frac{P \xrightarrow{\,}_t \quad \mathcal{E}(a)}{<\mathcal{E}, F, C, T^?, E, P>_n^{FT0} \xrightarrow{} <\mathcal{E} \dagger a, F', C, T^?, E, P>_n^{FT1}}$$

– The termination handler can compensate activities

$$(R_{TC}^1)\frac{T \xrightarrow{\$} T'}{<\mathcal{E}, F, C^?, T, E, S>_n^{FT1} \xrightarrow{\$} <\mathcal{E}, F, C, T', E, S^{-1}>_n^{TC}}$$

• The activity of a compensation handler is executed via the relation $\longrightarrow_c$ and it can be invoked only by a fault handler, a termination handler or another compensation handler.

$$(R_{TC}^2)\frac{<\mathcal{E}, F, C^?, T, E, P>_n^C \xrightarrow{a}_c <\mathcal{E}', F', C'^?, T', E', Q>_n^C}{<\mathcal{E}, F, C^?, T, E, P>_n^{TC} \xrightarrow{a} <\mathcal{E}', F', C''^?, T', E', Q>_n^{TC}}a \neq^{\Gamma}n \text{ and } Q \neq 1$$

• Once the compensation is successfully terminated, the control is turned back to the calling activity (fault handler).

$$(R_{TC}^3)\frac{<\mathcal{E}, F, C^?, T, E, P>_n^C \xrightarrow{a}_c 1}{<\mathcal{E}, F, C^?, T, E, P>_n^{TC} \xrightarrow{a} <\mathcal{E}, F, C^?, T, E, 1>_n^{TF1}}a \neq^{\Gamma}e$$

• If an error occurs during the execution of a compensation handler, its remaining activity is ignored and the control is turned back to the calling fault handler without reporting it.

$$(R_{TC}^4)\frac{<\mathcal{E}, F, C^?, T, E, P>_n^C \xrightarrow{\Gamma_n}_c S'}{<\mathcal{E}, F, C^?, T, E, P>_n^{TC} \xrightarrow{\tau} <\mathcal{E}, F, C^?, 1, E, 1>_n^F}$$

– The termination handler can run activities others than calling a compensation handler, but it can never signal an error.

$$(R_{TC}^5)\frac{<\mathcal{E}, F, C^?, T^?, E, T>_n \xrightarrow{a} <\mathcal{E}', F, C^?, T^?, E, T'>_n}{<\mathcal{E}, F, C^?, T, E, P>_n^{FT1} \xrightarrow{a} <\mathcal{E}', F, C, T', E, P>_n^{FT1}}a \neq^{\Gamma}e$$

3. Once the termination handler finished, the fault handler runs it own activity.

$$(R_F^5)\frac{T \xrightarrow{\,}}{<\mathcal{E}, F, C^?, T, E, P>_n^{FT1} \xrightarrow{\tau} <\mathcal{E}, F, C^?, T, E, P>_n^F}$$

– The fault handler can compensate an activity if this is specified in its activity.

$$(R_{FC}^1)\frac{F \xrightarrow{\$} F'}{<\mathcal{E}, F, C^?, T^?, E, P>_n^F \xrightarrow{\$} <\mathcal{E}, F', C^?, T^?, E, P^{-1}>_n^{FC}}$$

where

$$P^{-1} = \begin{cases} Q^{-1}.a & \text{if } P = a.Q \\ Q^{-1} + R^{-1} & \text{if } P = Q + R \\ Q^{-1} \parallel R^{-1} & \text{if } P = Q \parallel R \\ P & \text{else} \end{cases}$$

- The code of the compensation handler is executed by the relation $\longrightarrow_c$.

$$(R^2_{FC}) \frac{< \mathcal{E}, F, C^?, T^?, E, P >^C_n \quad \xrightarrow{a}_c \quad < \mathcal{E}', F', C'^?, T'^?, E', Q >^C_n}{< \mathcal{E}, F, C^?, T^?, E, P >^{FC}_n \quad \xrightarrow{a} \quad < \mathcal{E}', F', C'^?, T'^?, E', Q >^{FC}_n} a \neq^{\uparrow}e \text{ and } Q \neq 1$$

- Once a compensation handler terminate with success, the fault handler continues its activity.

$$(R^3_{FC}) \frac{< \mathcal{E}, F, C^?, T^?, E, P >^C_n \quad \xrightarrow{a} \quad 1}{< \mathcal{E}, F, C^?, T^?, E, P >^{FC}_n \quad \xrightarrow{\mathcal{E}(a)} \quad < \mathcal{E} \dagger a, F, C^?, T^?, E, 1 >^F_n} a \neq^{\uparrow}e$$

– A fault handler can run activities different from compensations.

$$(R^1_F) \frac{< \mathcal{E}, F, C^?, T^?, E, F >_n \quad \xrightarrow{a} \quad < \mathcal{E}', F, C^?, T^?, E, F' >_n}{< \mathcal{E}, F, C^?, T^?, E, P >^F_n \quad \xrightarrow{a} \quad < \mathcal{E}', F', C^?, T^?, E, P >^F_n} a \neq^{\uparrow}e$$

– A process or a scope that produces an error fails (i.e. becomes 0) regardless of its fault handler terminates with success or not as shown here after.
- If an error occurs inside a compensation handler, the fault handler propagates it to the parent scope and the current scope fails.

$$(R^4_{FC}) \frac{< \mathcal{E}, F, C^?, T^?, E, P >^C_n \quad \xrightarrow{\uparrow e}_c \quad Q}{< \mathcal{E}, F, C, T^?, E, P >^{FC}_n \quad \xrightarrow{\uparrow e} \quad 0}$$

- If an error occurs inside a fault handler itself, the error is propagated to the parent scope.

$$(R^2_F) \frac{F \quad \xrightarrow{\uparrow e} \quad F'}{< \mathcal{E}, F, C^?, T^?, E, P >^F_n \quad \xrightarrow{\uparrow e} \quad 0}$$

- If a fault handler terminates with success, its scope or process terminates in a fail mode (0).

$$(R^3_F) \frac{F \quad \xrightarrow{a} \quad 1}{< \mathcal{E}, F, C^?, T^?, E, P >^F_n \quad \xrightarrow{\mathcal{E}(a)}_c \quad 0} a \neq^{\uparrow}e$$

- **Event Handler:**
- Once an event is received, the activity of it corresponding event handler is executed in parallel with the principal activity of the scope.

$$(R_E) \frac{E \quad \xrightarrow{a?\vec{x}} \quad E' \quad D \quad \xrightarrow{a\uparrow\vec{v}} \quad D'}{< \mathcal{E}, F, C^?, T^?, E, P >^m_n \parallel D \quad \xrightarrow{a?\vec{v}} \quad < \mathcal{E} \dagger (\vec{x} \mapsto \vec{v}), F, C^?, T^?, E, E' \parallel P >^{m'}_n \parallel D'} \vec{v} \sqsubseteq \vec{x}$$

- Each error produced by an event handler is treated by the fault handler of the corresponding scope.

$$(R^{\uparrow}_E) \frac{E \quad \xrightarrow{\uparrow n} \quad E' \quad F \quad \xrightarrow{\uparrow n} \quad F'}{< \mathcal{E}, F, C^?, T^?, E, P > \xrightarrow{\tau} < \mathcal{E}, F', C^?, T^?, E, P >^{FT0}}$$

3   Related Work

Several interesting contributions were appeared during the last years to formalize the semantics of BPEL. Most of them tried to match the constructors of BPEL with some terms in an existing process algebra and only few works have attempted to define a new algebra that fit better with BPEL's features. In [7–9] the authors have presented a two-way mapping between a fragment of BPEL and the process algebra LOTOS. They have considered most of BPEL's activities including fault, compensation and event handlers. In [5] the authors have proposed a mapping from a BPEL process to a π-based calculus, named webπ∞. They advocated that the different mechanisms (fault handler, termination handler and compensation handler) for error handling are not needed and they proposed the idea of event notification to substitute them. The authors of [11] have proposed an approach based on two-way mapping between the π-based orchestration calculus and BPEL. [10] presented a formalization of BPEL 2.0 based on the π-calculus.The authors of [12] proposed an approach based RECATNet to model and verify a fragment of BPEL processes. The authors of [13] present a novel correct-by-construction formal approach based on refinement using the Event-B method. A Petri net sematics for BPEL has also been introduced in [14]. The main drawback of these works is that they are either too abstract to handle most of the interesting details related to BPEL or they lead to complex representation of some intuitive aspects like compensation. In [8,15,16], Pu et al. introduced an interesting process algebra to specify the activities of BPEL. Mostly, the authors focus on fault and compensation handling. Several other interesting formal semantics were proposed in the literature including [17,18] to formalize handlers in BPEL, but no one of them take into account all the details. Some of other advantages of AV-BPEL semantics are:

- Compensations can be executed in parallel in some cases as specified by the semantic of BPEL. But, this is not the case for [17,18].
- Receive action is blocking while send action is not which reflect better reality. Floating message give a simple way to integrate this kind of communication.

4   Conclusion

This paper introduces a process algebra called AV-BPEL to disambiguate some important but very confusing features of BPEL. These include fault handler, compensation handler, termination handler and event handler (EFCT). Despite that the global idea of these handlers can be easily understood, their full semantics hide many details making them the major source of difficulty behind BPEL. Compared to existing related work, the main advantage of our formalization is that it shows the real complexity hidden behind EFCT aspects by taking into account almost all details related to them.

References

1. Huhns, M.N., Singh, M.P.: Service-oriented computing: key concepts and principles. In: IEEE Internet Computing, pp. 75–81 (2005)
2. SOAP Version 1.2 Part 0: Primer, 2nd edn. (2007)
3. Web Services Description Language (WSDL 1.1) (2003)
4. UDDI Version 2.04 API Specification (2002)
5. Lucchi, R., Mazzara, M.: A pi-calculus based semantics for WS-BPEL. J. Logic Algebraic Program. **70**, 96–118 (2007)
6. Web Services Business Process Execution Language Version 2.0 (2007)
7. Salaün, G., Ferrara, A., Chirichiello, A.: Negotiation among web services using LOTOS/CADP. In: (LJ) Zhang, L.-J., Jeckle, M. (eds.) ECOWS 2004. LNCS, vol. 3250, pp. 198–212. Springer, Heidelberg (2004)
8. Mateescu, R., Poizat, P., Salaun, G.: Adaptation of service protocols using process algebra and on-the-fly reduction techniques. In: IEEE Transactions on Software Engineering. Institute of Electrical and Electronics Engineers (IEEE) (2012)
9. Ferrara, A.: Web services: a process algebra approach. In: Proceedings of 2nd ACM International Conference on Service Oriented Computing (2004)
10. Abouzaid, F., Mullins, J.: A calculus for generation, verification and refinement of BPEL specifications. In: Electronic Notes in Theoretical Computer Science, vol. 4421, pp. 43–65 (2008)
11. Yang, C., Zhong, F.: Towards the formal foundation of orchestration process. In: 5th ICCCNT- 2014 (2014)
12. Kheldoun, A., Ioualalen, M.: Transformation BPEL processes to recatnet for analysing web services compositions. In: Model-Driven Engineering and Software Development (MODELSWARD), pp. 425–430 (2014)
13. Guillaume BABIN, Y.A.A., PANTEL, M.: Formal verification of runtime compensation of web service compositions: a refinement and proof based proposal with Event-B. In: 2015 IEEE International Conference on Services Computing, vol. 978, pp. 7–15 (2015)
14. Stahl, C.: A Petri Net Semantics for BPEL, Humboldt-Universitat zu Berlin, Informatik-Berichte 188 (2005)
15. Pu, G., Zhu, H., Qiu, Z., Wang, S.-L., Zhao, X., Kleinberg, R.D.: Theoretical foundations of scope-based compensable flow language for web service. In: Gorrieri, R., Wehrheim, H. (eds.) FMOODS 2006. LNCS, vol. 4037, pp. 251–266. Springer, Heidelberg (2006)
16. Chirichiello, A., Salaun, G.: Encoding process algebraic descriptions of web services into BPEL. Web Intell. Agent Syst. Int. J. **5**(3), 419–434 (2007)
17. Lapadula, A., Pugliese, R., Tiezzi, F.: A calculus for orchestration of web services. In: Nicola, R. (ed.) ESOP 2007. LNCS, vol. 4421, pp. 33–47. Springer, Heidelberg (2007)
18. Spieler, D.: Scope-based fct-handling in WS-BPEL 2.0. Master's thesis, Saarland University (2008)

Intelligent Service Clouds

Context-Aware Personalization for Smart Mobile Cloud Services

Waldemar Hummer$^{(\boxtimes)}$ and Stefan Schulte

Distributed Systems Group, TU Wien, Wien, Austria
{Hummer,Schulte}@dsg.tuwien.ac.at

Abstract. The advent of the Internet of Things and the increasing sensorization of smart devices that surround us in our everyday lives are spurring the demand for context-aware applications to offer personalized services. With the rapid advances in sensor technology, distributed software architectures and backend infrastructures need to be able to systematically deal with increasing amounts of real-time context data. In this paper, we present an approach for intelligent service clouds to cater for the new challenges associated with complex context-aware applications. Based on an illustrative scenario from the connected car domain, we introduce a detailed system model and approach for context-based personalization of mobile services. Our solution focuses on a three-phase approach with context change analysis, context state management, and context-triggered adaptation actions. We discuss details of our prototype implementation and put the contributions into perspective with the related work. After discussing our preliminary results, we draw a roadmap for future work towards context-aware vehicle information systems.

1 Introduction

Over the past years, we have been witnessing a steep rise in the number of devices and sensors being connected to the so-called Internet of Things (IoT) [1], a phenomenon which spans across a multitude of industry verticals, including connected cars, smart homes, e-health, and more. Our increasingly connected world of cyberphysical systems and smart things opens up a wealth of unprecedented opportunities for applications that are specifically tailored towards the needs of mobile users with the ability to adapt to their current contextual environments.

Both the amount as well as the level of integration of context data in the IoT are rapidly increasing. In the automotive industry, real-time machine data from the vehicle (e.g., fuel level) is matched with driver-related biometrics data (e.g., fatigue sensor) and combined with other contextual information (e.g., time, location) in order to satisfy the driver's preferences (e.g., navigate to a gas station for coffee and fuel). This trend has been referred to as the *quantified car* [24], in a reference to this novel combination of *connected car* and *quantified self*. In light of the leaps in progress being made on the device and data collection layer,

© Springer-Verlag Berlin Heidelberg 2016
A. Norta et al. (Eds.): ICSOC 2015 Workshops, LNCS 9586, pp. 171–183, 2016.
DOI: 10.1007/978-3-662-50539-7_14

the cloud service and application providers need to catch up with the technical challenges introduced by the increased dynamism and context-awareness of smart applications for predominantly mobile, permanently connected users.

Catering for the personal preferences and individual user contexts is becoming a critical requirement for state-of-the-art cloud applications. The processing logic of applications that deal with user context requires integrated support from intelligent service clouds, which are able to capture and monitor user context, adapt to changing environments, and optimize the application delivery.

In this paper, we tackle this issue and discuss an approach for context-aware personalization of mobile cloud services. We illustrate our solution based on a scenario from the connected car domain, with a multitude of personalized services offered to the drivers in a vehicular information system. In particular, we follow a three-phase approach with context change analysis, context state management, and context-triggered adaptation actions.

The remainder of this paper is structured as follows. In Sect. 2 we introduce an illustrative scenario which serves as the basis for presentation. Section 3 introduces the assumed system model and details our proposed solution. Implementation details are covered in Sect. 4, and our work is evaluated in Sect. 5. In Sect. 6 we discuss previous work related to our approach. Section 7 concludes the paper and highlights topics for active ongoing research efforts.

2   Scenario

We consider a scenario from the *connected car* domain. Figure 1 illustrates a vehicle used by a driver under different user contexts over time ($t \in \{1, \ldots, 10\}$). The car operates a multitude of applications, including navigation, media streaming,

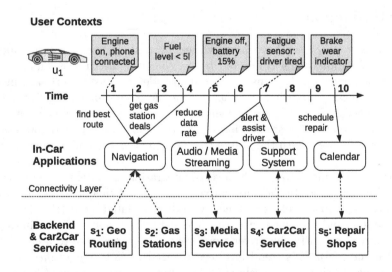

Fig. 1. Scenario: connected car with context-based personalized services

driver support system, and more. Additionally, the car is equipped with a multitude of sensors to regularly monitor the operational status (fuel, battery level, brake wear, etc.) as well as the behavior of the driver (e.g., fatigue sensor).

To enable seamless operation of the in-car applications, the continous context changes are reflected in the applications. At time $t = 1$, the engine is turned on, which triggers the navigation service to determine the target location and find the best route. At time $t = 4$, the fuel drops to a critically low level (< 5 L), hence the navigation app queries gas stations in the vicinity, and displays commercials for special deals. At $t = 5$, the engine is turned off and battery level is below 15 %, which causes the audio streaming application to reduce the data rate to save power. At $t = 7$, the fatigue sensor of the car alerts that the driver gets tired, which turns on driving assistance in the support system. Finally, at $t = 10$, the brake wear indicator reports that the brakes require maintenance, causing the calendar app to automatically schedule a service with a repair shop.

Table 1. Context-based service personalizations in scenario

Service	Context	Config. effect	Application action
Category: User Preferences			
Streaming	$timeOfDay = morning$	$station = news$	subscribe to respective media service
	$timeOfDay = afternoon$	$station = pop$	
	$timeOfDay = evening$	$station = jazz$	
Category: User Experience and Safety			
Navigation	$offTrack = true$	-	re-calculate route
Support System	$fatig = 1$	$assist = yes$	alert cars in vicinity
Category: Service Optimizations			
Streaming	$country = X$	$proxy = X$	use national proxy
Streaming	$battery > 20\%$	$dataRate = high$	adjust data rate and buffering
	$battery \leq 20\%$	$dataRate = low$	

Personalized configurations are applied depending on the current context. Table 1 contains an exemplary listing of context settings, plus the configuration effects and associated application actions. We distinguish between *user preferences* (explicitly defined by users), *user experience and safety* (predefined rules encoded within the respective services), as well as *service optimizations* (non-functional aspects). For instance, during morning hours ($timeOfDay = morning$) the driver prefers to listen to news radio, whereas the rest of the day she likes pop or jazz music. If the driver departs from the course ($offTrack = true$), the context triggers a re-calculation of the best route in the navigation service. Or, if the fatigue sensor alerts $fatigue = true$, the in-car driving assistance gets enabled.

Based on this illustrative scenario, we identify the following key challenges:

- **Manage Application-Level Context Changes**: Context data is often imprecise (e.g., precision radius of a GPS sensor) or prone to transient sensor errors. A mechanism is needed to reliably identify relevant context changes.
- **Application Actions and Adaptations**: Context changes result in application actions, which may also involve adaptation of the backend services. A systematic approach for reconfigurations at different levels is needed.
- **End-to-End Cloud Support**: Support for context handling and personalization should be offered on the Cloud layer. Integration with existing Cloud application development paradigms is desirable.

3   Approach

This section presents our approach for context-aware personalization of mobile Cloud services. We introduce the basic system model in Sect. 3.1, outline the approach in Sect. 3.2, and discuss selected details in Sects. 3.3, 3.4, and 3.5.

3.1   System Model

Table 2 lists the elements of the assumed system model with the respective symbols, description, and a brief example with reference to our scenario. In our formalization, $\mathcal{P}(Y)$ denotes the *power set* of a given set Y, and $[f] := \{f' : dom(f) \rightarrow codom(f)\}$ denotes the *function space* of a function f.

The model contains a set of services (S) which are consumed by different mobile service users (U). Each user is associated with a context (X) that changes over time (e.g., vehicle location). The context attributes are captured via a mapping from key (K) to value domain (V). The domain of time (T) is also encoded in the context. The current context of a user is determined by the function c. The function p represents user-specific service personalizations which apply at a certain point in time. Assuming user u_1 is currently driving in Austria, the media service (s_3) utilizes the local proxy $(proxy = AT)$ for music streaming.

Function d models derived context attributes, for instance if the fatigue sensor alerts $(fatig = 1)$ consecutively at time points $t \in T$ and $t + 1$, a warning event is issued and added to the user's context attributes $(fatigWarn = 1)$. This technique can be used to eliminate the impact of *false positives* caused by the fatigue sensor. Finally, function t defines a set of triggers where a certain context configuration leads to a change in a user's service personalization. In our example, if the driving user u_1 crosses the border to Germany $(country = DE)$, the local proxy $(proxy = DE)$ should be used for service s_3.

3.2   Approach Overview

Figure 2 illustrates an overview of our approach, based on the services and context data in our scenario. The figure depicts a timeline for three mobile service users, with different context changes.

Table 2. System model

Symbol	Description	Example
S	Set of services	$S = \{s_1, \ldots, s_5\}$
U	Set of mobile service users	$U = \{u_1, u_2, u_3\}$
$M : K \rightarrow V$	Domain of key-value maps, mapping a key (K) to a value domain (V)	-
$T \subset V$	Domain of time	$T = \{t = 1, \ldots, t = 10, \ldots\}$
$X \subset M$	Domain of user contexts, mapping context attributes (K) to values (V)	$ctx_1 = \{location \mapsto (47.1, 10.2)\}$
$c : U \rightarrow X$	Current context of a user	$c : u_1 \mapsto ctx_1$
$p : (U \times S) \rightarrow M$	Current service personalizations, mapping users (U) of a service (S) to a configuration map (M)	$(u_1, s_3) \mapsto \{proxy = AT\}$
$d : \mathcal{P}(T \times X) \rightarrow X$	Query rules for derived context attributes	$\{(t, fatig = 1), (t + 1, fatig = 1)\}$ $\mapsto (fatigWarn = 1)$
$t : U \times X \rightarrow [p]$	Context-based configuration triggers	$(u_1, country = DE) \mapsto \{(u_1, s_3) \mapsto \{proxy = DE\}\}$

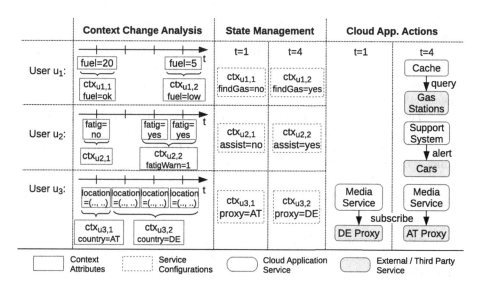

Fig. 2. Illustration of the overall approach

The first part in our three-stage approach is context change analysis, where context events are analyzed over time to derive higher-level context attributes (see Sect. 3.3). In the second stage, the context changes need to be propagated to the state management which tracks the current configurations for all users (see Sect. 3.4). Based on the state management, adaptations are performed to cater for the personalized service configurations (see Sect. 3.5).

3.3   Identification of Context Changes

We distinguish "raw" (or low-level) context changes which are typically measured by sensor devices, and "complex" (or higher-level) context changes which reflect the actual context information that is relevant to the application services.

In Fig. 2, the raw context changes for fuel level in liters ($fuel$), fatigue sensor ($fatig$), and current GPS location ($location$), need to be analyzed and enriched with additional information in order to have a meaningful impact on the service personalization. We distinguish the following mechanisms to derive relevant context changes:

- **Discretization**: Context attributes with a continuous value domain are mapped to a discrete value domain. For instance, a fuel level above 5 L is considered "*ok*", whereas levels below 5 L are considered "*low*". Evidently, the discretization varies from vehicle to vehicle, and also depends on the geographic area in which the vehicle is operated (in a deserted area, 5 L of fuel may be insufficient to reach the next gas station).
- **Sampling**: The raw context values should only be propagated to the application if they are deemed to properly represent the user's environment. The technique of sampling can be used to identify statistically significant context changes, and eliminate the impact of false positives in the sensor measurements. For instance, the fatigue warning in Fig. 2 ($fatigWarn = 1$) is only issued if there are two consecutive fatigue sensor measurements ($fatig = 1$ at time points 3 and 4). Clearly, this simple example can be extended to more meaningful statistical significance levels.
- **Pattern Detection**: For more sophisticated cases, we utilize complex event processing (CEP) [9] to derive high-level context changes from raw events. The context changes are modeled as a stream of events over time, and CEP window queries allow for complex pattern detection. In Fig. 2, if we combine the current GPS location of user u_3 with map data, we can derive the current country (AT) and anticipate the entry into a new country (DE) if the event pattern indicates that the driver approaches the country border.

Currently, rules and CEP queries are defined manually, yet for convenience we offer a set of predefined rule templates which can be parameterized according to individual scenarios. For instance, a *geo fence* template reports whether any tracked objects are within a circular geographical region; parameterizations are (1) the center location, and (2) the radius of the geo fence. In future work, we envision a hybrid approach, mixing manually specified rules for identifying context changes with automatically learned rules for predicting context changes. The necessary underlying machine learning techniques are readily available, as evidenced, for instance, by the Prediction API[1] in the Google Cloud offering. A specialized module to learn rules for deriving context changes will become an important offering as part of intelligent service clouds.

3.4   Multi-user Context Propagation and State Management

Having a mechanism to identify application-relevant changes (Sect. 3.3), we need to propagate the context information and maintain user-specific configuration states for the Cloud services. The context propagation happens in multiple steps, as demonstrated in the connected car scenario: the values from multiple sensors within the car need to be collected to form the user context (step 1), which is transmitted to the Cloud and transformed into user-specific service personalizations (step 2), and then combined into optimized configurations and variants of the Cloud services shared among the users (step 3).

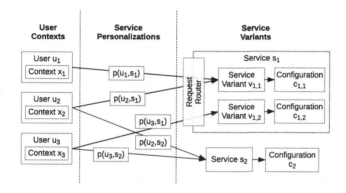

Fig. 3. Propagation of context values and management of configuration state

Figure 3 illustrates the approach based on exemplary context request flows from three service users (u_1, u_2, u_3). The contexts (x_1, x_2, x_3) on the left hand side are transmitted and transformed into service personalizations, via function t in our system model in Sect. 3.1. Any interaction of a user u_m with a backend service s_n carries the service personalization state $p(u_m, s_n)$ that helps the request router to select the respective service variant. A service variant is an instance of the service that has a particular configuration associated, yet this configuration is shared by a multitude of users (as opposed to service personalizations, which are user-specific). For example, in our scenario the media service is configured with two variants for high-quality and low-quality streaming, respectively. Detailed discussion of service variability engineering are out of the scope of this paper, and for details we refer to specialized literature [21].

---

[1] https://cloud.google.com/prediction/.

Currently, we apply state management for single services and their service variants only, and do not take into account the interactions between groups of services or business processes. In future work, we plan to integrate support for more comprehensive service ontologies [23] allowing to model service workflows.

3.5 Context-Triggered Actions and Adaptations

Based on changes in the service configurations, application actions are triggered which result in adaptation of the Cloud environment. We distinguish three types:

- **Application**: Any actions encoded in the business logic of the application.
- **Infrastructure**: Any adaptations related to current allocation of resources on the infrastructure layer (e.g., virtual machines, disk volumes, databases).
- **Topology**: Any changes in the relationships and interconnections of the components (e.g., master-slave election in a clustered service).

Table 3 contains three examples of context-triggered adaptations, applied to our scenario. If a driver is running out of fuel, a cache infrastructure component is configured before the application starts querying for gas stations. To adjust the *dataRate* for the streaming service, an adaptation is required in the request router to pick the respective service variant. Finally, switching to a different streaming proxy induces a topology change with a new service variant. Our approach also integrates previous work on *service prefetching* [18], an application adaptation that is necessary to handle unreliable connectivity (e.g., in tunnels).

Table 3. Context-triggered adaptations (Examples)

Trigger	Type(s)	Adaptation
findGas = true	Infrastr., Application	Instantiate cache, query gas stations
dataRate = high|low	Topology, Application	Configure request router to pick respective variant of media service
proxy = X	Topology	Create a service variant that subscribes to the stream proxy of country X

4 Implementation

We are currently working towards a full-stack implementation of our approach, embedded in Google's scalable services cluster management tool *Kubernetes*[2]. Here we discuss the architectural design and selected details of our prototype.

Figure 4 depicts the architecture of the deployed system (third-party tools are in grey boxes). On the client side (e.g., in-car application platform) each user

---

[2] http://kubernetes.io/.

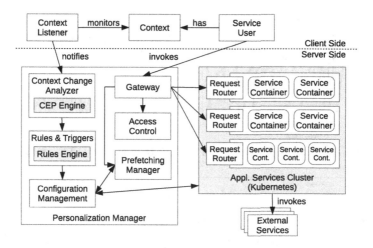

Fig. 4. System architecture

operates under a specific Context, which is monitored by the Context Listener. For the external client-server connectivity, we assume a cellular network connection (e.g., UMTS/HSPA). Upon notification, the Context Change Analyzer uses a CEP engine (*Esper* [5]). We build on our previous work and develop a Domain Specific Language (DSL) for specifying rules to derive application-relevant context changes, based on the MONINA language [19]. The context changes are fed into the Rules & Triggers component, which incorporates a Rules Engine.

Our implementation caters for the principles of the *12-factor app* [20], which has gained high popularity for scalable Cloud applications. Application services are mostly stateless, the state (e.g., current user context) is maintained in a configuration management tool (we use the distributed key-value store *etcd* provided by *CoreOS*). For deployment, we utilize DevOps automation scripts which deploy the services and reliably bring the infrastructure into the desired state [17].

The user accesses the services via a Gateway which is responsible for performing Access Control, deciding over service prefetching (via the Prefetching Manager [18]), and finally forwarding requests. The Request Routers select among the available service variants (each deployed in a separate service container). Currently, this is tailor-made, because Kubernetes merely performs simplistic round-robin load balancing; we plan to integrate our context-based routing directly into the Kubernetes code base, which we deem a highly useful extension.

5   Evaluation

In this section we evaluate our approach and discuss some of the preliminary results that we have collected. We have set up a test bed on a machine with quad-core 2.5 GHz CPU and 16 GB RAM. For experimentation, we utilize a real-life data set published by Volkswagen as part of a programming contest[3]. The data

---

[3] Volkswagen CodeFest[8], http://group-it.volkswagenag.com/codefest/codefest.html.

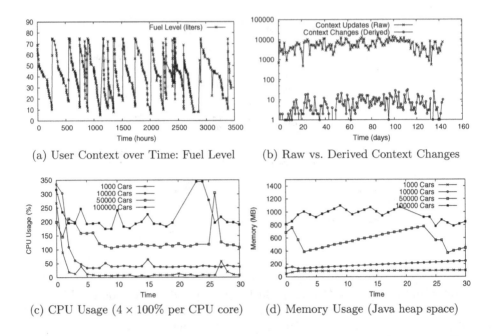

(a) User Context over Time: Fuel Level   (b) Raw vs. Derived Context Changes

(c) CPU Usage ($4 \times 100\%$ per CPU core)   (d) Memory Usage (Java heap space)

Fig. 5. Evaluation results

set contains traces of eight driving cars with a rich set of context attributes (including: speed, battery, fuel, fatigue sensor, brake wear sensor, etc.).

Context snapshots of the vehicles are recorded approximately every 5–30 s, resulting in a total of roughly 800K data points with some 25M context attribute values. Figure 5a plots the fuel level of one of the car traces, recorded over a period of 143 days (apprx. 3500 h). The values are aggregated over periods of one hour; in fact, for our scenario we are not interested in the detailed fuel levels, but only in the critically low levels. The same applies for the fatigue sensor where we only need to monitor the application-relevant transition from $fatig = no$ to $fatig = yes$, or vice versa. This ratio of raw events to derived context changes is illustrated in Fig. 5b (note the logarithmic scale on the y-axis). That is, the majority of context data can be pre-processed inside the car (by the Context Listener) and need not be transmitted to the server, which leaves huge space for optimization of network utilization, as well as energy usage.

Yet, with increasing numbers of cars, the burden on the infrastructure can become significant. In our experiments we have evaluated the end-to-end stress to the backend, for increasing number of cars (1K, 10K, 50K, 100K), assuming each car sends one context update (e.g., location) every 5 s. Figure 5c and d depict the CPU usage and memory usage of the Personalization Manager, which hosts the CEP Engine, Rule Engine, Configuration Management etc. The CPU spikes at the beginning due to high initialization efforts for the CEP engines, and the intermittent CPU spikes (e.g., time points 23/24) are due to Java garbage collection (see corresponding drops in heap space memory). We observe that for 100K cars the single-node deployment operates almost at its limit; currently, we are extending our implementation with a distributed setup, to evaluate even larger scenarios. In a large-scale setup we further need to evaluate the reliability of the system under different faults during processing of the context events [15].

6   Related Work

In this section, we discuss related work in the areas of context-aware computing, Web service personalization, and adaptive service-oriented systems.

Early work on context-aware systems [2] and pervasive/ubiquitous systems [3] dates back to the early 2000s, with seminal contributions achieved in various areas, including ontologies for context monitoring [8], service-oriented middlewares for context-based computing [12], intelligent context dissemination in vehicular networks [10], as well as context-based human-computer interaction [4]. Recently, topics revolving around context-aware computing have found new application in the area of IoT in general, and the domain of connected vehicles in particular. Gansel et al. [11] introduce a context-aware access control concept for automotive systems, focusing on human interactions with the car computer. Bolchini et al. [6] discuss a taxonomy of context models, along different dimensions like context attributes, representations, and management. The approach by Ouedraogo et al. [22] uses *models@run.time* techniques for contextualized deployment of security policies in intelligent service clouds. Their approach discusses the design of context-based security mediators, while our focus is on end-to-end context propagation and context-triggered adaptations in service clouds.

Previous approaches to Web service personalization have focused on rules modeling, service matching, and personalized adaptation. Yu et al. [26] present a framework for rules-based personalization in Web service workflows, which uses aspect-oriented programming (AOP) with hooks to allow dynamic switching between user contexts. Hella et al. [13] use Semantic Web technologies to perform service matching based on user preferences. Wang et al. [25] propose *rule nets* as a technique to express rules for personalized needs. While their work presents a formal model and language for expressing rules, our focus is on applying CEP and rules for analysis of context changes in adaptive cloud applications.

A large body of research has been done in the area of adaptive service-based systems. Hu et al. [14] discuss a rule-based approach for dynamic adaptation of business processes based on context changes. Their assumed model is a business process definition, whereas we target cloud applications with service variants and context-triggered configuration changes. Inzinger et al. [19] introduce event-based monitoring and adaptation of application configurations, which has influenced our technical solution. Brogi et al. [7] discuss dynamic contextual adaptation for behavioural interfaces, e.g., between a client and server process. Their contextual environments provide interface mappings, but do not take complex patterns of context updates into account, which is at the core of our work.

7   Conclusion

The advance of the Internet of Things poses novel challenges with regards to massive amounts of real-time context data generated by devices and sensors surrounding us in our everyday lives. The ubiquity of contextual information opens up novel opportunities for personalization in modern user-centric applications. Built-in support for personalization is hence becoming a critical requirement for intelligent service clouds. In this paper we introduce and discuss techniques for context-aware personalization of mobile cloud services.

Based on our illustrative scenario from the connected cars domain, we provide a detailed system model and outline our solution, following a three-stage approach. First, we utilize CEP techniques to aggregate raw context events into higher-level information, in order to identify application-relevant context changes. Second, we apply triggers to propagate context changes into user-specific service configurations. Third, we illustrate the integration with cloud services to apply context-triggered adaptation actions. We discuss our prototype implementation which is embedded into Kubernetes, a state-of-the-art cloud technology for cluster management of service containers. In our future work, we extend our approach with various advanced aspects of context processing and service personalization, including high scalability, multi-tenant optimization of the event processing logic [16], as well as privacy and data protection aspects.

Acknowledgements. This work is partially supported by the European Union within the SIMPLI-CITY FP7-ICT project (Grant agreement no. 318201).

References

1. Atzori, L., Iera, A., Morabito, G.: The internet of things: a survey. Comput. Netw. **54**(15), 2787–2805 (2010)
2. Baldauf, M., Dustdar, S., Rosenberg, F.: A survey on context-aware systems. Int. J. Ad Hoc Ubiquit. Comput. **2**(4), 263–277 (2007)
3. Bellavista, P., Corradi, A., Fanelli, M., Foschini, L.: A survey of context data distribution for mobile ubiquitous systems. ACM Comput. Surv. **44**(4), 24 (2012)
4. Bellotti, V., Edwards, K.: Intelligibility and accountability: human considerations in context-aware systems. Hum.-Comput. Interact. **16**(2–4), 193–212 (2001)
5. Bernhardt, T., Vasseur, A.: Esper: event stream processing and correlation. ONJava, in OReilly (2007). http://www.onjava.com/lpt/a/6955
6. Bolchini, C., Curino, C.A., Quintarelli, E., Schreiber, F.A., Tanca, L.: A data-oriented survey of context models. ACM Sigmod Rec. **36**(4), 19–26 (2007)
7. Brogi, A., Cámara, J., Canal, C., Cubo, J., Pimentel, E.: Dynamic contextual adaptation. Electron. Notes Theoret. Comput. Sci. **175**(2), 81–95 (2007)
8. Chen, H., Finin, T., Joshi, A.: An ontology for context-aware pervasive computing environments. Knowl. Eng. Rev. **18**(03), 197–207 (2003)
9. Cugola, G., Margara, A.: Processing flows of information: from data stream to complex event processing. ACM Comput. Surv. (CSUR) **44**(3), 15 (2012)
10. Eichler, S., Schroth, C., Kosch, T., Strassberger, M.: Strategies for context-adaptive message dissemination in vehicular ad hoc networks. In: MOBIQUITOUS (2006)

11. Gansel, S., Schnitzer, S., et al.: An access control concept for novel automotive HMI systems. In: ACM SACMAT 2014, pp. 17–28. ACM (2014)
12. Gu, T., Pung, H., Zhang, D.Q.: A service-oriented middleware for building context-aware services. J. Netw. Comput. Appl. **28**(1), 1–18 (2005)
13. Hella, L., Krogstie, J.: Using Semantic Web for Mobile Services Personalization. Int. J. u-and e-Serv. Sci. Technol. **7**(2), 221–238 (2014)
14. Hu, G., Wu, B., Chen, J.: Dynamic adaptation of business process based on context changes: a rule-oriented approach. In: PACEB Workshop @ ICSOC (2014)
15. Hummer, W., Inzinger, C., Leitner, P., Satzger, B., Dustdar, S.: Deriving a unified fault taxonomy for event-based systems. In: 6th ACM DEBS Conference (2012)
16. Hummer, W., Leitner, P., Satzger, B., Dustdar, S.: Dynamic migration of processing elements for optimized query execution in event-based systems. In: DOA (2011)
17. Hummer, W., Rosenberg, F., Oliveira, F., Eilam, T.: Testing idempotence for infrastructure as code. In: Eyers, D., Schwan, K. (eds.) Middleware 2013. LNCS, vol. 8275, pp. 368–388. Springer, Heidelberg (2013)
18. Hummer, W., Schulte, S., Hoenisch, P., Dustdar, S.: Context-aware data prefetching in mobile service environments. In: BDCloud Conference, pp. 214–221. IEEE (2014)
19. Inzinger, C., Hummer, W., et al.: Generic event-based monitoring and adaptation methodology for heterogeneous distributed systems. SPE **44**(7), 805–822 (2014)
20. Kemp, C., Gyger, B.: Professional Heroku Programming. Wiley, Chichester (2013)
21. Kumar, A., Yao, W.: Design and management of flexible process variants using templates and rules. Comput. Ind. **63**(2), 112–130 (2012)
22. Ouedraogo, W., Biennier, F., Merle, P.: Contextualised security operation deployment through mds@run.time architecture. In: ISC Workshop @ ICSOC (2014)
23. Pahl, C., Casey, M.: Ontology support for web service processes. ACM SIGSOFT Softw. Eng. Notes **28**, 208–216 (2003)
24. Swan, M.: Connected car: quantified self becomes quantified car. JSAN **4**(1), 2–29 (2015)
25. Wang, W., Zong, S., Yu, J., Yongchareon, S.: Modelling web service personalization with rule nets. In: Liu, C., He, J., Huang, G., Huang, Z. (eds.) WISE Workshops 2013. LNCS, vol. 8182, pp. 228–238. Springer, Heidelberg (2014)
26. Yu, J., Han, J., Sheng, Q.Z., Gunarso, S.O.: PerCAS: an approach to enabling dynamic and personalized adaptation for context-aware services. In: Liu, C., Ludwig, H., Toumani, F., Yu, Q. (eds.) Service Oriented Computing. LNCS, vol. 7636, pp. 173–190. Springer, Heidelberg (2012)

Information Governance Requirements for Architectural Solutions Supporting Dynamic Business Networking

Mohammad R. Rasouli[✉], Rik Eshuis, Jos J.M. Trienekens, and Paul W.P.J. Grefen

School of Industrial Engineering, Eindhoven University of Technology,
P.O box: 513, 5600 Eindhoven, The Netherlands
{M.Rasouli,H.Eshuis,J.J.M.Trienekens,P.W.P.J.Grefen}@tue.nl

Abstract. The competition in the globalized markets highlights the need for the formation of dynamic business networks to provide mass-customized integrated solutions for customers. However, dynamic interoperations among parties within a business network results in emerging information governance (IG) requirements. In previous research different architectural solutions have been developed to support dynamic business networks. In this paper we investigate in the extent to which the emerging IG requirements in dynamic business networks are covered by developed architectural solutions. This investigation reflects required future developments to enrich architectural solutions in order to support IG requirements in dynamic business networks.

1 Introduction

The competition in the globalized markets forces organizations to co-create mass customized integrated solutions for customers through the formation of dynamic business networks [1]. These business networks need to handle dynamic interactions among parties within a value network in order to respond to an expected customer experience [2]. The interactions among parties can be seen as inter-organizational business processes that exchange information among parties. The formation of business networks, however, necessitates dealing with information exchange related issues resulting from the autonomy, the distribution, and the heterogeneity of information products [3, 4]. These issues highlight the need for considering information governance (IG) in the context of dynamic business networking.

Different architectural solutions have been developed in previous work to support dynamic formation of business networks (e.g. [5, 6]). Recent proposals [7] are targeting cloud computing systems as implementation platform [8]. In this position paper, we aim to investigate in the extent to which IG requirements in the context of dynamic business networking are covered by these existing architectural solutions. This gives us directions for further research to investigate how IT can support information governance for dynamic business networks.

The plan of this paper is as follows. In Sect. 2, we enumerate IG requirements that need to be attended to in architectural solutions in the context of dynamic business networking. In Sect. 3 we investigate how the enumerated IG requirements are addressed in the developed architectural solutions. A discussion is represented in Sect. 4 on the

© Springer-Verlag Berlin Heidelberg 2016
A. Norta et al. (Eds.): ICSOC 2015 Workshops, LNCS 9586, pp. 184–189, 2016.
DOI: 10.1007/978-3-662-50539-7_15

required architectural developments to support IG requirements in dynamic business networks. The paper is concluded in Sect. 5 by the delineation of future work.

2   IG Requirements in Dynamic Business Networking

IG can be characterized as a holistic approach to different mechanisms that are required to enable high quality information exchange [9]. IG can be seen within three main domains, respectively, the information quality (IQ), the information security, and the metadata domain [10]. The IQ indicates the extent to which information provided within a business network fits with stakeholders' needs [11]. The IQ points out the information product quality as well as the information service quality. The former considers information as a product that needs to be produced by a manufacturing process with as end-product the information stored in a database. But, information service quality focuses on the activities occurring after information is stored as an end-product in a database, i.e. to enable consumers to obtain and use information. Information security underlines the protection of information confidentiality, integrity and availability [12]. Metadata reflects information about the data processed in an information service that enhances the usability and understandability of the service [10].

Dynamic business networking that entails dynamic partnering as well as dynamic operating among parties results in the emergence of new IG requirements. These IG requirements reflect the necessities of high quality information exchange. A list of IG issues resulting from dynamic business networking has been explored in [4]. A business network governor should effectively respond to these issues through different types of possible solutions like organizational solutions, architectural solutions, or computational solutions. In this paper we evaluate how well existing architectural solutions for dynamic business networks support IG. Based on the explored IG issues in dynamic business networking [4, 13], the IG requirements that need to be covered by an architectural solution are enumerated below:

- *Information product quality requirements:* these requirements point out the quality issues of information products that are stored in distributed databases in a business network. Some examples of such pertaining requirements can be described as handling information product repetition and information product synchronization, and linkage of relevant information products.
- *Information service quality requirements:* these requirements address the modification of the syntactic and semantic inconsistency of information services.
- *Information security requirements:* these requirements underline the necessities for safeguarding added-value information assets.
- *Metadata requirements:* These requirements imply the need for shared and generally accepted metadata in a business network to support a consistent understanding of the exchanged information.

3 Architectural Solutions Supporting Dynamic Business Networking

In this section we investigate to which extent the aforementioned IG requirements are addressed by architectural solutions that are developed in previous research to support dynamic business networking. For this purpose we concentrate on related works that consider interactions among collaborating parties as process-view based interoperations (see [14]). We found 8 related architectural solutions in previous work that address the formation of dynamic business networking. While most of them have been developed before cloud computing emerged, reference [8] explicitly targets a cloud computing implementation platform. We investigate how IG requirements have been attended in these related architectural solutions; see Table 1. For this investigation we rely on the requirements that have been identified for the development of these architectures as well as the components introduced within the architectural designs. The investigation is based on a 4-level assessment that is outlined in the legend of Table 1.

Table 1. IG requirements in architectural solutions supporting dynamic business networking

Architectural solution supporting dynamic business networking	IG requirements			
	Information product quality	Information service quality	Information security	Metadata
[15]	○	◐	⊕	⊕
[16]	○	◐	⊕	⊕
[14]	○	◐	⊕	○
[17]	○	◐	◐	○
[18]	○	⊕	○	○
[7]	○	⊕	⊕	○
[6]	○	◐	○	○
[19]	○	◐	⊕	⊕

○ requirements have not been addressed   ⊕ requirements have been addressed partially/implicitly in an abstract level
◐ requirements have been addressed clearly, but in an abstract level   ● requirements have been addressed clearly and concretely

The architecture proposed in [15, 16] assume syntactic consistency of information services within dynamic inter-organizational business processes. In this work, however the necessity for domain knowledge integration is addressed as an approach for metadata governance, but concrete relevant components are not reflected in the proposed architecture. The architecture developed in [14] focuses on the development of adapted process views to facilitate interoperability in dynamic supply networks. In this way, the proposed architecture addresses syntactic misalignment between process views; other IG requirements are not considered. Citation [17] modifies the syntactic inconsistencies among flexible distributed business processes through an Wf-XML message handler. It also clearly points out the reliability and security of the exchanged messages. Citation [18] represents an abstract architecture to overcome the heterogeneity of business process views; all other aspects of IG requirements are neglected. The architecture developed in the WISE project [7] provides a comprehensive view on business process management in virtual enterprises. But it doesn't clearly address the IG requirements and its approach to deal with syntactic inconsistency and security issues does not offer concrete guidance. Using protocol adaptors to deal with the syntactic heterogeneity of information services is clearly addressed in [6]. However the proposed architecture remains quite abstract and does not address information governance. Citation [19] proposes the e-sourcing concept for interoperability in a business network. The proposed architecture in this work that refines the e-sourcing concept addresses syntactic and semantic inconsistency by a component supporting negotiation for setting up a collaboration configuration. It also handles information security through a trusted third part. However these components remain quite abstract and high-level solutions.

4   Discussion on Related Work

The investigation of related work, as reflected in Table 1, shows that from the IG requirements point of view the developed architectural solutions supporting dynamic business networking mostly concentrate on the information service quality. This might be due to the dominance of the service-oriented architecture that underlines the separation of the service functionality from the service internal logic. In this way, it can be conceived that in most of the developed architectural solutions the governance of information product is seen as the internal responsibility of information service providers. However, most of the information product quality requirements resulting from dynamic business networking (like information product repetition, synchronization, and pooling) cannot be met by information service providers and need to be addressed by a network governor. A central support by a network governor is required to enable information product quality in the whole value network. This central support should be aided by relevant components in architectural solutions.

Among the information service quality requirements, the developed architectural solutions have mostly focused on the modification of the syntactic and semantic inconsistencies between information services. The provision of integrated solutions for customers through dynamic business networking necessitates the collaboration of parties from different business contexts. The context-aware semantic modification of information services requires further development of the architectural solutions.

Although different solutions have been developed to support information security in dynamic business networks (e.g. [20]), a comprehensive and well-established view on security in dynamic business networking context needs further development. For instance, the modification of inconsistent security policies established by autonomous parties cannot easily be responded to by conventional dynamic trust management mechanisms. The architectural solutions supporting dynamic business networking require a more comprehensive view on information security.

Architectural solutions enhancing collaborative ontology management as a support for the metadata governance have been developed in previous research (e.g. [21]). However, this domain of information governance requirements has not been addressed clearly in aforementioned architectural designs. Indeed, it can be said that substantial developments is required in order to address metadata governance in the formation of dynamic business networks.

Architectural designs to support information governance in the context of the integrated information systems (e.g. [3, 22]), on the other hand, do not clearly address the requirements of formation of dynamic business networking. More specifically, these architectures reflect required components to support the information quality lifecycle in cooperative information systems, but a comprehensive view on IG requirements as represented in Sect. 2 is not addressed by these architectures. However, as a general idea, the composition of proposed components in these architectures with architectures supporting dynamic business networking would be an appropriate direction to respond to the aforementioned IG requirements.

Meanwhile, business scenarios that are considered for developing the investigated architectural solutions need to be updated to address emerging business visions like the service dominant logic of marketing and the product-service transition. These emerging visions underline the role of the customer as a co-developer and a co-creator in a value network. In this way, the dynamic B2B interactions need to be integrated with dynamic B2C interactions. Information governance in this emerging business situation deals with new requirements like customer information privacy. These emerging requirements may fundamentally transform all B2B interactions to B2C or actor to actor (A2A) relations. These emerging requirements may point out a revolutionary change in the aforementioned architectural designs.

5   Conclusion and Future Work

In this paper, from the IG point of view we critically investigated a number of proposed architectural solutions that support dynamic business networking. This investigation reflects required future developments in architectural designs to respond to IG requirements in emerging business networking scenarios. The findings show that substantial developments are required to enhance information governance requirements, particularly in emerging customer centric business networking scenarios.

As a next step, we aim to specify more concrete requirements of information governance in customer centric dynamic business networks. These requirements can be a well-established basis for the enrichment of the aforementioned architectural solutions through the development of new components.

References

1. Rasouli, M.R., Kusters, R.J., Trienekens, J.J., Grefen, P.W.: Service Orientation in Demand-Supply Chains: Towards an Integrated Framework. In: Camarinha-Matos, L.M., Afsarmanesh, H. (eds.) Collaborative Systems for Smart Networked Environments. IFIP AICT, vol. 434, pp. 182–193. Springer, Heidelberg (2014)
2. Rasouli, M.R., Trienekens, J.J., Kusters, R.J., Grefen, P.W.: A dynamic capabilities perspective on service-orientation in demand-supply chains. Procedia CIRP 30, 396–401 (2015)
3. Mecella, M., Scannapieco, M., Virgillito, A., Baldoni, R., Catarci, T., Batini, C.: Managing data quality in cooperative information systems. In: CoopIS 2002, DOA 2002, and ODBASE 2002. LNCS, vol. 2519, pp. 486–502. Springer, Heidelberg (2002)

4. Rasouli, M.R., Eshuis, R., Trienekens, J.J., Kusters, R.J., Grefen, P.W.: Information quality in dynamic networked business process management. In: CoopIS 2015, ODBASE 2015, and C&TC 2015. LNCS, vol. 9415, pp. 202–218. Springer, Switzerland (2015)

5. Grefen, P., Aberer, K., Hoffner, Y., Ludwig, H.: CrossFlow: cross-organizational workflow management in dynamic virtual enterprises. Comput. Syst. Sci. Eng. **1**, 277–290 (2000)

6. Seguel, R., Eshuis, R., Grefen, P.: Architecture support for flexible business chain integration using protocol adaptors. Int. J. Coop. Inform. Syst. **23**, 1450008 (2014)

7. Alonso, G., Lazcano, A., Schuldt, H., Schuldt, C.: The WISE approach to electronic commerce. Int. J. Comput. Syst. Sci. Eng. **15**, 343–355 (2000)

8. Rimal, B.P., Jukan, A., Katsaros, D., Goeleven, Y.: Architectural requirements for cloud computing systems: an enterprise cloud approach. J. Grid Comput. **9**, 3–26 (2011)

9. Kooper, M.N., Maes, R., Lindgreen, E.R.: On the governance of information: Introducing a new concept of governance to support the management of information. Int. J. Inf. Manage. **31**, 195–200 (2011)

10. Khatri, V., Brown, C.V.: Designing data governance. Commun. ACM **53**, 148–152 (2010)

11. Wang, R.Y.: A product perspective on total data quality management. Commun. ACM **41**, 58–65 (1998)

12. Bishop, M.: What is computer security? IEEE Secur. Priv. **1**, 67–69 (2003)

13. Rasouli, M.R., Kusters, R.J., Trienekens, J.J., Grefen, P.W.: Information governance requirements in dynamic business networking. In: Industrial Management and Data Systems Special Issue on IT Governance for IoT Supply Chains (2016)

14. Liu, D.-R., Shen, M.: Business-to-business workflow interoperation based on process-views. Decis. Support Syst. **38**, 399–419 (2004)

15. Mehandjiev, N., Grefen, P. (eds.): Dynamic business process formation for instant virtual enterprises. Springer, London (2010)

16. Grefen, P., Eshuis, R., Mehandjiev, N., Kouvas, G., Weichhart, G.: Internet-based support for process-oriented instant virtual enterprises. Internet Comput. IEEE **13**, 65–73 (2009)

17. Jung, J.-Y., Kim, H., Kang, S.-H.: Standards-based approaches to B2B workflow integration. Comput. Ind. Eng. **51**, 321–334 (2006)

18. Jiang, P., Shao, X., Qiu, H., Gao, L., Li, P.: A Web services and process-view combined approach for process management of collaborative product development. Comput. Ind. **60**, 416–427 (2009)

19. Norta, A., Grefen, P., Narendra, N.C.: A reference architecture for managing dynamic inter-organizational business processes. Data Knowl. Eng. **91**, 52–89 (2014)

20. Blaze, M., Kannan, S., Lee, I., Sokolsky, O., Smith, J.M., Keromytis, A.D., Lee, W.: Dynamic trust management. Computer **42**, 44–52 (2009)

21. Fensel, D., Facca, F.M., Simperl, E., Toma, I.: Semantic Web Services. Springer, Heidelberg (2011)

22. Scannapieco, M., Virgillito, A., Marchetti, C., Mecella, M., Baldoni, R.: The DaQuinCIS architecture: a platform for exchanging and improving data quality in cooperative information systems. Inform. Syst. **29**, 551–582 (2004)

Big Data Services
and Computational Intelligence

An Evolutionary Multiobjective Approach for the Dynamic Multilevel Component Selection Problem

Andreea Vescan[✉]

Computer Science Department, Babes-Bolyai University,
1, M. Kogalniceanu, Cluj-Napoca, Romania
avescan@cs.ubbcluj.ro
http://cs.ubbcluj.ro/~avescan

Abstract. The architecture of a systems changes after the deployment phase due to new requirements thus the software architect must make decisions about the selection of the right software components out of a range of choices. This work deals with the component selection problem with a multilevel system view in an dynamic environment. We are approaching the problem as multiobjective using the Pareto dominance principle. The model aims to minimize the cost of the final solution while satisfying new requirements (or having available new components) keeping the complexity of the system as minimum as possible (in terms of used components). To validate our approach we performed experiments using a case study, a *Reservation System* application example. We have compared our approach with a random search algorithm using the Wilcoxon statistical test. The tests performed show the potential of evolutionary algorithms for the dynamic multilevel component selection problem.

Keywords: Component selection · Dynamic · Multilevel · Multiobjective optimization

1 Introduction

The problems of identification and selection the right software components out of a range of choices to satisfy a set of requirements have received considerable attention in the field of component-based software engineering during the last two decades [4,10].

Identification of a software architecture for a given system may be achieve in two ways: (1) Component Identification [7] and (2) Component Selection [9]. Component Identification has the scope to partition functionalities of a given system into non-intersecting logical components to provide the starting points for designing the architecture. The aim of Component Selection methods is to find suitable components from repository to satisfy a set of requirements under various constraints/criteria (i.e. cost, number of used components, etc.). This paper has focused on the component selection process, the goal being to provide the suitable existing components matching software requirements.

© Springer-Verlag Berlin Heidelberg 2016
A. Norta et al. (Eds.): ICSOC 2015 Workshops, LNCS 9586, pp. 193–204, 2016.
DOI: 10.1007/978-3-662-50539-7_16

After the deployment phase, the maintenance phase requires more attention and the software architects need assistance in the decisions of the frequent
changes of the software system, either for adding new requirements or for removing some of the requirements. So, the other perspective concerning *component
configurations* refers to updating/adding/removing one or many requirements
from an already constructed system. This represents the *reconfiguration problem* [15], transforming the structural view of a component system, changing the
system's functionality [13].

The major contribution to this paper is **the combination of the two
perspectives: the multilevel configuration [12] of the component selection problem combined with the dynamical changing requirements,
i.e. updating/adding/removing requirements (or components) from
an already constructed system** [13]. Another contribution contained in this
paper is the consideration of a non-functional requirement, **the cost of a component, and therefore the cost of the entire solution.**The configuration problem considers the multilayer view with additional cost objective. The
reconfiguration problem considers the following dynamics: system requirements
change over time and the component repository varies over time.

The paper is organized as follows: Sect. 2 contains configuration and reconfiguration description problems, and presents the used component model. The
optimisation process of the dynamic multilevel component selection problem is
described in Sect. 3. In Sect. 4 we apply to a real world case study our approach to
validate it. Some experiments are performed considering two dynamics: requirements changes over time and component repository varies over time. Section 5
introduces the current state of art regarding the component selection problem
and analysis the differences compared with our present approach. We conclude
our paper and discuss future work in Sect. 6.

2   Background: Configuration/Reconfiguration Problem and Component Model

To provide a discussion context for the dynamic multilevel component selection process, we first describe the configuration/reconfiguration problems and
then the assumptions about components and their compositions, i.e. the used
component model.

2.1   Component Systems, Configurations and Reconfigurations

A component is an independent software package that provides functionality via
defined interfaces. The interface may be an export interface through which a
component provides functionality to other components or an import interface
through which a component gains services from other components.

A configuration [15] of a component system is described as the structural
relationship between components, indicated by the layout of components and
connectors. A reconfiguration is to modify the structure of a component system in
terms of additions, deletion, and replacement of components and/or connectors.

2.2   Component Model

A graphical representation of our view of components is given in Fig. 1. There are two type of components: *simple component* - is specified by the inports (the set of input variables/parameters), outports (the set of output variables/parameters) and a function (the computation function of the component) and *compound component* - is a group of connected components in which the output of a component is used as input by another component from the group.

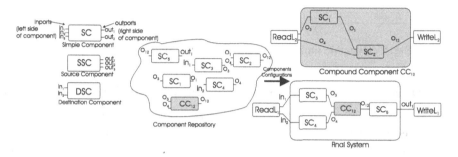

Fig. 1. Components graphical representation and components assembly construction reasoning

In Fig. 1 we have designed the compound component by fill in the box. We have also presented the inner side of the compound component: the constituents components and the interactions between them. For details about the component model please refer to [12].

3   Dynamic Multilevel Component Selection Optimisation Process

To present our optimisation approach, we first give an overview.

Our approach starts by considering a set of components (repository) available for selection and the specification of a final system (input and output). The optimisation process begins with the *Dynamic Multilevel Component Selection Problem Formulation* (see Fig. 2 for details). The result of this step is the transformation of the final system specification as the set of required interfaces (and the set of provided interfaces). In the second step, the construction of the multilevel configurations is done by applying the evolutionary optimisation algorithm (from the fourth step, see Fig. 2) for each time steps (from the Dynamic Changing Requirements or Dynamic Changing Components step). The evolutionary optimisation algorithm is applied for each time steps (i.e. if there are still changing requirements or components) and for each compound component from each level. The solution with best fitness value is selected at each level. The fifth step presents the results.

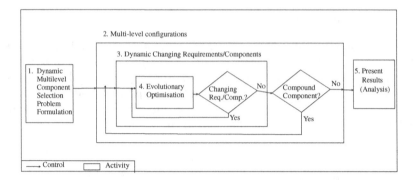

Fig. 2. Dynamic multilevel component selection optimisation process

3.1   Dynamic Multilevel Component Selection Problem Formulation

A formal definition of the *configuration problem* [12] (seen as a compound component) is as follows. Consider SR the set of final system requirements (the provided functionalities of the final compound component) as $SR = \{r_1, r_2, ..., r_n\}$ and SC the set of components (repository) available for selection as $SC = \{c_1, c_2, ..., c_m\}$. Each component c_i can satisfy a subset of the requirements from SR (the provided functionalities) denoted $SP_{c_i} = \{p_{i_1}, p_{i_2}, ..., p_{i_k}\}$ and has a set of requirements denoted $SR_{c_i} = \{r_{i_1}, r_{i_2}, ..., r_{i_h}\}$. The goal is to find a set of components Sol in such a way that every requirement r_j $(j = \overline{1, n})$ from the set SR can be assigned a component c_i from Sol where r_j is in SP_{c_i} $(i = \overline{1, m})$, while minimizing the number of used components and the total cost of assembly. All the requirements of the selected components must be satisfied by the components in the solution. If a selected component is a compound component, the internal structure is also provided. All the levels of the system are constructed.

The *reconfiguration problem* [15] is define similar to the *configuration problem* but considering the dynamical changes of either requirements or component. Regarding the *reconfiguration problem* [13], the dynamics of the component selection problem can be viewed in two ways:

1. The system requirements change over time. The operations allowed to take place in this dynamic situation are:
   (a) new requirements are introduced, in addition to the existing ones;
   (b) some of the requirements are removed;
   (c) a combination of the two above: some of the requirements are removed while new ones are added.
2. The repository containing the components varies over time. A set of possible components is initially considered. The operations allowed are similar to the ones above, i.e. adding new components, or removing existing ones, or a combination of adding and removing components. At each time step some new components may be available, either with cost lower or higher than the existing ones or with more or less number of provided interfaces (required by the system under development).

3.2   Multilevel Configurations

The second step from the dynamic multilevel component selection process consists in the construction of the multilevel configurations of the system. Components are themselves compositions of components. This give rise to the idea of composition levels. In other words, in an hierarchical system, a subsystem of higher level components can be the infrastructure of a single component at a lower level [12].

3.3   Evolutionary Optimisation

The approach presented in this paper uses principles of evolutionary computation and multiobjective optimization [5]. First, the problem is formulated as a multiple objective optimization problem having 5 objectives, The percentage importance of each objective to the fitness functions are: 30 % number of distinct used components, 30 % number of new requirements, 5 % number of provided interfaces, 5 % number of initial requirements that are not in solution, and 30 % cost value. We have selected these percentages because of their impact in finding the final solution. There are several ways to deal with a multiobjective optimization problem. In this paper the Pareto dominance principle is used.

Solution Representation. The current solution representation was used in [13] paper. A solution (chromosome) is represented as a 5-tuple ($lstProv$, $lstComp$, $lstInitReq$, $lstNewReq$, $cost$) with the following information: list of provided interfaces ($lstProv$); list of components ($lstComp$); list of initial requirements ($lstInitReq$); list of new requirements ($lstNewReq$); cost (sum of the cost of each component in the chromosome). The value of $i - th$ component represents the component satisfying the $i - th$ provided interface from the list of provided interfaces. An example is given in what follows.

A valid chromosome may be structured as follows:

$Crom_0 = ((3, 4), (12, 24), (1, 2), (5, 7, 8, 11, 33, 30), (67))$. This chromosome does not represent a solution, it is only an initialized chromosome without any applied genetic operator. The provided interfaces (3, 4) are offered by the components (12, 24). The set of initial requirements are: (1, 2). By using a component we need to provide it's requirements: component 12 requires the (5, 7, 8, 11) new requirements and component 24 requires the (33, 30) new requirements.

Genetic Operator. Because the current paper uses the same genetic algorithm as in [13] paper, the mutation operator keeps the computation method. There are two types of mutations that can be applied to a chromosome, depending of the chromosome "status": the chromosome still has new requirements to satisfy or the chromosome representations does not have any other new requirements to be satisfied. See details in [13].

3.4   Evaluation

When comparing [6] two algorithms, the best fitness values obtained by the searches concerned are an obvious indicator to how well the optimisation process performed. Inferential statistics may be applied to discern whether one set of experiments are significantly different in some aspect from another. Usually we wish to be in a position to make a claim that we have evidence that suggests that Algorithm A (Genetic Algorithm) is better than Algorithm B (Random Search). The Wilcoxon signed ranks test [3] is used for answering the following question: do two samples represent two different populations? It is a nonparametric procedure employed in hypothesis testing situations, involving a design with two samples. It is a pairwise test that aims to detect significant differences between two sample means, that is, the behavior of two algorithms. The best fitness value (from the entire population) was used for comparing the two algorithms.

The Wilcoxon signed ranks test has two hypothesis:

1. Null hypothesis H_0: The median difference is zero versus.
2. Research hypothesis H_1: The median difference is not zero, $\alpha = 0.05$.

Steps of the Wilcoxon signed ranks test: compute W_- and W_+; check if $W_- + W_+ = n(n+1)/2$; select the test statistic (for the two tailed test the test statistic is the smaller of W_- and W_+); we must determine whether the observed test statistic W_t supports the H_0 or H_1, i.e. we determine a critical value of W_c such that if the observed value of W_t is less or equal to critical value W_c, we reject H_0 in favor to H_1.

Due to stochastic nature of optimisation algorithms, searches must be repeated several times in order to mitigate against the effect of random variation. How many runs do we need when we analyze and compare algorithms? In many fields of science (i.e. medicine and behaviour science) a common rule of thumb [1] is to use at least $n = 30$ observations. We have also used in our evaluation 30 executions for each algorithm.

Our Research Question: How and Why do Search-based Algorithms (in our case a Genetic Algorithm and a Random Search Algorithm) provide different results for the Dynamic Multilevel Component Selection Problem?

4   Reservation System Case Study

To better illustrate the components selection optimisation approach proposed in this paper, a real case study for building a *Reservation System* is developed. The system allows booking several types of items (hotel, car, ... etc.), by different types of customers, having thus different types of offers. A possible (first level) architecture (created by a software architect) of the system may be as follows. Four modules that define the business logic of this system are identified: *Offer Module* (provides transactions on making a reservation and getting a notification), *LoyaltyPrg Module* (responsible for the loyalty program for old clients), *ReservationType Module* (managing different types of booking offers) and *Customer Module* (provides information about customers). Two of the four modules mentioned above, *LoyaltyPrg Module* and *Offer Module*, are described at level 1 as compound components which are further decomposed at next levels whereas, the modules *ReservationType* and *Customer Module* are simple components and remain unchanged over modules decomposition. The components and the structure of (one) solution may be found at [14].

4.1 Component Selection Problem Formulation

Having specified two input data (customerData, calendarData) and two output data (doneReservation, requestConfirmation) needed to be computed, and having a set of 126 available components, the goal is to find a subset of the given components such that all the requirements are satisfied considering the optimisation criteria specified above. The set of requirements $SR = \{r_3, r_4\}$ (view as provided interfaces $\{p_3, p_4\}$) and the set of components $SC = \{c_0, c_1, c_2, c_3, c_4, c_5, c_6, ..., c_{126}\}$ are given. The final system has as input data (transformed in required interfaces) the set $\{r_1, r_2\}$.

Remark. Due to lack of space the component repository is not described in this paper but may be found at [14]. There are many components that may provide the same functionality with different requirements interfaces. The components from the repository system have been numbered for better management and utilization of the algorithm.

4.2 Experimental Studies - Case 1: Dynamic Changing Requirements

We consider two types of dynamics and, consequently two experiments corresponding to each of them: the requirements of the problem change over time, and the components available at a certain time step change.

The algorithm was run 100 times and the number of nondominated solutions and the number of distinct nondominated solutions were recorded for all situations. Also, the cost and the number of distinct used components in a solution were logged. Also, the best, worse and average fitness values were recorded for all situations.

In order to analyze the behavior of the algorithm, we performed a few tests. Their role is to see if the number of iterations and the population size play a role in finding the Pareto solutions. For each time step we report the number of non-dominated solution in the final population and the number of distinct solutions (some of them will have multiple copies and we consider in the end the singular solutions). We use the average value for both number of nondominated solutions and the number of distinct nondominated solutions (over 100 runs).

The final system requirements change from one step to another. There are a few possible scenarios: adding new requirements to the ones at the previous step (the stakeholder needs some new requirements to be added, for example, in the considered case study a requirement related to special offers due to certain holidays is requested by the stakeholder to be implemented); removing some of the requirements from the previous step (the development team found out that some requirements were not correctly specified first or even not needed, for example in the considered case study, it may be the case that the developers considered *individual reservation* as a distinct requirement but this can be reduced to *group reservation* as a particular case); a combination of the previous two: adding new requirements and removing some of the ones at the previous step (in this situation we always ensure that the added components are different from the removed ones). We do not treat each of these situations in particular due to the fact that we did not observe a particular behavior for a particular situation. It appears that the complexity is same no matter the sort of dynamics involved in this case. Four different time steps are built using artificially generated data and the dynamics at each of these steps are: T=1 (The initial requirements), T=2 (Add one new requirement), T=3 (Remove one requirement and add one new requirement), T=4 (Add one new requirement).

Remark. It is worth noticing that we have multiple time steps only for the first level of the final system. The next levels just construct the compound components from the first level and modifications (either removing or adding new requirements at these levels) will result in construction components not compatible with the previous levels. Also, the repository containing the components is unchanged for the entire duration of the algorithm and time steps.

Performed Tests. Some remarks can be derived from the experiments performed. We are interested in finding as many nondominated solutions as possible, but, on the other had we look for diversity as well and we wish to have a large number of distinct solutions among the nondominated ones.

Multilevel Configurations. Until now we have obtained the final system but it still has some compound components, that means we need to construct them as well by applying the same algorithm but with different requirements and input data. The best obtained solution from Level 1 (time step 4) has the fitness value 5.40 (6 provides, 6 components, and cost 11, $L1 = \{60, 14c, 11, 12, 38, 53\}$). This "best" solution is from the set of final nondominated solutions from Level 1. This solution has a compound component with id 14. This compound component forms the second level of the final system. The solution with the best fitness value 3.55 (from level 2) has 4 distinct components, 5 providers and cost 7: $L2 = \{67, 71c, 82, 79\}$. This solution has a compound component, id 71. This compound component forms the third level of the final system. The solution with the best fitness value 4.15 has 4 distinct components, 5 providers and cost 9: $L3 = \{91, 97, 88, 104\}$ has no compound component.

Wilcoxon Statistical Test. In Sect. 3.4 we have described in details the Wilcoxon statistical test that we have use to compare our Genetic Algorithm with the Random Search Algorithm. In Table 1 we have the test results for the Case Study 1 - Dynamic Changing Requirements. The Wilcoxon statistical test shows that we have statistically significant evidence at $\alpha = 0.05$ to show that the median is positive, i.e. the H_0 Null-Hypothesis is rejected in favor of H_1 for all levels and for all time steps.

Table 1. Wilcoxon statistical test - *changing requirements* experiment.

L-T	W_-	W_+	W_{test}	N	W_{critic}	H_0	H_1
L1-T0	-5	185	5	19	46	×	✓
L1-T1	-131.5	333.5	131.5	30	137	×	✓
L1-T2	-30.5	404.5	30.5	29	126	×	✓
L1-T3	-23	383	23	28	116	×	✓
L2-T0	0	465	0	30	137	×	✓
L3-T0	-340	95	95	29	126	×	✓

4.3   Experimental Studies - Case 2: Dynamic Changing Components

In this case, the repository containing components changes over time. This modification of the available components may be seen as an update of the COTS market, new components being available or other being withdrawn from the market.

Five different time steps are built using artificially generated data and the dynamics at each of these steps are: T=1 (The initial components), T=2 (Add two new components), T=3 (Remove one component), T=4 (Remove one component and add one new component), and T=5 (Add three new components).

It is worth noticing that the requirements are unchanged for the entire duration of the algorithm and time steps. But we have multiple time steps for all levels for the dynamic changing components case, unlike the changing requirements case. This make sense because we only change the component repository and not the requirements of the compound components from the previous levels.

Performed Tests. In order to analyze the behavior of the algorithm, we performed a few tests. Their role is to see if the number of iterations and the population size play a role in finding the Pareto solutions. Next, a discussion about the obtained solutions on Level 1 (only for the last time step due to page limitation) and the influence of changing the available components for the obtained solutions follows. The best obtained solution from Level 1 (time step 5) has the fitness value 4.45 (5 provides, 5 components, and cost 9, $L1 = \{64,\ 65,\ 53,\ 57,\ 67c\}$). The new components that were added to the repository at this time step improved the final solution from the structure perspective, that means a solution with a less number of components (and provides) was discovered than the solutions obtained at the previous time steps.

Multilevel Configurations. Until now we have obtained the final system but it still has some compound components, that means we need to construct them as well by applying the same algorithm but with different requirements and input data. The obtained solution from Level 1, time step 5 has a compound component, id 67. This compound component forms the second level of the final system. For the second level we have three time steps. The modifications for each step are presented next: $T = 1$ (No modifications of the component repository), $T = 2$ (Adding two new components), and $T = 3$ (Adding three new components and removing an old component). The best obtained solution from Level 2 (time step 3) has the fitness value 4.4 (4 provides, 3 components, and cost 11, $L2 = \{75, 85, 79c\}$). The new components that were added to the repository at this time step improved the final solution from the structure perspective but not from the cost perspective. For example, the solution $L2 = \{84, 83\}$ has a less number of components and providers but has a higher cost 14 (fitness values is 4.95). The obtained solution from Level 2, time step 3 has a compound component, id 79. This compound component forms the third level of the final system. For the third level we have four time steps. The modifications for each step are presented next: $T = 1$ (No modifications of the component repository), $T = 2$ (Adding two new components), $T = 3$ (Removing two old components), and $T = 4$ (Adding two new components and eliminating one old component). The best obtained solution from Level 3 (time step 4) has the fitness value 4.75 (5 provides, 4 components, and cost 11, $L3 = \{103, 96, 90, 87\}$). The new components that were added to the repository at this time step improved the final solution from the structure perspective but not from the cost perspective. For example, the new added component 104 has cost 7, therefore the solution constructed containing this component has a fitness equal to 5.0 due to 4 providers, 3 components but cost 14. The obtained solution from Level 3, time step has no compound components, therefore no other execution of the algorithm is needed: all the compound components were configured.

Wilcoxon Statistical Test. In Sect. 3.4 we have described in details the Wilcoxon statistical test that we have use to compare our Genetic Algorithm with the Random Search Algorithm. In Table 2 we have the test results for the Case Study 1 - Dynamic Changing Components. The Wilcoxon statistical test shows that we have statistically significant evidence at $\alpha = 0.05$ to show that the median is positive, i.e. the H_0 Null-Hypothesis is rejected in favor of H_1 for all levels and for all time steps.

Table 2. Wilcoxon statistical test - *changing components* experiment.

L-T	W_-	W_+	W_{test}	N	W_{critic}	H_0	H_1
L1-T0	-93.5	341.5	93.5	29	126	×	✓
L1-T1	-21	385	21	28	116	×	✓
L1-T2	-46.5	388.5	46.5	29	126	×	✓
L1-T3	-8.5	397.5	8.5	28	116	×	✓
L1-T4	0	435	0	29	116	×	✓
L2-T0	0	231	0	21	58	×	✓
L2-T1	-17	448	17	30	137	×	✓
L2-T2	-33	345	33	27	107	×	✓
L3-T0	-386	49	49	29	126	×	✓
L3-T1	-394	71	71	30	137	×	✓
L3-T2	-338	97	97	29	126	×	✓
L3-T3	-369	96	96	30	137	×	✓

5   Related Work Analysis

This section presents the current state of art regarding the component selection problem and analyzes the differences compared with our present approach. Component selection methods are traditionally done in an architecture-centric manner. *In relation to existing component selection methods, our approach aims to achieve goals similar to* [4]. All the above approaches did not considered the multilevel structure of a component-based system; our previous research has studied this problem in [12]. Various genetic algorithms representations were proposed in [8,10]. The authors proposed an optimization model of software components selection for CBSS development. *We argue that our model differs by the fact that components interactions are computed automatically* based on required and provided component interface specification. Also, regarding the function ratings, *our approach discovers automatically the constituent components for each module of the final system.* In [11] a hybrid approach for multi-attribute QoS optimization of component-based software systems has been proposed. *In relation to this existing approach, ours aims to achieve similar goals, being capable of obtaining multiple solutions in a single run and it can be scaled to any number of components and requirements.* Another perspective refers to updating requirements (components) from an already constructed system [15]. Our previous research regarding this perspective was proposed in [13]. *Our current approach considers dynamic modifications of the requirements, investigating different ways of modifying them, by adding new ones or deleting existing ones.* A similar approach considering evolution of software architecture was proposed by [2]. It suggests the best actions to be taken according to a set of new requirements. In relation to this approach, *our current approach also discovers the optimal solution minimizing the final cost when new requirements are needed. But it also considers the case that the component repository changes over time.*

6   Conclusion

The current work investigated the potential of evolutionary algorithms in a particular case of multiobjective dynamic system: multilevel component selection problem. Two types of dynamics have been considered: the requirements of the system change over time and the components available in the repository change over time. The Wilcoxon statistical test was used to compare our Genetic Algorithm approach with a Random Search Algorithm: we have statistically significant evidence at $\alpha = 0.05$ to show that the median is positive, i.e. we obtain better results with our approach.

With respect to the state-of-art the following major aspects characterize the novelty of the approach presented in this paper: this is among the first papers that supports the evolution of a software architecture using an optimization model that automatically construct the entire architecture of a multilevel system; the components interactions are computed automatically based on required and provided component interface specification, and finally, our approach can facilitate the work of a maintainer.

References

1. Arcuri, A., Briand, L.: A practical guide for using statistical tests to assess randomized algorithms in software engineering. In: International Conference on Software Engineering, pp. 1–10 (2011)
2. Cortellessa, V., Mirandola, R., Potena, P.: Managing the evolution of a software architecture at minimal cost under performance and reliability constraints. Sci. Comput. Program. **98**, 439–463 (2015)
3. Derrac, J., Garcia, S., Molina, D., Herrera, F.: A practical tutorial on the use of nonparametric statistical tests as a methodology for comparing evolutionary and swarm intelligence algorithms. Swarm Evol. Comput. **1**, 3–18 (2011)
4. Fox, M.R., Brogan, D.C., Reynolds, P.F.: Approximating component selection. In: Conference on Winter Simulation, pp. 429–434 (2004)
5. Grosan, C.: A comparison of several evolutionary models and representations for multiobjective optimisation. In: ISE Book Series on Real Word Multi-Objective System Engineering. Nova Science (2005)
6. Harman, M., McMinn, P., de Souza, J.T., Yoo, S.: Search based software engineering: techniques, taxonomy, tutorial. In: Meyer, B., Nordio, M. (eds.) Empirical Software Engineering and Verification. LNCS, vol. 7007, pp. 1–59. Springer, Heidelberg (2012)
7. Hasheminejad, S.M.H., Jalili, S.: CCIC: clustering analysis classes to identify software components. Inf. Softw. Technol. **57**, 329–351 (2015)
8. Jhaa, P., Balib, V., Narulaa, S., Kalra, M.: Optimal component selection based on cohesion and coupling for component based software system under build-or-buy scheme. J. Comput. Sci. **5**(2), 233–242 (2014)
9. Khan, M.A., Mahmood, S.: A graph-based requirements clustering approach for component selection. Adv. Eng. Softw. **54**, 1–16 (2012)
10. Kwong, C., Mu, L., Tang, J., Luo, X.: Optimization of software components selection for component-based software system development. Comput. Industr. Eng. **58**(1), 618–624 (2010)
11. Martens, A., Ardagna, D., Koziolek, H., Mirandola, R., Reussner, R.: A hybrid approach for multi-attribute QoS optimisation in component based software systems. In: Heineman, G.T., Kofron, J., Plasil, F. (eds.) QoSA 2010. LNCS, vol. 6093, pp. 84–101. Springer, Heidelberg (2010)
12. Vescan, A., Grosan, C.: Evolutionary multiobjective approach for multilevel component composition. Studia Univ. Babes-Bolyai. Informatica, vol. LV(4), pp. 18–32 (2010)
13. Vescan, A., Grosan, C., Yang, S.: A hybrid evolutionary multiobjective approach for the dynamic component selection problem. In: International Conference on Hybrid Intelligent Systems, pp. 714–721 (2011)
14. Vescan, A., Serban, C.: Details on case study for the dynamic multilevel component selection optimisation approach (2015). http://www.cs.ubbcluj.ro/~avescan/?q=node/202
15. Wei, L.: QoS assurance for dynamic reconfiguration of component-based software systems. IEEE Trans. Softw. Eng. **38**(3), 658–676 (2012)

Dependability Issues
in Services Computing

A Reusable Architecture for Dependability and Performance Benchmarking of Cloud Services

Amit Sangroya[1(✉)] and Sara Bouchenak[2]

[1] TCS Innovation Labs, Mumbai, India
amit.sangroya@tcs.com
[2] INSA de Lyon, Villeurbanne, France
sara.bouchenak@insa-lyon.fr

Abstract. With the increasing demand and benefits of cloud computing services, new solutions are needed to benchmark the dependability and performance of these services. Designing a dependability and performance benchmark that covers a variety of fault and execution scenarios, poses various architectural challenges. In this paper, we present a generic software architecture for dependability and performance benchmarking for cloud computing services. We provide the details of this generic architecture i.e. various components and modules, that are responsible for injecting faults in cloud services in addition to the components responsible for measuring the performance and dependability. We make use of this architecture to build two software prototypes: MRBS and MemDB. These prototypes are used to benchmark two popular cloud services: MapReduce and Memcached. The case studies with the use of software prototypes demonstrates the benefits of building a generic architecture.

1   Introduction and Related Work

Guaranteeing reliability, availability and performance are one of the major challenges for cloud service providers such as Amazon, Google, Salesforce and Microsoft. Primary motivation for introducing a benchmarking framework for cloud services is that there is no scientific approach or framework so far in the existing literature that could help users to evaluate the important quality aspects such as dependability for cloud computing services. MapReduce is a well known example of such services that provides a convenient means for distributed data processing and automatic parallel execution in cloud computing environments. Various benchmark programs are often used to evaluate the specific frameworks such as Hadoop MapReduce. However, they are mainly micro level benchmarks measuring specific Hadoop properties.

Most of the times, the cloud service users are more interested in knowing the performance and associated costs rather than measuring low level statistics such as CPU behaviour and memory. Here, it is to be noted that we do not mean that low level system statistics are not important to analyze the quality aspects.

© Springer-Verlag Berlin Heidelberg 2016
A. Norta et al. (Eds.): ICSOC 2015 Workshops, LNCS 9586, pp. 207–218, 2016.
DOI: 10.1007/978-3-662-50539-7_17

Rather, we argue that as a cloud service are used even by naive users and for these users or service providers, most important question is how an application performs in a realistic environment (e.g. in the presence of failures) and what is the associated cost? Dependability benchmarking is a promising approach to understand a system behaviour in the presence of faults. For a benchmark suite to enable a thorough analysis of a wide range features of cloud service, it must provide the following. First, it must enable the empirical evaluation of the performance and reliability of cloud services, two key properties of a cloud service.

Furthermore, with the advent of pay-as-you-go model, a benchmark suite must allow the evaluation of the costs of the running a representative workload in cloud environments. Second, it must cover a variety of application domains and workload characteristics, ranging from compute intensive to data-intensive applications, online real-time applications as well as batch-oriented applications. Moreover, in order to stress reliability and performance, the benchmark suite must enable different fault injection rates, and it must allow the generation of different workloads (i.e. #clients, clients request distribution). Building complex benchmarks such as dependability benchmarks is difficult, since these benchmarks are composed of diverse fault types, different ways to inject the faults in a running system and diverse metrics to understand the dependability levels. New services such as cloud computing services add an additional layer of complexity because of virtualization and sharing of the resources.

Key features for a dependability benchmark are as follows: Representativeness; Repeatability; Portability; and Scalability [1,2]. Dependability benchmarks have been proposed in various domains of computing such as hardware; cluster computing; operating systems; database systems; web servers; and web services among others [3,4]. Various works aim to propose a standard approach for dependability and performance benchmarking. *DBench* project aims to provide a basic foundation for dependability benchmarking and performs a detailed study on dependability benchmarks [1]. *Barbosa et al.* [5] introduced a dependability benchmark to evaluate dependability of operating systems. *Vieira et al.* [6] proposed a dependability benchmark for Online transaction processing (OLTP) systems. *Duraes et al.* [7] present a benchmark for the dependability of web-servers.

One of the limitations of these approaches is that they do not discuss a generic software architecture that can be extended by the users to develop dependability benchmarks for their systems. A generic architecture might be a key factor in reducing cost to build a new benchmark and also improve the overall quality of benchmarking process. This is possible using generic components which can be reused in building the new benchmark. In addition, it must be able to support a diverse set of workload and fault injection scenarios. Of course, the benefits of reuse would be maximum if the new benchmark to be built is closer to the application domain of the previous benchmark. For example, using the case studies conducted in this thesis, we demonstrate two software prototypes built using the generic architecture in PaaS domain of cloud computing.

We also observed that state of the art dependability benchmarks do not address the challenges raised by cloud computing systems. This is mainly due to the fact that cloud computing is a relatively new domain. Some of the terms such as faultload, workload, and dataload are not clearly defined for cloud computing use cases. The literature lacks the specific knowledge to build a benchmark for cloud computing services. Therefore, it is not possible to extend any existing benchmark easily for a cloud computing service. However, we argue that the general definitions and principals can still be extracted from the existing works and adapted to build a generic dependability and performance benchmarking architecture for cloud computing services.

In this paper, we make following key contributions:

1. We discuss various components of a dependability benchmark in detail. The major components of the dependability benchmark architecture, i.e. workload, faultload, statistics analysis, etc. are generic and can be easily adapted to build a new dependability benchmark.
2. We provide the details of various classes of our architecture API. The classes can be easily adapted for designing a benchmark for a new service.
3. We provide a detailed illustration of instantiating the proposed architecture in the domain of cloud service. We choose the two widely used cloud service models: MapReduce and Memcached service. The proposed architecture is used in each of these service models to define the components of the dependability benchmark such as faultload, injection of the faultload and measuring the performance and dependability.

Rest of the paper is organized as follows. Section 2 describes the proposed generic architecture and software framework of dependability benchmarking. In Sect. 3, we instantiate the proposed architecture for cloud services. Section 4, highlights the benefits of architecture. In Sect. 5, we present the conclusions.

2 Architecture and General Software Framework

In the first phase i.e. load generation phase, workload and faultload specified by dependability benchmark user are generated. This phase might also include an optional dataload generation, if it is needed by any of the benchmark workload application. Users of the benchmark must describe the loads that they want to inject during the benchmark run. Once the loads are defined by the users, in the second phase i.e. load injection phase, they are injected to the system under test according to the time described by the users. Normally, there is a warm-up period before a run time period. Normally, the warm period is used for starting various processes such as warming up caches, etc., so that the system is in a relatively steady state. This provides a better estimate of system's dependability and performance compared to a scenario where no warm-up period is used. After the warm-up period, the benchmark runs for a particular time as specified by the user. During this run time period, workload is run with the given dataload and faults are injected.

In the third phase i.e. monitoring phase, various statistics such as response time, throughput, availability, reliability etc. are computed and stored. During this phase, the system counters can be used to generate the desired statistics. For example, the number of failed jobs, number of successful jobs can be calculated to plot the reliability statistics. In the final phase i.e. statistics measurement phase, statistics outputs are produced in the form of user friendly graphs or files. During this phase, the statistics values obtained in the preceding phase are computed to plot easy to read charts/html files. These charts/html files provide an easy to understand view of system's performance and dependability.

One of the most important benefit of this architecture is that we can leverage large scale reuse of the components. The design of most of the components of architecture is kept generic. *Faultload, faultload injector, benchmark, workload injector* are independent from the system under test. To build a new benchmark, these components do not need any modifications. The system dependent components such as *faulttype, workload* and *SystemUnderTestAPI* are the ones where due to various dependencies it is difficult to reuse them. The architecture consists of generic classes such as faultload, benchmark, workload injector and statistics. The other classes can also be adapted easily according to the system under test. Various classes and associated methods of the generic architecture are explained as follows:

2.1 Benchmark

A workload might consist of a number of benchmark applications. The client can send requests according to different rules and combinations. For example, in FIFO case, there will be method to create concurrent client, wait for the completion of the request (or the end of run time of benchmark if it comes before) and send the next request. The next client request may be chosen either randomly or according to a probability distribution. This is explained as follows: A benchmark consists of a set of client requests. This class contains request distribution functions. The requests might be uniformly distributed or some requests may have higher probabilities of occurrence than others. The motivation for this is that all these client requests can be different in terms of data and computation behaviour. Therefore, to get a better understanding of system's dependability and performance, a user can set the probability for the occurrence of the next client request. Benchmark class calls the *Request* class for issuing a new client request.

2.2 Faultload

This class includes method that reads the particular faultload and provide description of the locations of these faults. Faultload can be described using a file according to various criterion like *random, trace based* or *synthetic*. This class includes methods to generate the faultload based on the criteria specified by the user of the benchmark. For example, in the simplest case, if a user wants to inject a random faultload, this class invokes the method which is responsible for generating a set of random fault types, timestamps etc. in the faultload file.

2.3   Faultload Injector

This class includes a method that injects a given faultload in a running system. For example, it will read the timestamps and fault types in the faultload file and would inject a particular fault type at the specified time.

2.4   Workload

This class includes methods to initialize, prepare and destroy a benchmark. As we discussed earlier, a dependability benchmark needs an application that a user run on the top of dependability benchmark. The workload class includes specific methods that are needed to start these applications, run for the given run time of the benchmark and stop when the time to run the benchmark is over. There might be some optional methods to prepare any input data, if it is needed by the benchmark workload application.

2.5   Workload Injector

This class contains methods to send client requests that are described by the workload. In case, where a user wants to emulate a multi-clients behaviour, this class would create the concurrent clients that will send requests. In a simplest First in First out (FIFO) case, there will be a method to create concurrent clients, wait for the completion of the request (or the end of run time of benchmark if it comes before) and send the next request.

2.6   Statistics

This class contains methods for calculating the statistics. For example, it includes methods that count the number of successful and failed jobs to measure the availability and reliability that are used to build the dependability metrics. Moreover, it is also responsible to invoke methods that measure the response time of different client requests. Response time and throughput are used to build the performance metrics. In addition, this class also has methods to monitor the time for upload of the data.

2.7   System Under Test API

This class is responsible of injecting the workload and faultload into the system under test. This class contains methods that identify the nodes in the distributed system. It might also differentiate between master and slave nodes, e.g. in the case of Hadoop cluster or server and clients in the case of Memcached system. The identification of nodes is important because a user might want to select where he/she wants to inject a particular fault. For example, in the Hadoop version 1.0.0, master node is not fault tolerant [8]. Therefore, he/she might want to skip the master node for fault injection.

Moreover, this class has methods that are responsible for starting and stopping the nodes at the beginning and at the end of a benchmark respectively. There might be some additional services that might need a start and stop such as Hadoop services. This class also communicates with *Statistics* class to send the information from system counters to build the required statistics.

2.8   Dependability Benchmark

This is the main class which is primarily responsible for uploading the data, and calling other methods of classes discussed before. This class orchestrates all the classes to perform the operation as specified by the user in the configuration file.

3   Case Studies

This section presents the details of two case studies that are conducted to validate the proposed architecture.

3.1   MapReduce Benchmark Suite (MRBS)

MRBS is a comprehensive benchmark suite for evaluating the dependability of MapReduce systems [9]. MRBS achieve the following design objectives:

1. **Multi-criteria analysis.** MRBS aims to measure and analyze the performance *and* dependability of MapReduce systems. In particular, we consider several measurement metrics such as reliability, availability, financial cost, request response time (i.e. latency), and request throughput. We also consider low-level MapReduce metrics, such as throughput of MapReduce jobs and tasks, task and job failures, I/O throughput (data reads/writes), etc.
2. **Diversity.** MRBS covers a variety of application domains and programs with a wide range of MapReduce characteristics. This includes data-oriented applications vs. compute-oriented applications. Furthermore, whereas MapReduce was originally used for long running batch jobs, modern MapReduce cluster is shared between multiple users running concurrently [10]. Therefore, MRBS considers batch applications as well as interactive applications. Moreover, MRBS allows to characterize different aspects of application load such as the *faultload*, the *workload* and the *dataload*. Roughly speaking, the faultload describes MapReduce fault types and fault arrival rates. The workload is characterized by the number of clients (i.e. users) sharing a MapReduce cluster, the types of client requests (i.e. MapReduce programs), and request arrival rates. The dataload characterizes the size and nature of MapReduce input data.

3. **Usability.** MRBS is easy to use, configure and deploy on a MapReduce cluster. It is independent from any infrastructure and can easily run on different public clouds and private clouds. MRBS provides results which can be readily interpreted in the form of monitored statistics and automatically generated charts.

MRBS allows to inject various faultloads, workloads and dataloads in MapReduce systems, and to collect information that helps testers understand the observed behavior of MapReduce systems. MRBS comes with a benchmark suite, that is a set of five benchmarks covering various application domains: recommendation systems, business intelligence, bioinformatics, text processing, and data mining. Conceptually, each benchmark implements a service running on a MapReduce cluster, and each service has several types of requests that are issued by users (i.e. clients). A client request executes one or a series of MapReduce jobs. MRBS may emulate multiple clients implemented as external entities, that concurrently access the MapReduce cluster.

MRBS benchmarks were chosen to exhibit different behaviours in terms of computation pattern and data access pattern: the Recommendation System is a compute-intensive benchmark, the Business Intelligence system is a data-intensive benchmark, and the other benchmarks are relatively less compute/data-intensive.

Experiments with MRBS: Comparing Performance of MapReduce Frameworks. We compared the two Hadoop v0.20.2 and Hadoop v1.0.0 MapReduce frameworks with regard to their performance. These experiments were conducted on Amazon EC2, hosting, on the one hand, a 10-node Hadoop v0.20.2 (blue bar), and on the other hand, a 10-node Hadoop v1.0.0 (red bar). Each MapReduce cluster is used by one client at a time with default dataloads. An experiment consists of a 15 min run-time phase, after a 5 min warm-up phase. No faultload was injected.

Figure 1 compares the client response times with the different MapReduce framework implementations. Surprisingly, Hadoop v1.0.0 provides lower performance (i.e. higher client response times) than Hadoop v0.20.2, whatever the benchmark is. Here, the average client response time with Hadoop v1.0.0 is higher than with Hadoop v0.20.2 by 34 % for Recommendation System, 29 % for Bioinformatics, 34 % for Business Intelligence, 39 % for Text Processing, and 27 % for Data Mining benchmark.

3.2   Dependability and Performance Analysis in MemDB

MemDB allows to inject various faultloads, workloads and dataloads in a Memcached system and to collect information helping testers understand the observed behavior of Memcached system. The overall architecture of MemDB is presented in Fig. 2.

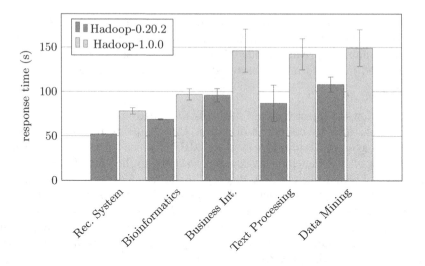

Fig. 1. Performance of two MapReduce frameworks.

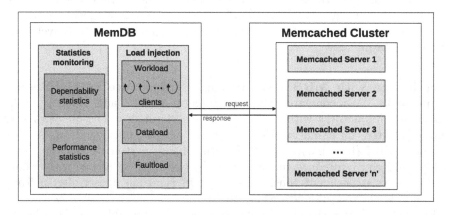

Fig. 2. Overview of MemDB

MemDB comes with a benchmark, Brutis [11] that is a tool designed to test memcached instances by providing reproducible performance data for comparison purposes. We adopt *Brutis* and perform two key operations: The *set* operation that store our generated data in Memcached and the *get* operation that retrieve the data given according to a key. These operations can be mixed to emulate more complicated scenarios.

Experiments with MemDB: Performance and Dependability of Memcached. Following experiments were conducted on a four-nodes Memcached cluster. One node is used to host MemDB which emulates workload that consists of 10 clients per node sending client requests in a random manner. 10 % of the requests are *set* requests and 90 % of the requests are *get* requests. The

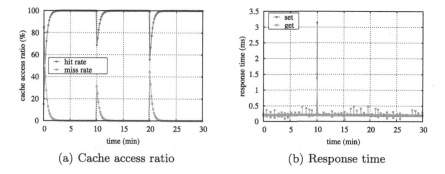

(a) Cache access ratio   (b) Response time

Fig. 3. Dependability and performance of Memcached under network faults and node crashes

experiment is conducted during a run-time phase of 30 min, including a warm-up phase. We consider a synthetic faultload that consists of network faults and hardware faults as follows: first, network faults are injected 10 min after the beginning of the run-time phase, and then node crashes are injected 10 min later.

To better explain the behavior of the Memcached cluster, we will analyze statistics, as presented in Fig. 3(a) and (b). Figure 3(a) presents successful Memcached hits and misses over time. When network faults occur, the server node on which we injected the fault, fails to send and receive the packets within the timeout limit (a value configured in the Memcached). As a result of this, after certain number of server retries, the node which was taking long time to respond, is marked as failed. Memcached removes this node from the list of available nodes. Thereafter, Memcached client copies the data (keys) on the other live nodes in the cluster.

We can observe from Fig. 3(b) that at the time of network fault injection (at 10 min), there is an impact on the response time of client requests. High response time during this period is due to the injected latency, because of which some client requests are successful but they took long time to respond. On the contrary, with node crash fault injection (at 20 min) we observe a slightly similar behaviour of cache access ratio. This is because, similar to the network fault where the node was marked as failed due to timeout, after a node crash, Memcached removes the faulty nodes from the list of available nodes. We also observe that number of hits decrease and number of misses increase when we injected the node crash fault (compared to the period when we inject network fault). This is because of higher load on the servers after one node was removed after network fault. There was one less node after network fault and load per server was higher.

4   How the General Architecture Supports Building New Benchmarks

In this section, we demonstrate how the proposed architecture helps to reduce the cost and effort in building a benchmark for a new cloud computing service.

We consider various dimensions for evaluation: cost of software development; design complexity; usability and adaptability.

4.1   Reduced Development Costs

This section includes the software development effort (focused on code reuse) needed to develop a new dependability benchmark for the previous use cases following the architecture proposed in this chapter. Obviously, there is a part of the dependability benchmark that depends on the workload to be injected, application dependant, that will require more or less effort based on the semantics of the application. We focus thus on the effort needed to inject the different types of faults. Of course, this will depend again on the number of different faults that are considered to evaluate the dependability of a specific application. Table 1 shows the details of the software prototypes developed for performance and dependability benchmarking of MepReduce and Memcached i.e. MRBS and MemDB respectively. For both prototypes, we provide the details of total lines of code and performance and dependability specific components.

Table 1. Comparison of effort to build a new benchmark

Evaluation Parameter	MRBS	MemDB
Total lines of code	10,606	454
Performance application dependant	1,183	104
Performance application independent	6,394	0
Dependability application dependant	979	41
Dependability application independent	673	0
# lines per fault injector	35	3

Effort Needed to Inject Faults in MapReduce. The MRBS benchmark was built using 10,606 lines of code. Among them, 1,183 correspond to the platform independent modules for workload generation, 6,394 correspond to the platform dependant modules for workload generation, 979 for the generic part of dependability benchmarking, 673 for the platform specific dependability benchmark and 1,377 for statistics generation. In the platform specific dependability benchmark, 535 lines correspond to the generation of faultloads from previous execution traces, and 138 to the fault type definitions and their injectors (80 lines to inject *Task Software Fault* and *Hanging Task* faults, and 58 to inject *Node Crash* and *Task Process Crash* faults).

Effort Needed to Inject Faults in Memcached. The MemDB benchmark was build using 454 lines of code. This benchmark also includes various third party libraries. Among the total lines of code, 104 correspond to the platform dependent modules for workload generation, 41 for the platform specific dependability benchmark and 309 for statistics generation. In the platform specific dependability benchmark, 41 lines correspond to inject *Node Crash* and *Network Fault*.

4.2 Better Usability

The architecture possesses better usability from the point of view of benchmark designers and also benchmark users. Due to standard design of components, it is always easier to develop a new benchmark. The use of configuration files for tuning the parameters makes it easier to use and run the benchmark. The benchmark outputs such as graphs and HTML files provides an easier way to visualize the performance and dependability metrics. Most of the code of benchmark prototypes such as MRBS is in Java which makes it robust and platform independent.

4.3 Higher Adaptability

The architecture is also flexible and adaptable. The addition of new features such as new fault types is not difficult. This can be done without modifying the generic components of the architecture. The addition of new workloads and dataloads also do not require major modifications to the existing code. The interfaces for faultload addition, injection, and workload injection are flexible.

5 Conclusions and Perspectives

In this paper, we have presented the generic architecture to build performance and dependability benchmarks for cloud services. We described various components and modules responsible for injecting faults in cloud services in addition to the components responsible for measuring the performance and dependability. We demonstrated with case studies that this architecture helps in reducing the efforts to build a new dependability benchmark. We believe that this study would greatly benefit the designers of dependability benchmark solutions or cloud services

References

1. Dependability Benchmarking Project (2004). http://webhost.laas.fr/TSF/DBench/
2. Gray, J.: Benchmark Handbook: For Database and Transaction Processing Systems. Morgan Kaufmann Publishers Inc., San Francisco (1992)
3. Mauro, J., Zhu, J., Pramanick, I.: The system recovery benchmark. In: Proceedings of the 10th IEEE Pacific Rim International Symposium on Dependable Computing (PRDC 2004), pp. 271–280 (2004)

4. Brown, A., Patterson, D.A.: Towards availability benchmarks: a case study of software RAID systems. In: Proceedings of the Annual Conference on USENIX Annual Technical Conference. ATEC 2000, p. 22 (2000)
5. Barbosa, R., Karlsson, J., Yu, Q., Mao, X.: Toward dependability benchmarking of partitioning operating systems. In: IEEE/IFIP 41st International Conference on Dependable Systems Networks (DSN 2011), pp. 422–429 (2011)
6. Vieira, M., Madeira, H.: A dependability benchmark for OLTP application environments. In: Proceedings of the 29th International Conference on Very Large Data Bases, VLDB 2003, vol. 29, pp. 742–753 (2003)
7. Durães, J., Vieira, M., Madeira, H.: Dependability benchmarking of web-servers. In: Proceedings of 23rd International Conference on Computer Safety, Reliability and Security (Safecomp 2004), pp. 297–310 (2004)
8. Hadoop 1.0.0 Release Notes (2013). http://hadoop.apache.org/docs/r1.0.0/releasenotes.html
9. Sangroya, A., Serrano, D., Bouchenak, S.: Benchmarking dependability of MapReduce systems. In: IEEE International Symposium on Reliable Distributed Systems (SRDS) (2012)
10. Condie, T., Conway, N., Alvaro, P., Hellerstein, J., Elmeleegy, K., Sears, R.: MapReduce online. In: USENIX Symposium on Networked Systems Design and Implementation (NSDI) (2010)
11. Brutis Memcache benchmarking tool written in PHP (2009). http://code.google.com/p/brutis/wiki/Readme

Safe Configurations of Replica Voting Processes in Fault-Resilient Data Collection Services

Kaliappa Ravindran$^{(\boxtimes)}$ and Arun Adiththan

Department of Computer Science, City College of CUNY, Graduate Center,
New York, NY 10031, USA
ravi@cs.ccny.cuny.edu

Abstract. Voting among replicated sensor devices achieves a timely delivery of correct data to the end-user in a hostile environment. Enforcement of this *safety prescription* by the voting system depends on the hostility of environment, system parameters & resources (network bandwidth and device replication), and input data characteristics. How severely the faulty devices induce data corruptions and timeliness errors impacts the quality of information (QoI) in data delivery. We consider situations where the network bandwidth varies dynamically, device replication faces operational constraints, and environment parameters change unpredictably. An adaptation management module H exercises control of the voting system based on application context and external threats. H determines the safe configurations of voting system: i.e., the device replication and system resource allocation, to sustain an acceptable QoI.

1 Introduction

In a networked system S, sensing errors may arise in the form of inaccurate and/or delayed reporting of the events occurring at various sub-system interfaces. An event depicts, for instance, the changes in external object space under surveillance (e.g., radar detection of a plane, software anomaly detection). A sensing error may skew the control actions exercised therein on the physical world [1]. Component replication is often used as a means to reduce the sensing errors [2]. A high sensing accuracy combined with suitable control actions (as computed by models of the external world) steer S towards a desired output behavior [3]. This paper provides a framework for autonomic management of replication-based sensor configurations to guarantee safe operations of S.

In the absence of knowledge about event occurrences reported from a sensed data (i.e., ground truth) and/or device-level failures, *majority voting* on the data fielded by various replicas is employed to decide on a correct data delivery to the end-user (i.e., reach consensus about event occurrences). Figure 1 illustrates the voting algorithm processes. A management entity H observes the flow of algorithm activities and the external environment conditions, to suitably adjust the parameters of voting system: such as the number of replicas invoked and the amount of system resources allocated (e.g., CPU cycles and bandwidth).

© Springer-Verlag Berlin Heidelberg 2016
A. Norta et al. (Eds.): ICSOC 2015 Workshops, LNCS 9586, pp. 219–230, 2016.
DOI: 10.1007/978-3-662-50539-7_18

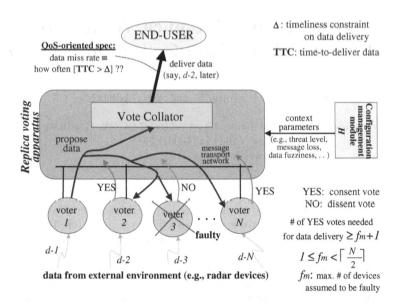

Fig. 1. Data collection system with replicated sensing (service-oriented view)

The goal is to lower the latency and message overhead & energy usage incurred to effect a data delivery (i.e., improve the system QoS)[1].

Given N replicated devices ($N \geq 3$), the correctness of data delivery is contingent on a *majority* of the replicas surviving failures. Suppose f_a is the actual number of failed devices and f_m is the maximum number of devices that the voting algorithm believes as might be failing. The algorithmic assumption: $1 \leq f_m < \lceil \frac{N}{2} \rceil$ should always hold — under the premise that $0 \leq f_a \leq f_m$. An enforcement of this condition is needed for a safe operation of the voting system, despite the intrinsic difficulty of measuring f_a. In other words, a scenario of $f_a > f_m$ can lead to safety violation: i.e., the delivery of a corrupted data to the end-user without an easy algorithmic mechanism to detect the incorrect delivery. Thus, a safe operation of the voting system sets $f_m \gg f_a'$ and $N \gg (2f_m+1)$ — where f_a' is an approximate estimate of f_a. Here, $|f_m - f_a'|$ and $(\lceil \frac{N}{2} \rceil - f_m)$ depict the safety margins in the voting system. H estimates f_a' from computational models of the voting processes and the observations of external environment.

A larger N — i.e., $N \gg (2f_m + 1)$ — lowers the latency of data delivery to the end-user. This improved QoS is due to increased parallelism in the device operations, in the face of computational asynchrony among devices. A higher latency diminishes the user-level QoI (quality of information) associated with data delivery. H exercises a microscopic control of the voting system to sustain an acceptable QoI, while meeting the safety condition $f_a \leq f_m$ and $f_m < \lceil \frac{N}{2} \rceil$.

---

[1] With field-deployed sensor devices, a low message overhead of the voting system reduces the energy drain on device batteries — and hence improves system operational life-time [4]. So, message overhead is a QoS attribute of the voting service.

A larger N should however be seen in the light of device-level heterogeneity that is infused as a deterrent to attacks [5]. The heterogeneity, which can be at the hardware, algorithm, and/or platform levels, however incurs a high cost of replication: such as software development, platform maintenance, and device deployment. H weighs this operational cost of replication, which is $\mathcal{O}(N^2)$, against the benefits of improved QoI and fault-tolerance.

Our paper focuses on the autonomic management techniques to enforce safe configurations of a replica voting system, in the face of dynamically changing environment situations. H monitors the hard-to-measure fault parameter f_a using state-based estimators (e.g., Kalman Filter), and then adjusts the system parameters $[N, f_m]$ to adequately meet the QoI specs. H employs a computational model of the voting system to generate a reference QoS trajectory, and then iteratively refine $[N, f_m]$ based on the observed QoS deviations.

The paper is organized as follows. Section 2 gives a service-oriented view of data collection systems that deal with sensor errors and faults. Section 3 discusses the existing control frameworks to manage the dependability of network services. Section 4 describes model-based engineering techniques to manage the replication process in data collection systems. Section 5 concludes the paper.

2   Service-Level View of Component Faults

A data collection system S presents the sensed events to an application module for processing. In the face of data errors and functional faults occurring in the infrastructure, the algorithmic processes in S are controlled by a management module H to provide a calibrated quality of the events reported — as suggested in [6]. H maintains a computational model of S that treats the faults and errors as emanating from an uncontrolled external environment. See Fig. 2-(A).

2.1   Failure Impact of System Components

Given an ensemble of K devices in the infrastructure, the management entity H deploys N devices to participate in the voting algorithm execution, where $3 \leq N \ll K$. The choice of N is tied to an assumption by H that at most f_m devices can fail and a failed device exhibits a fault severity of r — where $1 \leq f_m < N$ and $0 < r \leq 1.0$. The external environment, which may include attackers, does not have knowledge of the algorithm parameters $[N, r, f_m]$.

In an actual scenario however, f_a of the K devices fail disrupting the system output — where $0 \leq f_a \ll K$. Furthermore, a failed device exhibits a fault severity of r'', which depicts the probability of erroneous behavior when an input trigger occurs (i.e., how many operations the failed device performs correctly before responding erroneously to the trigger). Note here that $[f_a', r]$ is the aggressiveness of a faulty device as estimated by H — which reflects the belief of H about the hostility of external environment. For high accuracy of management decisions, H strives to keep $f_a' \approx f_a$ and $r \approx r''$.

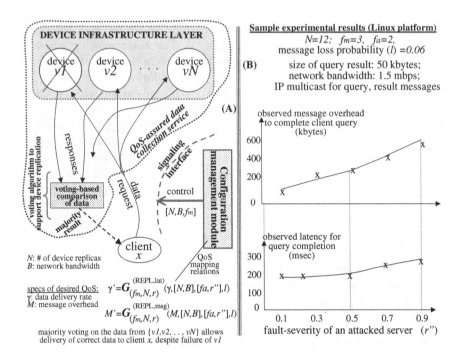

Fig. 2. System structure to manage device replication for fail-safe data delivery

We reason that a higher N lowers the data delivery latency L but increases the message overhead M, *albeit*, in a non-linear fashion. Intuitively, over a region of small N (say, $N = 3 \cdots 5$), an increase of N has a strong impact on lowering L, because the higher device-level asynchrony increases the likelihood of receiving the needed $f_m + 1$ consent votes quicker. But, over a region of large N (say, $N = 9 \cdots 11$), the increased device-level asynchrony results only in a marginal reduction in L (assuming that f_m does not change with N). Our experimental results in Fig. 2-(B) show how L and M vary with respect to r'' for a case of $[f_a = 2, f_m = 3]$. That L and M increase with r'' is due to the faulty devices sending corrupted data with high probability, which requires more messages from non-faulty devices to counter the errors. The increase in L and M exhibits a monotonic convex behavior: a useful property for reasoning and prediction.

Since the parameters of actual failures $[r'', f_a]$ are not known to H, the system designer needs to model the external environment to get a probabilistic estimate of $[f_a, r'']$: say, treating them as random variables with appropriate distributions and correlations. Such a modeling of environment parameters allows determining their impact on the accuracy and timeliness of event reports (i.e., QoI).

2.2 QoI Aspects of Sensor Replication

Processing and communication delays are incurred as the raw input data moves through various system elements. The composite delays incurred therein manifest as the event reporting latency L. The QoI associated with data delivery is high when $L \in (0, \Delta]$, and decays exponentially in the range $L \in (\Delta, \Delta_m]$. Data delivery is useless when $L > \Delta_m$: which reduces 'data availability' from end-user perspective. Thus, the QoS specs (Δ, Δ_m) for timeliness directly maps onto the user-level QoI. H strives to sustain a reasonable QoI, while meeting the safety condition $f_a \leq f_m$ and $f_m < \lceil \frac{N}{2} \rceil$.

An excessive sensor delay due to the heterogeneity in data processing skews the control actions triggered therein at the application level. In an example of collision avoidance system for automobiles, a combination of sensors (e.g., microwave radar, Lidar, infrared) are employed to detect the presence of road obstacles and fuse their results by voting — for improved vehicle safety [7]. The system-level cost of such device replication: both in design complexity and field deployment, increases exponentially with N.

The adaptation logic of applications, as programmed in the management module H, takes cognizance of the quality of event reporting (i.e., QoI) to reduce action errors [6]. A suitable resource allocation B in the voting system (network bandwidth, device CPU cycles) supports the sensor replication parameter setting $[N, f_m]$ — c.f. Fig. 2-(A). H thus views sensor replication as a pervasive activity that can be suitably controlled to meet the application needs[2].

An autonomic management of the replication process strives to keep the QoI and system resource usage at acceptable levels while meeting the safety requirements. It manifests as a constrained optimization problem to balance the cost of replication vis-a-vis the QoI utility rewards. The problem can be solved by machine-intelligence tools & methods: such as model-based reasoning [9].

2.3   Management View of Voting Algorithm

A non-faulty device incurs a time T_c to process the raw input data collected from the environment. T_c may randomly vary based on the dimensionality of data being processed and the amount of CPU cycles and bandwidth in the device. Given the asynchrony in data generation (arising from device heterogeneity) and system-level communication & processing, the voting process may go through multiple iterations — where each iteration involves the voting on a candidate data produced by one of the devices (i.e., proposal). Therein, each of the remaining $(N-1)$ devices casts a consent (YES) or dissent (NO) vote, based on whether its locally computed data matches with the candidate proposal or otherwise. A candidate data x is delivered to the end-user if at least $f_m + 1$ consent votes are received; otherwise, x is discarded and a next candidate data x' is taken up for voting. The ability of voting protocol to deliver a data without always having to wait for $\lceil \frac{N}{2} \rceil$ YES votes lowers the data delivery latency L. See [10] for details

---

[2] Sensor replication is subject to the physical constraints imposed by the target system. For e.g., it may be difficult to replicate the ECUs in an automobile due to the electrical bus load, logistics limitations, and/or revenue considerations. Such constraints are enforced by the management module H as part of application-specific policy functions (say, the cost function for replication) — as suggested in [8].

of the algorithm-internal adaptation mechanisms (such as when/how to solicit votes, adjusting timeout parameters, etc.).

For management purposes, the voting system incorporating the above algorithm is represented as a black-box with the mapping functions:

$$B = \mathcal{G}(\gamma, [f_a, r, l], N, [f_m, r'']); \quad \gamma' = \mathcal{G}^*(\gamma, B, [f_a, r, l], N, [f_m, r'']).$$

This depicts the realization of QoI specs γ under the environment conditions $[f_a, r, l]$ and device replication N (l: message loss probability). If γ' is the fraction of collected data that actually gets delivered to the end-user (i.e., $L < \Delta_m$ with probability γ'), the QoI requirement is: $\gamma' \geq \gamma$ — typically, $\gamma \approx 0.90$. The unknown external inputs $[f_u, r, l]$ impact the actual delivery probability γ'. $\mathcal{G}(\cdots)$ is a non-separable function of B, N, γ, l, $[f_a, r]$, and $[f_m, r'']$.

In earlier works, we have studied the engineering of voting protocol mechanisms for improved QoS and performance: i.e., lower the latency L and message overhead M [11]. The system-level protocol mechanisms include time-out based message retransmissions (to deal with network loss), coordinated broadcast of candidate proposals (to reduce redundant exchange of large-sized data), and selective vote solicitation for a candidate data (to reduce the implosion of vote messages). $\mathcal{G}(\cdots)$ captures the voting protocol rules for various message exchanges over the network to counter malicious acts of faulty devices.

The allowed operating range of voting system is determined by QoI optimality needs against the cost constraints imposed by the replica deployment (such as hardware/software, physical maintenance, and security). H may dynamically find the optimal point by an iterative search of the γ-space vis-a-vis the resource allocation $[B, N]$ and the associated cost constraints.

3   A Perspective on Related Works

[12] advocates a probabilistic approach to manage the dependability of services in a distributed system. Our work follows this trait by treating fault-tolerance as a QoS attribute. This is reflected in our management of data collection services that employ functional redundancy of devices to handle the data sensing errors.

[6] describes a system architecture that allows prescribing the QoI (quality of information) needs of application in suitable metrics. The system captures the QoI expectations in a prescriptive notation and matches them with various system configurations (assembled from base component specs) to provide the QoI capabilities. Our work draws from this QoI-based approach in a specific domain of replication based sensor data collection.

Existing safety verification methods based on static specs of a target system [13] are restrictive for our reconfigurable voting system — given the hard-to-measure external environment parameters (such as f_a). There have been however system-level tools developed elsewhere to aid middleware management software: such as probabilistic monitoring [14] and controlled fault-injection [15]. These tools can be used in our management module H.

At a meta-level, our management module H orchestrates the reconfiguration activities without domain-specific knowledge about the voting system (the domain knowledge is captured in the underlying software stubs). This is in contrast from existing paradigms for network QoS adaptation [16,17] which, if employed, would require domain-specific knowledge about the replica voting processes to be hard-wired in H. Our approach reduces the cost of software development for adaptive network systems by re-use of the model-based control architecture.

4 Model-Predictive Autonomic Control of Voting System

The domain-knowledge needed in H to orchestrate reconfiguration activities in the voting system S is based on: (i) the closed-form mapping relations between the QoI indices and algorithmic & environment parameters, and (ii) the software stubs underneath the programming interfaces for QoI monitoring & control.

4.1 State-Dependent Operational Analysis

Given that a voting round can spread over at most $(f_a + f_m + 1)$ iterations to deliver a data, a short-hand check to verify the timing constraint is:

$$[\mu(T_c) + (f_m + f_a + 1).\delta] < \Delta \quad \text{for } f_a \leq f_m,$$

where δ is the time spent on a voting iteration. The probability distribution of T_c strongly influences the number of iterations L' executed in a voting round.

To determine L', consider the state where a jth voting iteration has passed without success $(1 \leq j \leq f_a + f_m)$. Data delivery then occurs in a wth iteration, where $(j+1) \leq w \leq (f_a + f_m + 1)$. This is captured by the correctness assertion:

$$\forall j = 1, 2, \cdots, f_a + f_m \ [\ \sum_{w=j+1}^{f_a+f_m+1} \text{prob}(D_w | \neg D_j) = 1.0\ ]; \tag{1}$$

where D_w is the delivery of a data in wth iteration. It means that if a data delivery has not occurred in j^{th} iteration (i.e., state $\neg D_j$), a delivery will occur in a future iteration $j + 1, \cdots, w, \cdots, f_a + f_m + 1$. Thereupon, the algorithmic execution of current voting round terminates[3]. Our model-based treatment of the voting system then involves computing the probability density:

$$\text{prob}(D'_w) \equiv \text{prob}(D_w \cap \neg D_0)|_{w=1,2,3,\cdots,f_a+f_m+1}. \tag{2}$$

This probabilistic flow of algorithm-level events for data delivery is captured in the estimation of voting service-level performance indices: L and M.

---

[3] In the conditional probability: $\text{prob}(D_w | \neg D_j) = \frac{\text{prob}(D_w \cap \neg D_j)}{\text{prob}(\neg D_j)}$, the term $\text{prob}(D_w \cap \neg D_j)$ indicates the probability density of data delivery in wth step for a scenario where j^{th} step has not succeeded. Given that $\text{prob}(\neg D_j) \equiv \text{prob}(\neg D_j | \neg D_{j-1})$, the term $\text{prob}(\neg D_0) = 1.0$ depicts a degenerate case of probability assignment to kick-start the first iteration of algorithm (i.e., $w = 1$).

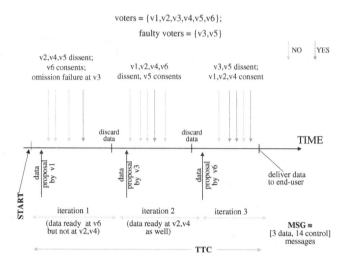

Fig. 3. Impact of voter asynchrony on latency and overhead (an illustration)

The computation of state probabilities is anchored on estimating the probability of a good proposal versus a bad proposal in a voting iteration j $(1 \leq j \leq f_a + f_m)$. It considers various scenarios of $(N - j + 1)$ of the devices eligible to propose from an ensemble of faulty and non-faulty devices. A voter generating good data attempts to propose in j^{th} step with a probability q_j, where $q_j = \frac{j}{2f_m + 1}$. We assume an uniformly distributed T_c over the time-span of $(2f_m + 1)$ voting steps. The number of propose-abort steps (i.e., iterations) in a voting round indicates how far the voter failures impede a data delivery. See Fig. 3.

4.2 Estimation of Performance Indices

The mean number of iterations elapsed for data delivery: $L' = \sum\limits_{w=1}^{f_a + f_m + 1} \text{prob}(D'_w) \times w$,

is an observational state in the voting system that is indicative of L and M — where $\frac{(f_m + 1)}{2} < L' < (f_a + f_m + 1)$ for $\frac{\sigma(T_c)}{\mu(T_c)} \gg 0.0$. Our model-based estimation of L and M factors other influential system-internal parameters also: such as device speeds, algorithmic work-flows (and device-level parallelism therein), network characteristics (broadcast/unicast, topology, etc.), and external environment conditions. The latency L is thus computed as:

$$L = \sum_{w'=1}^{f_a + f_m + 1} \text{prob}(D'_{w'}) \times [w'.\delta + \sum_{i=1}^{w'} (\overline{T}_{c(i)} - \overline{T}_{c(i-1)})], \qquad (3)$$

where $\overline{T}_{c(i)}$ is the mean time to compute good data by at least $(f_m + 1)$ of the N devices in a run up to i^{th} voting step — note that $\overline{T}_{c(0)}$ is set to $T_{c_{min}}$: the minimum time expended to compute a data. The time δ taken by the voting algorithm to carry out a single iteration is given as: $\delta = (T_{dcmp} + \frac{\alpha.d_R+(N+1).d_c}{B})$ — where T_{dcmp} is the time-to-compare for a candidate data proposal with the locally computed data for a device to decide on its YES/NO vote ($T_{dcmp} \gg 0$). A moderation factor α accounts for the multiplicity of proposal messages generated in a voting step when more than one device attempt to propose ($1 < \alpha \ll N$). $\overline{T}_{c(i)}$ is obtained from a probability distribution capturing the device-level computational spread parameters $[\mu(T_c), \sigma(T_c)]$.

Similar to L, the message overhead M can be estimated from the probability $\text{prob}(D'_{L'})$. The L and M formulas[4] constitute the system model $\mathcal{G}(.)$.

4.3   Analytical Results on Voting System

We study the influence of the device redundancy parameter N on the QoS achieved (while keeping the other parameters fixed). We reason that a higher N increases γ', *albeit*, in a non-linear fashion. Intuitively, over a region of small N (say, $N = 3 \cdots 5$), an increase of N has a strong impact on increasing γ', because the higher device-level asynchrony increases the likelihood of receiving $f_m + 1$ consents quicker — thereby lowering L' (and hence L). But, over a region of large N (say, $N = 9 \cdots 11$), the device-level asynchrony induced by an increase of N results only in a marginal reduction in L' — assuming that f_m does not change with N. Our analytical results, as shown in Fig. 4, corroborates this observation. It also aligns with the experimental results — c.f. Fig. 2-(B).

The performance parameter L' critically depends on the external environment parameters: $[f_a, r, l]$, the device-level asynchrony parameter $[\mu(T_c), \sigma(T_c)]$, and the network bandwidth B allocated for the voting operations. The graphs in Fig. 4 shows how L' varies with respect to f_a and r — note: L' can be directly mapped onto a QoS-related parameter: data miss ratio $\zeta = (1 - \gamma)$. The results are obtained from our probabilistic analysis of replica voting system. The exponential increase in L' with an increase of $[f_a, r]$ arises from a potentially large increase in the wasteful operations caused by faulty behavior of devices.

The behavior: $\frac{dL'}{dr} < 0$ for $r \in (0.0, r_0]_{0.45 < r_0 < 0.6}$ (Fig. 4), stems from a *bio-inspired* feature incorporated in our model of voting protocol. Here, an unsuccessful iteration in a voting round, which indicates the likelihood of a quickly generated bad data proposal from a faulty device, causes the non-faulty devices to jack up their computational resources (e.g., allocation of more VM cycles for sensor tasks hosted on a cloud) and increase the probability of a good proposal q_j in the next iteration. This smart behavior of voting system lowers L', when compared to a non-intelligent behavior[5]. In the region $r_0 < r \leq 1.0$ however,

---

[4] Given the complexity of state-space analysis for adaptive systems, we employ model slicing [18] to simplify the voting system formulas (for tractability). For brevity, we omit the estimation of state probabilities for generating good/bad data proposals.

[5] A biological analogy is the vaccination to develop body immunity: namely, the injection of a very small dosage of semi-dead disease-causing virus that stirs up the body defense system to launch immunological actions !! Here, L' corresponds to the bad effects of disease-causing virus that the body gets exposed to (e.g., fever).

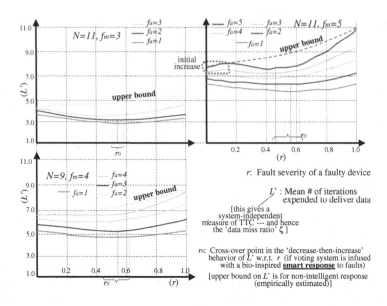

Fig. 4. QoS-related parameter L' versus fault parameters $[f_a, r]$

the smart response of voting system cannot fully subdue the negative effects of increased bad behavior (the latter is measurable as $f_a.r$).

The latency and resource costs depict a monotonic convex increase with respect to the external parameters $[f_a, r]$ (for given algorithm parameters $[N, B, f_m]$) — c.f. Figs. 2-(B) and 4. This mathematical property, combined with a monotonic concave decrease in the system utility with respect to latency, poses the optimization problem for QoS γ' with a unique optimal solution: $[N, f_m, B]$.

4.4   Sample Reconfiguration Scenario

Figure 5 illustrates our model-computed reconfigurations in pertinent time-scales. The changes occur in the algorithm parameters $[N, (f_m, r)]$. A reconfiguration is triggered by the estimated external conditions (f_a, r''). Potentially, multiple runs of the voting algorithm occur between two successive reconfigurations. For brevity, we show only the observations of M as triggers.

A configuration with $[N = 12, (f_m = 3, r = 0.4)]$ and $(f_a = 0, \_)$ is used as a base case incurring 1 message unit, i.e., $M = 1$. The overhead M for arbitrary configurations is expressed as normalized units relative to the base case. Our model-based analysis yields $M = 2.55$ for $(f_a = 4, r'' = 0.3)$, 1.96 for $(3, 0.3)$, and 1.55 for $(2, 0.4)$. The change in fault parameters from $(2, 0.4)$ to $(5, 0.3)$ is quite significant, increasing N to 11 and then to 15, with M estimated as 3.11 and 3.88 respectively. A lower confidence in estimating $f_a = 4$ in the next interval however forces H to keep $f_m = 6$ and $N = 13$, which incurs a high M at 3.15. A decrease in N, as triggered by a spontaneous reduction of QoS specs in the meanwhile, lowers M to 2.38. When the sensed fault is lower from $f_a = 4$

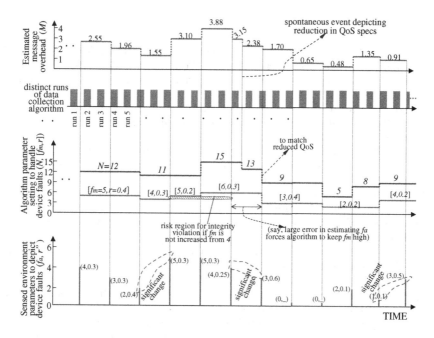

Fig. 5. Sample scenario of voting system reconfigurations

to $f_a = 3$, M reduces correspondingly to 1.70. A lower M: 0.65 and 0.48, occurs when there is no faulty behavior, i.e., $f_a = 0$, and 0.91 when $f_a = 1$.

Our management module H orchestrates reconfigurations without explicit domain-knowledge. This reduces the software development costs for adaptive network systems in general, by reuse of the structure of H in different domains.

5   Conclusions

Functional redundancy at various sub-system levels improves the performance, QoS, and fault-tolerance aspects of a networked system. However, algorithm-level message exchanges between replicated sensors and logistics & physical constraints on sensor replication incur operating costs and management overhead. In this light, we considered a system for voting among replicated sensors.

A sustainable QoI of data delivery in the face of faulty devices inducing data corruptions and/or timeliness errors requires a dynamic reconfiguration of the voting system parameters. Reconfiguration is guided by a safety prescription that stipulates the degree of sensor replication and the algorithm parameter settings needed to meet the QoI needs. The paper described the management of safe reconfigurations of a voting system, despite the knowledge uncertainty about the faulty behavior of sensors. The adaptation control processes in our management module can also be re-used in other application domains.

References

1. Kopetz, H., Verissmo, P.: Real time dependability concepts. In: Mullender, S. (ed.) Distributed Systems, pp. 411–446. Addison-Wesl. Co., New York (1993). Chapter 16
2. Leveson, N.G.: Software challenges in achieving space safety. J. Br. Inter Planet. Soc. **62**, 265–272 (2009)
3. Filieri, A., Ghezzi, C., Leva, A., Maggio, M.: Autotuning control structures for reliability-driven dynamic binding. In: IEEE Conference on Decision and Control (2012)
4. Wu, J., Ravindran, K., Sabbir, A., Kwiat, K.A.: Engineering of replica voting protocols for energy-efficiency in data delivery. In: Proceedings of IEEE WOWMOM, Niagara Falls (NY), pp. 458–460, June 2006
5. Forrest, S., Somayaji, A., Ackley, D.H.: Building diverse computer systems. In: Proceedings of the 6th Workshop HotOS-VI, IEEE (1997)
6. Frischbier, S., Pietzuch, P., Buchmann, A.: Managing expectations: runtime negotiation of information quality requirements in event-based systems. In: Franch, X., Ghose, A.K., Lewis, G.A., Bhiri, S. (eds.) ICSOC 2014. LNCS, vol. 8831, pp. 199–213. Springer, Heidelberg (2014)
7. Amditis, D.A., et al.: Multiple sensor collision avoidance system for automotive applications using an IMM approach for obstacle tracking. In: Fusion 2002, Proceedings of the International Society of Information Fusion (2002)
8. Keeney, J., Cahill, V.: Chisel : a policy-driven, context-aware, dynamic adaptation framework. In: Proceedings of the IEEE International Workshop on Policies for Distributed Systems and Networks (POLICY 2003), June 2003
9. Eberhart, R.C., Shi, Y.: Computational Intelligence: Concepts to Implementations, Chapter 2. Morgan Kaufman Publ, San Francisco (2007)
10. Kwiat, K.A., Ravindran, K., Wu, J., Sabbir, A.: Adaptive QoS mechanisms for dependable data delivery in replication-based voting systems. In: Proceedings of SCS-SPECTS 2006, Calgary (Canada), June 2006
11. Ravindran, K., Kwiat, K.A., Sabbir, A., Cao, B., Voting, R.: A distributed middleware service for real-time dependable systems. In: Proceedings of the IEEE/ACM COMSWARE 2006, New Delhi (India), January 2006
12. Avizienis, A., Laprie, J.C., Randell, B., Landwehr, C.: Basic concepts and taxonomy of dependable and secure computing. IEEE Trans. Dependable Secure Comput. **1**(1), 11–33 (2004)
13. Yi, J., Woo, H., Browne, J.C., Mok, A.K., Xie, F., Atkins, E., Lee, C.G.: Incorporating resource safety verification to executable model-based development for embedded systems. In: IEEE-RTAS, pp. 137–146 (2008)
14. Brunner, M., Dudkowski, D., Mingardi, C., Nunzi, G.: Probabilistic decentralized network management. In: Proceedings of IM-2009, June 2009
15. Lanigan, P.E., Narasimhan, P., Fuhrman, T.E.: Experiences with a CANoe-based fault injection framework for AUTOSTAR. In: IEEE/IFIP Conference on Dependable Systems and Networks (DSN 2010) (2010)
16. Li, B., Nahrstedt, K.: A control-based middleware framework for quality of service adaptations. IEEE JSAC **17**(9), 1632–1650 (1999)
17. Bridges, P.G., Hiltunen, M., Schlichting, R.D.: Cholla: a framework for composing and coordinating adaptations in networked systems. IEEE Trans. Comput. **58**(11), 1456–1469 (2009)
18. Schaefer, I., Heffter, A.P.: Slicing for model reduction in adaptive embedded systems development. In: Workshop on Software Engineering for Adaptive and Self-managing Systems (SEAMS 2008), May 2008

On Composition of Checkpoint and Recovery Protocols for Distributed Systems

Soumi Chattopadhyay[1], Ansuman Banerjee[1], and Himadri Sekhar Paul[2(✉)]

[1] ACMU, Indian Statistical Institute, Kolkata, India
{soumi_r,ansuman}@isical.ac.in
[2] Innovation Labs, TCS Ltd., Kolkata, India
HimadriSekhar.Paul@tcs.com

Abstract. Rollback recovery has been studied as a low-cost fault tolerance mechanism for ensuring dependability of critical distributed applications. There is a rich variety of recovery protocols proposed in literature and they are broadly classified as *checkpoint-based recovery protocols* and *message-log based recovery protocols*. In this paper we attempt to model composition of protocol and check whether such composition is consistent with recovery. The composition of protocols in important in a system whether resources are hierarchically organized, for example grid or cloud systems.

1 Introduction

Distributed systems have always been looked at as a powerful computation platform for addressing and mitigating the resource limitations of a single-node system in terms of compute power or available memory. Over the past few years, distributed systems have evolved into the grid and then the cloud, imparting more control and ease of access to such distributed infrastructures. Such infrastructures have often been defined as a federation of resources from multiple administrative domains.

A distributed system like a grid or cloud, which is termed here as a *global infrastructure* or simply a *global system*, is composed of multiple smaller distributed installations, termed here as *native systems* or *native clusters*. Each native system is a conglomeration of basic resources, like computing nodes. Typically a native cluster is located in a constrained geography, for example, in the department of some university. But the clusters themselves can be geographically dispersed. Although the resources are managed in a hierarchical manner, the whole system is presented as a single system to the user. At the same time, it is important to maintain administrative segregation among the participating native systems to honor their own administrative policies. To maintain a single system view of the global infrastructure, it becomes important that some of the system level services of the constituent native systems may need to be combined to provide a system-wide, single, consistent service.

Fault tolerance remains a critical aspect of such systems and is being addressed in various ways depending on the services they provide. In this paper,

A. Norta et al. (Eds.): ICSOC 2015 Workshops, LNCS 9586, pp. 231–242, 2016.
DOI: 10.1007/978-3-662-50539-7_19

we assume that the native clusters employ some rollback recovery mechanisms as fault tolerance. These native recovery protocols are combined by some global recovery protocol to ensure system-wide consistent recovery. In this paper, we investigate the problem of composing different recovery protocols in a cluster-based distributed system. Section 2 presents discussions on definitions and models related to distributed systems. In Sect. 3, we present a model of a recovery protocol. Analysis of composition consistency of recovery protocols based on this model is presented in Sect. 4. Finally, Sect. 5 concludes this paper with directions for future work.

2   Background

A distributed system is a collection of independent resource nodes connected over a network. Since node failures and communication link malfunctions are assumed to be independent events, larger the system - higher is the probability of failure. Fault tolerance is, therefore, an important issue in distributed systems and is critically linked to reliability, availability, and throughput. Fault tolerance, however, can only be achieved through some form of redundancy. There are different levels of guarantees for different forms of redundancy and with different associated cost. Rollback recovery is a form of temporal redundancy which has been proposed as a cost-effective mechanism of fault tolerance for non-critical distributed applications. The following section presents a model of distributed systems which we use for the illustration of our key concepts.

2.1   Model of Distributed System

A distributed system consists of a set of n processes $\mathcal{P} = \{P_1, P_2, \ldots P_n\}$. The processes are connected by underlying communication channels, $\mathcal{C} = \{C_{ij} \mid 1 \leq i, j \leq n\}$, where channel $C_{i,j}$ denotes a uni-directional channel from P_i to P_j. Execution of a single process P_i is modelled as a state transition system $\mathcal{S}_i$. State transitions are triggered by events. Events in distributed systems are classified as two types: (1) *local events* like computation events, message send events; and (2) *external events*, like message receive events. A *local checkpoint* of a process P_i is a concrete realization of its execution state.

The execution model of the distributed system is the composition of the state transition systems of the constituent processes, *i.e.* $\mathbf{S} = \mathcal{S}_1 \times \mathcal{S}_2 \times \cdots \times \mathcal{S}_n$. The global state of a distributed system is represented as the tuple $DS = (SP, SC)$, where $SP = \{s_i | s_i$ is the state information for $p_i \in P\}$ and $SC = \{c_{ij} | 1 \leq i, j \leq n\}$ where, c_{ij} is a set of in-transit messages from p_i to p_j. A *global checkpoint* is a composition of local checkpoints, one taken from each of the processes and also the state of the channels, which essentially represent the in-transit messages in the channels.

A recovery process uses information recorded during the failure-free execution of the system to construct a consistent global state. The necessary condition that a recovery is consistent is that, for every message received by some process in the system, the corresponding send events are recorded in the state of the sender. In the next section, we present a model of consistent recovery, which we use for protocol composition.

3   Recovery Consistency Model

Protocols that employ temporal redundancy for fault tolerance, can be broadly classified into two categories, namely checkpoint-based rollback recovery and message-log-based roll-forward recovery. Checkpoint-based recovery ensures *rollback* of system state to some past consistent state. Message-log based recovery uses *roll-forward* in conjunction with rollback recovery, where the processes are assumed to follow the Piece-Wise Deterministic (PWD) model [12]. According to the model, execution of a process is divided into series of deterministic executions, each terminated by a non-deterministic event or external event, like a message receive event. For example, Fig. 1 depicts one execution instance where a process has passed through the states s_1, s_2, s_3, s_4, and s_5 in sequence. The state transitions were triggered by events e_1, e_2, e_3, and e_4 in that order. Events $e_1 = receive(m_1)$ and $e_2 = receive(m_2)$ are non-deterministic events. The deterministic executions are highlighted with rectangular boxes. The non-deterministic events are logged and are replayed during recovery. In message passing distributed systems, the log consists of messages. We now define an operation PWD which, given the local state of a process and a set of non-deterministic event logs, determines the state at which the process can finally be rolled forward following the PWD model.

Definition 1. Reachable by PWD*: The reachability of a state s_s with respect to an event log M in the PWD model is defined as $PWD(s_s, M) = s_f$ where, s_s is the start state, s_f is the final state reached by PWD model from s_s by replaying events from M.*

We also use an alternative notation $s_s \leadsto^M s_f$ for $PWD(s_s, M) = s_f$. If a process is not assumed to follow PWD model, we say $PWD(s, \cdot) = s$.

With reference to Fig. 1, consider the message log $M = \{m_1\}$. The state of the system can be rolled-forward from s_1 to s_2 by replaying the receive event e_1 from M. In fact, by PWD, the system can be rolled forward up to s_4, but not beyond s_4 since $m_2 \notin M$. Hence $s_1 \leadsto^M s_4$, but $s_1 \not\leadsto^M s_5$.

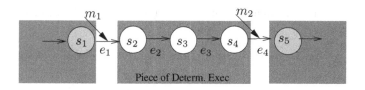

Fig. 1. Roll-forward by PWD model

3.1   Consistency of Global Recovery

In the event of a failure, processes need to be restarted. However, we can start processes from some intermediate state instead of re-starting them from their initial states. A global checkpoint represents such a state of the system and the recovery protocol computes such a state from available local checkpoints of the processes. However, any composition of local states does not guarantee consistency of the global checkpoint. In this section, we derive consistency conditions which are applicable for both checkpoint-based recovery protocols, as well as log-based recovery protocols. The essential idea of consistency is to capture the condition that no message becomes *orphan* after completion of the recovery process. We formalize the concept of the orphan message in the discussion below. This condition for consistency of a global checkpoint is a necessary condition. However, in an environment where the underlying communication channel is reliable, the recovery process must also ensure that there is no *lost message*, which essentially means that for every message whose send event is captured in the log, the corresponding receive event is present as well. Based on this discussion, the condition of consistency can be derived as follows.

No Orphan Message: Given local states or checkpoints of a pair of processes p_s and p_r, denoted as c_s and c_r respectively, and a message m whose sender is the process p_s and the receiver is p_r; the message is said to be *orphan* w.r.t. the states $\{c_s, c_r\}$, if the receive event is recorded in c_r but the corresponding send event is not recorded in c_s. In a consistent recovery, there cannot be any orphan message present in the recovered global state. The condition is defined here as *No Orphan Message* (*NOM*). Given a global state $DS = (SP, SC)$ as defined earlier, for every pair of local checkpoints, $SP_i, SP_j \in DS$, the NOM criterion denotes *either* there is no orphan message for (SP_i, SP_j) *or* P_i can be rolled forward from SP_i to a state s such that there is no orphan message for the pair $< s, SP_j >$. Formally, this is defined as,

Definition 2. *Given a global checkpoint* $\mathfrak{C} = (SP, SC)$, *No Orphan Message* *(NOM) constraint for a pair of local checkpoints,* $SP_i, SP_j \in SP$ *is defined as,*

$$NOM(SP_i, SP_j) = \begin{cases} true & if\ \forall receive(m) \in SP_j : \\ & (send(m) \in PWD(SP_i, M_i)) \\ false & otherwise \end{cases}$$

where, M_j is the event log of receive messages at process P_j, $send(m)$ denotes the send event of a message m, and $receive(m)$ denotes the receive event of a message m,

Definition 3. *No Orphan Message constraint for a global checkpoint,* $\mathfrak{C}$, *is defined as:*

$$NOM(\mathfrak{C}) = \bigwedge_{\forall i,j} NOM(SP_i, SP_j) \quad | \quad SP_i, SP_j \in \mathfrak{C}$$

No Lost Message. Given local states or checkpoints of a pair of processes p_s and p_r, denoted as c_s and c_r respectively, and a message m whose sender is the process p_s and the receiver is p_r; the message is said to be *lost w.r.t.* the states $\{c_s, c_r\}$, if the send event is recorded in c_r but the corresponding receive event is not recorded in c_s. In a system, where the underlying communication channels are reliable, a recovery protocol must ensure that there are no lost messages in the recovered state to ensure consistency. Given a global state $DS = (SP, SC)$ as defined earlier, the condition of *No Lost Message* (NLM) is described for a pair of local checkpoints $SP_i, SP_j \in DS$ as follows:

- *Either,* there is no lost message for (SP_i, SP_j)
- *Or,* for every in-transit message m from P_i to P_j, $m \in SC_{ij}$, where $SC_{ij} \in DS$
- *Or,* P_j can be rolled forward to a state s such that for the state pair $< SP_i, s >$, there is no lost message or every in-transit message is included in the channel state SC_{ij}.

Definition 4. *Given a global checkpoint* $\mathfrak{C} = (SP, SC)$, *the No Message Loss constraint for a pair of checkpoints* $SP_i, SP_j \in SP$, *can be defined as follows:*

$$NLM(SP_i, SP_j) = \begin{cases} true & if \quad \forall send(m) \in SP_i : \\ & \left(receive(m) \in PWD(SP_j, M_j) \right. \\ & \left. \oplus \quad (m \in SC_{ij} \mid SC_{ij} \in SC) \right) \\ false & otherwise \end{cases}$$

Definition 5. *No Lost Message (NLM) constraint for the global checkpoint,* $\mathfrak{C}$, *is defined as:*

$$NLM(\mathfrak{C}) = \bigwedge_{\forall i,j} NLM(SP_i, SP_j) \mid SP_i, SP_j \in \mathfrak{C}$$

3.2   Consistency of Global Checkpoint

A failure free run of a distributed system is one of its many valid execution paths. Consistency of a global checkpoint ensures reachability of a global state which could have been reached by the system in some failure free run. However in none of these possible execution paths, an orphan message generation is possible. Consistency criterion of a global state must ensure that such conditions are not violated. Any arbitrary composition of local checkpoints into a global checkpoint does necessarily make it consistent. We now define the consistency criterion for a global checkpoint.

Definition 6. *Given a global checkpoint* $\mathfrak{C} = (SP, SC)$

$$consistent(\mathfrak{C}) \Leftrightarrow \begin{cases} NOM(SP_p, SP_q) & \forall SP_p, SP_q \in SP \\ \quad \dots when\ the\ channels\ are\ unreliable \\ NOM(SP_p, SP_q) \wedge NLM(SP_p, SP_q) & \forall SP_p, SP_q \in SP \\ \quad \dots when\ the\ channels\ are\ reliable \end{cases}$$

Intuitively, the definition above signifies that a collection of local checkpoints, as a global checkpoint, is consistent only when there is no orphan message, given any pair of local checkpoints from this collection. However, if the underlying communication channels are reliable, the consistency criterion is more stringent and must additionally satisfy 'no lost message' constraint.

3.3 Fault and Recovery Model

We now present a discussion on the fault and recovery model of the system following Hoare's logical notations denoting logical derivation from a set of given expressions [4]. For example, $\frac{P\quad Q}{R}$ expression denotes logical derivation of the expression R from given expressions P and Q. Fault and recovery can be modelled as processes. A fault takes the system to an unknown, possibly inconsistent state. A fault can occur at any time, therefore,

$$\frac{\{*\}}{I\,\{F\}\,\blacksquare}$$

where I is a consistency invariant condition, F denotes the fault. We denote unknown or unspecified condition as $\blacksquare$. The numerator denoted by $*$ stands for the fact that the fault can manifest at any state, denoted by the symbol $*$.

The recovery process takes the system from an unspecified state to a state where the consistency criterion holds. We assume that no fault occurs during the recovery procedure. Therefore,

$$\blacksquare\,\{R\}\,I$$

where I is a consistency invariant condition as above, R denotes the recovery process.

In these cases, I can be the global state condition tuple $\{NOM, NLM\}$, denoted in our usual representation of (process state, channel state) when the underlying channels are lossless or $\{NOM\}$ when the underlying channels are lossy.

When a fault process is triggered, a recovery process must be subsequently triggered, and the objective of the recovery process is to restore the system to a consistent state. Therefore, under the composition operator ($\circ$), the final system remains in a consistent state.

$$\frac{I\,\{F\}\,\blacksquare,\quad \blacksquare\,\{R\}\,I}{I\,\{F \circ R\}\,I}$$

Assumption 1. *Given a consistent global state $\mathfrak{C}$, recovery with $\mathfrak{C}$ leads to a consistent recovery.*

$$\frac{consistent(\mathfrak{C})}{\blacksquare\,R(\mathfrak{C})\,I}$$

4   Hierarchical Protocol Analysis

A cluster-based distributed system is composed of several clusters of machines where the clusters may be geographically dispersed and administered by independent organizations. As a consequence, different clusters can employ different checkpoint and recovery protocols. Figure 2 shows a snapshot of execution of processes in two different clusters. The figure shows the communication pattern and local checkpoints of the processes. Each of the clusters employ checkpoint and recovery protocols independent of each other. For a simple case, we assume both the clusters employ the same protocol. We analyze the consistent recovery phenomenon under this most simple setup. We also present an analysis of scenarios involving two and three protocols being composed. Composition involving more than one protocol is more complex than composing two instances of the same protocol since the requirements of the individual checkpointing protocols and their corresponding recovery protocols may be very different.

In a general framework of hierarchical protocols, there are two key elements, a *global protocol* which interacts with nodes outside its own cluster and a *local protocol* which implements the native checkpoint and recovery protocol inside the cluster. Native protocols are well known protocols found in literature. The global protocol is used to combine natives protocols running in different clusters so that a consistent recovery can be ensured across the whole system. Each cluster may have a node specially designated as the *leader* node, which usually acts as the local coordinator whenever coordination is demanded by the global protocol.

4.1   Composition with Un-Coordinated Protocol

We begin our analysis with the simplest case of hierarchical composition of checkpoint and recovery protocols, where all the clusters in the system use a

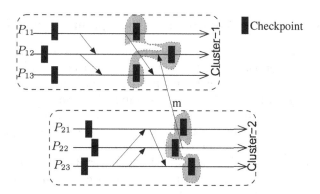

Fig. 2. Communication pattern involving two clusters

completely un-coordinated checkpointing protocol cite. The checkpointing protocol in this case is trivially composed where the global protocol has no role to play. However, the corresponding recovery protocol requires coordination among all nodes to construct a consistent global recovery state and this objective needs to be achieved by the global protocol. The global recovery line can be computed from partial Rollback Dependency Graphs (RDGs) maintained by all nodes in the system [13]. Algorithm 1 presents an outline of the global recovery protocol. The proof of the recovery is trivial and is guaranteed by the native recovery protocol and is not elaborated here.

Algorithm 1. Global Recovery Protocol

1: **procedure** GLOBALRECOVERYCOORD
2:     The failed process initiates recovery by sending *Recovery Request Message* to all the *leader* processes in the system.
3:     All *Leaders* on receipt of the *Recovery Request Message* broadcast the *Recovery Request Messages* to all nodes in its own cluster.
4:     All nodes on receipt of the *Recovery Request Message* construct RDGs based on their partial view of the dependency of the checkpoints and send to the their leader process (native recovery procedure)
5:     The *leader* combines the RDGs and sends to the failed processes
6:     The failed process on receive of responses from all *leader* processes combines the RDGs and identifies the recovery line (native recovery process)
7:     The failed process sends the recovery line to all *leaders*
8:     The *leader* broadcasts the recovery line in its cluster
9:     All nodes, on receipt of the recovery line roll back to the checkpoint identified in the recovery line and delete all local checkpoints beyond the recovery line (native recovery process)
10: **end procedure**

4.2   Composition with Coordinated Checkpointing Protocol

We address another scenario where all the clusters use a coordinated checkpoint and recovery protocol based on the two-phase commit protocol [3] as the native protocol. This allows them to work independently without any global protocol. It can be easily shown that this simple composition cannot guarantee a consistent recovery and a counter-example is depicted in Fig. 2 in support of this claim. The recovery lines in the individual clusters are highlighted. However, these two recovery lines are not consistent with each other due to the presence of the inter-cluster message m. If the global state recovers to the yellow recovery line highlighted in the figure, then m becomes an orphan message, *i.e.* $NOM(SP_{12}, SP_{22})$ does not hold, where SP_{12} and SP_{22} are the checkpoints of P_{12} and P_{22} respectively on the recovery line.

In general, due to consistency of native recovery protocols, $NOM(SP_{ki}, SP_{kj})$: $1 \leq i, j \leq n_k$ holds, where SP_{ki} and SP_{kj} are checkpoints of processes $P_{ki} \in K_k$ and $P_{kj} \in K_k$ respectively, K_k represents the kth cluster, and n_k is the number of nodes in K_k. However, trivially $NOM(SP_{ki}, SP_{lj})$ does not hold, where SP_{ki} and SP_{lj} are checkpoints on the recovery line of clusters K_k and K_l respectively. This violation is usually due to the inter-cluster message as depicted in the example above.

One possible method of composition to eliminate orphan inter-cluster messages is to impose coordination of checkpointing activities among clusters through a global protocol. However, this translates to the fact that all checkpointing and recovery activities become a global event and by the guarantees of the coordinated checkpointing protocol, the recovery is always consistent. Another way of composition is by selectively blocking clusters, during global level coordination. Paul *et al.* proposed this solution, where a process is blocked whenever it attempts to send an inter-cluster message during a global level coordination for checkpointing [10]. They implement the rule as *Policy B*, which, when in force, blocks the process on receipt of any inter-cluster message. The message can only be processed once the policy is revoked at the termination of global checkpoint coordination.

In the later sections, we explore more complex scenarios where multiple native checkpoint and recovery protocols are used among clusters.

4.3   Composition of Two Heterogeneous Protocols

In this section, we consider the composition problem in the context of two clusters, each employing its own checkpoint & recovery protocol. The case can be generalized to any number of clusters, where there are two different protocols being employed, with some processes running the first protocol and some running the second. We analyze the case of composition of coordinated checkpointing [5] and a pessimistic message-log-based recovery protocol [1]. Initially, we assume that they are trivially composed with no global protocol to coordinate activities between two different clusters. We have already shown that without global coordination, two clusters with coordinated checkpointing protocol cannot ensure consistent recovery. Also, without global coordination, a cluster with coordinated checkpointing cannot be consistent with the cluster employing message-log based recovery. Consider Fig. 2 and let us assume *cluster-1* employs a log-based recovery protocol and *cluster-2* employs coordinated checkpointing. In the event of a failure, by the native recovery protocol, the coordinated cluster rolls back to its previous checkpoint, while the log-based recovery protocol only restarts the failed process and rolls forward its state by replaying messages from its message log. Consider a failure in *cluster-2* which, by its native recovery protocol, rolls back to the state highlighted in the figure. However, the processes in *cluster-1* continue execution. Now, after recovery of the processes in *cluster-2*, it becomes inconsistent since $NOM(SP_{12}, SP_{22})$ does not hold due to the presence of m, which now is an orphan message.

In a cluster with log-based recovery protocol, only the failed process recovers by restart and roll-forward mechanism. No other process takes part in the recovery activity. So after recovery, by the guarantee of the native recovery process, the recovered process becomes consistent with the states of rest of the processes in the system. In order to eliminate any possibility of generation of orphan message in the event of a rollback in a cluster with coordinated checkpointing, the global protocol must ensure that the cluster does not rollback beyond any send event of an inter-cluster message. A forced checkpoint in the clusters with coordinated checkpointing after every send event of an inter-cluster message, was proposed as a solution in [11]. Due to this enforcement by the global protocol, in the event of a recovery, a cluster with coordinated checkpoint never rolls back beyond any send event of an inter-cluster message. Therefore, after recovery $NOM(SP_{ki}, SP_{lj})$ holds, where SP_{ki} is the recovered state of a process in the kth cluster and SP_{lj} is the same for the lth cluster, and $k \neq l$. Again by the guarantees of native recovery protocol of a cluster, $NOM(SP_{ki}, SP_{kj})$ holds for intra-cluster messages. Therefore, NOM holds for any two processes in the system and hence the recovery is consistent.

4.4   Composition of Three Protocols

In this section, we attempt to compose three different protocols, namely coordinated checkpointing and recovery [5], receiver-based pessimistic message log-based recovery [1], and quasi-synchronous checkpointing protocol [6]. We assume each cluster employs one of these three types of protocol. The recovery consistency guarantee provided by the protocols are as follows:

$$NOM(SC_{ki}, SC_{kj}) \quad k^{th} \text{ cluster employs coordinated checkpointing}$$
$$NOM(s_{li}, PWD(\ominus, M_{kj})) \quad k^{th} \text{ cluster employs log-based recovery and } k \neq l$$
$$\ominus \text{ represents the restarted state}$$
$$NOM(SC_{ki}, SC_{kj}) \quad k^{th} \text{ cluster employs quasi-synchronous}$$
$$\text{checkpointing}$$

The composed global checkpoint and recovery protocol must ensure the NOM condition for local states of all processes after recovery. A failure in the cluster employing log-based recovery is trivially consistent with states of all other processes by the guarantee of the protocol. Since violations of NOM condition arises due to inter-cluster messages, processes in clusters employing coordinated checkpointing or quasi-synchronous checkpointing must force extra checkpoints so that these processes never roll back beyond the send event of any inter-cluster message. The message send procedure is shown in Algorithm 2.

Algorithm 2. Message Send Event Handler for Clusters with Coordinated and Quasi-Synchronous Checkpointing

---

procedure MSGSENDHANDLER(m : Message to be send)
    Buffer m
    Initiate coordinated checkpointing protocol
    On completion of the native checkpointing successfully, release m to be
    sent through network.
end procedure

We now prove that the global protocol with the message handler described in Algorithm 2 ensures consistent recovery in all clusters.

Proof. We need to prove that after rollback, the states of the processes are consistent with respect to each other. There can be two cases for a pair of processes, (1) both belong to the same cluster, and (2) both belong to different clusters. For the first case, the consistency of the states of the processes are guaranteed by the consistency of the native recovery protocol. We prove the second case by contradiction. Let the processes be P_{ki} and P_{lj} and they belong to clusters C_k and C_l respectively and $k \neq l$. Let the states of the processes after recovery be s_{ki} and s_{lj} respectively. We assume $NOM(s_{ki}, s_{lj})$ does not hold. Without loss of generality, there must be an inter-cluster message m sent before s_{ki} and received before s_{lj}. There can be the following cases.

Case 1: C_l employs log-based protocol and C_k employs Coordinated checkpointing. During recovery, by native recovery protocols, P_{li} does not rollback and continues with its normal operation. P_{kj} recovers to its latest checkpoint. But, due to the Algorithm 2, there cannot be any send event of an inter-cluster message recorded after s_{kj}. Hence a contradiction.

Case 2: C_l employs log-based protocol and C_k employs Quasi-Synchronous checkpointing. Same argument as in case 1 holds.

Case 3: C_l and C_k both employ either Coordinated or Quasi-Synchronous checkpointing. By the application of Algorithm 2, there cannot be any inter-cluster message send event beyond the recovered state of either P_{ki} or P_{lj}. Hence a contradiction.   □

4.5 Related Work

The first work towards composition of protocols for hierarchical distributed systems was by Paul et al. [9] where they demonstrated that cluster-based systems running a coordinated checkpointing protocol and a communication induced checkpointing (CIC) protocol can be combined by a higher level checkpoint and recovery protocol to provide a consistent recovery. Monet et al. worked in the same direction and presented a more detailed protocol where they combined clusters running coordinated checkpointing with the method of the CIC protocol as global protocol [7]. Paul et al. also proposed a method to combine a coordinated checkpointing protocol with a message logging protocol [11]. Bhatia et al. proposed a hierarchical causal logging protocol that addresses the scalability problems of causal logging [2]. Ndiaye et al. present a comparison of these protocols obtained through composition by simulation using OmNet+ [8]. To the best of our knowledge, a formal treatment of protocol composition as discussed in this paper, is missing in literature.

5 Conclusion

In this paper, we discuss a model of checkpoint and recovery protocols for message passing distributed systems and extracted consistency criterion of a recovery process. The model we present is extended for inclusion of message-log based recovery protocols. The motivation behind the model is to apply the same for protocol compositions and deduce the consistency of the recovery. Such composition is meaningful in a cloud or grid computing scenario, where multiple clusters from multiple administrative domains participate in the system. We apply the model on simple compositions involving various checkpoint and recovery protocols. We believe that this study will open up future research avenues on more protocol variants.

References

1. Alvisi, L., Murzullo, K.: Message logging: pessimistic, optimistic, causal and optimal. IEEE Trans. Softw. Eng. **24**, 149–159 (1998)
2. Bhatia, K., Marzullo, K., Alvisi, L.: Scalable causal message logging for wide-area environments. Concurency Comput. Pract. Exp. **15**(3), 873–889 (2003)
3. Gray, J.N.: Notes on database operating systems. In: Bayer, R., Graham, R.M., Seegmüller, G. (eds.) Operating Systems. LNCS, vol. 60, pp. 393–481. Springer, Berlin (1978)
4. Hoare, C.A.R.: Communicating sequential processes. Commun. ACM **21**(8), 666–677 (1978)
5. Koo, R., Toueg, S.: Checkpointing and rollback-recovery for distributed systems. IEEE Trans. Softw. Eng. **SE–13**(1), 23–31 (1987)
6. Manivannan, D., Singhal, M.: A low-overhead recovery technique using quasi-synchronous checkpointing. In: Proceedings of the 16th International Conference on Distributed Computing Systems, pp. 100–107, May 1996
7. Monnet, S.: Hybrid checkpointing for parallel applications in cluster federations. In: Proceedings of 4th IEEE/ACM International Symposium on Cluster Computing and the Grid, pp. 773–782 (2004)
8. Ndiaye, N.M., Sens, P., Thiare, O.: Performance comparison of hierarchical checkpoint protocols grid computing. Intl. J. Interact. Multimedia Artif. Intell. **1**, 46–53 (2012)
9. Paul, H.S., Gupta, A., Badrinath, R.: Combining checkpoint and recovery algorithm for distributed systems. In: 3rd Workshop on Distributed Computing, pp. 68–72 (2001)
10. Paul, H.S., Gupta, A., Badrinath, R.: Hierarchical coordinated checkpointing protocol. In: IASTED PDCS, pp. 235–240 (2002)
11. Paul, H.S., Gupta, A., Badrinath, R.: A heterogeneous checkpoint and recovery protocol in cluster-based distributed systems. In: PDPTA, pp. 1224–1230 (2003)
12. Strom, R., Yemini, S.: Optimistic recovery in distributed systems. ACM Trans. Comput. Syst. **3**(3), 204–226 (1985)
13. Wang, Y.M.: Reducing message logging overhead for log-based recovery. In: Proceedings of IEEE International Symposium on Circuits and Systems, pp. 1925–1928 (1993)

A Proactive Solution to Manage Web Service Unavailability in Service Oriented Software Systems

Navinderjit Kaur Kahlon[1(✉)], Salil Vishnu Kapur[1], Kuljit Kaur Chahal[1], and Sukhleen Bindra Narang[2]

[1] Department of Computer Science, Guru Nanak Dev University, Amritsar, Punjab, India
navinderjitkahlon@gmail.com
[2] Department of Electronics Technology, Guru Nanak Dev University, Amritsar, Punjab, India

Abstract. A service oriented application consists of component web services which cooperate with each other to offer the desired functionality. Due to the distributed and unpredictable nature of the underlying environment, the component web services have uncertain dependability characteristics. This paper looks into the issue of web service availability. The paper proposes a proactive framework to manage the situation when third party web services become unavailable. Software agents are employed to monitor web services on the provider side. The framework is implemented in J2EE, using JADE environment for creating and deploying software agents. Experimental analysis shows that the proposed solution is effective and behaves considerably well when availability of component web services is varied from 0 % to 100 %.

Keywords: Web service availability · Proactive solutions · Reactive solution · Software agents

1 Introduction

In service oriented architecture, composite web services are dependent upon third party atomic or composite web services for fulfilling a client's request. However, due to the distributed nature of service oriented systems, the component services may not always respond back to every invocation request. A component service may become unavailable (due to service, server, or network failures) and fail to give a response to the client. Failure of a component web service may lead to abrupt termination or degraded performance of the composite web service. This could lead to loss of business or sometimes human lives as well if the composite web service implements a business ecosystem or some critical application such as healthcare [6]. Therefore, the challenge lies in ensuring availability of component services that cooperate to implement a service oriented system. It is important to track up-to-date information regarding changes in status of component services and implement change reaction decisions (e.g. replacement of a failed service) as soon as possible to improve the dependability of service oriented applications.

This paper discusses the availability issue of web services. Service availability is defined as a situation in which a web service responds to client requests as often as 24/7.

© Springer-Verlag Berlin Heidelberg 2016
A. Norta et al. (Eds.): ICSOC 2015 Workshops, LNCS 9586, pp. 243–254, 2016.
DOI: 10.1007/978-3-662-50539-7_20

A web service may become unavailable due to software/hardware/network failures. The challenge is to ascertain the service failure as soon as possible so that a remedial action just-in-time can be taken without compromising the performance of the composite web service. The unavailability of a web service can be handled in reactive way i.e. detecting the unavailability at runtime. This often leads to halt of execution and time goes in searching for candidate web services for replacement to complete the execution. A reactive approach often provides user and business dissatisfaction, money and business loss [1]. A proactive approach is an alternative that requires finding the alternative services or replacement services before the problem occurs. Some prediction based solutions for proactive adaptation already exist in the research literature [2]. Proactive solutions are advocated to be more suitable for web services which are composed for long term [10]. As web services with long term are invoked repeatedly in comparison to web services with short term. A short term web service is created to satisfy a business goal for a limited number of users.

This paper proposes a proactive approach for handling web service availability issue. It uses the concept of mobile agents, which run at service provider side and provide latest information regarding the service to the service user. Therefore, service user can arrange alternatives of a failed service even before invoking it. In addition, it also proposes service replacement strategies for optimizing the process execution. The key advantages of proactive approach lie in timely action taken before the invocation of an unavailable web service. We assume that mobile agents do not violate any security requirements of the service provider.

The paper is organized as follows. Section 2 describes some preliminary information regarding the concepts used in this study - web services and software agents. Section 3 describes the proactive framework. Section 4 gives results of the framework evaluation. Section 5 presents related work and the last section concludes the paper.

2   Preliminaries

2.1   Web Services

Web services are autonomous, self-contained, self-describing, modular applications that can be published, located and invoked over the Web [17]. Web-services have been extensively used for developing business or enterprise process workflows. They are simple, loosely coupled, platform independent and are based upon standards like Simple Object Access Protocol (SOAP), Web Services Description Language (WSDL) [13], Universal Discovery Description and Integration (UDDI).

Web service monitoring ensures verification of a service's properties from functional as well non-functional aspects [5]. Functional property verification ensures that the web service delivers the functions as per the expectations. On the other hand, non-functional or Quality of Service (QoS) verification ensures how efficiently the service performs its functions. Some of the most common QoS properties are availability, performance, and security. Web service monitoring makes service users aware of the problems so that they can take corrective decisions and avoid performance degradation of their applications.

2.2 Software Agents

Software Agents [7] are autonomous and self contained software systems that reside in some environment aiming to fulfill certain objectives. A mobile agent can migrate across a network. It can reduce the interactions required between remote machines, and hence reduce the network traffic. There is research work in this direction to combine the capabilities of software agents and web services to create intelligent autonomous solutions [12].

3   The Proposed Framework

We suggest a proactive solution to handle a situation when a component service becomes unavailable. The solution attempts to avoid invocation of web services which have already become unavailable. This can maintain the performance of a service oriented application; otherwise it may degrade as time may be wasted in invoking the web service and then finding a substitute of the service after realizing the invocation failure. However, this approach does not handle the invocation failures of web services which may not be due to unavailability.

Figure 1 shows the overall architecture of the framework with the main components namely - workflow manager, service manager, service repair, service monitor agent and client monitor agent. It also shows the inputs and outputs (represented as documents) connected to every component of the framework. The description of each component is as:

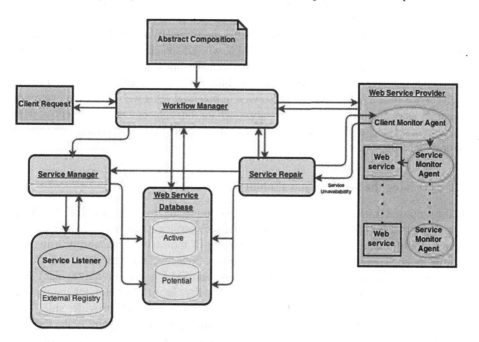

Fig. 1. Architecture of the proactive framework

The *abstract composition* module provides a predefined abstract process which involves a sequential and parallel flow. Corresponding concrete web services are chosen by the service manager module. We assume existence of services instances for each task in the abstract process.

The *workflow manager* is the main component of our framework. It coordinates all the components of the framework. It acts as a controller to execute the services using centralized orchestration. It receives a client request from an Android based interface and responds back with the result; gets the corresponding abstract composition; initiates service manager to select corresponding web services from the services database; initiates service repair to dispatch agents to the service provider sites to monitor the availability of the chosen web services; and invokes the web services for preparing the results.

The *service manager* module creates the services database in the form of two tables – Active Services and Potential Services. It populates the tables from an external service registry. Service manager, when asked, retrieves not only the top most service from the service registry as per the selection criteria, rather it fetches a bag of services corresponding to an abstract service. It keeps the top most service of the set in Active Service table, and rest of the retrieved services (next best) are stored in Potential services table. Active Services table contains information about the services that are currently being used in the software application. Potential Services table has information about the services available for replacement in case an active service fails.

The *service repair* module is responsible for the maintenance of web services database. To begin with it dispatches mobile agents, called the Client Mobile Agent (CMA), to the service provider's sites corresponding to all the services in the Active Service table. On the provider side, every web service is monitored by a provider deployed agent, called Service Monitor Agent (SMA). A CMA, when dispatched subscribes to the SMA. When a web service becomes unavailable, the SMA notifies the CMA and the CMA then sends message to the Service Repair module. The service repair also substitutes the web service in active set with a web service in potential set if web service in active set becomes unavailable. It uses proactive approach for the replacement of web service with the help of service monitor agent and client monitor agent that monitors the web service at provider side.

3.1   Tracking the Service Unavailability

In the proposed framework, every web service is monitored by an agent called the SMA. The SMA that is continuously monitoring the web service at the provider side detects unavailability of the web service. It keeps track of the service availability using the heartbeat mechanism. Web service and the SMA both reside on the same host. So no network communication cost is involved. Moreover, SMA helps to avoid regular client monitoring calls that may disrupt the service quality. In order to monitor the service availability, a service consumer deploys a mobile agent at service provider side. This mobile agent communicates with the service monitor agent to know status of the service. All the mobile agents deployed by service consumers subscribe to the SMA. When the service does not respond to the ping requests of the SMA, it broadcasts service unavailable status to all the subscribed CMAs. Every CMA notifies the status about the change proactively to its respective client executing on the service consumer side. No acknowledgement of receiving is expected for a trap by an agent.

The execution process of the proactive framework is depicted using the sequence diagram in Fig. 2. It describes the entire process flow of execution for our framework.

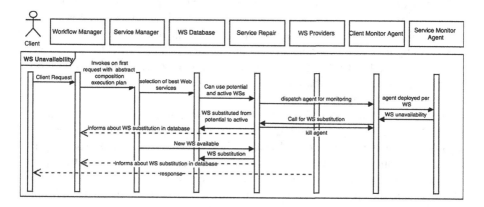

Fig. 2. Sequence diagram of proactive framework execution process

3.2   The Adaptation Process

The adaptation process of proactive framework will be triggered when a web service becomes unavailable at the provider side. The SMA notifies the CMA, which in turn sends a message to the Service Repair module. The Service Repair Module replaces the web service in the Active Service Table with the next best service (of the same category) available in the Potential Service Table. It also informs the Workflow Manager, lest the Workflow Manager may invoke the service which has now become unavailable. The Workflow Manager postpones the invocation. In the worst case, it may have to wait till an alternate service is put in the Active Service Table, a CMA is dispatched to the service provider side, and service becomes ready for invocation.

It is the responsibility of the Service Repair Module to maintain the potential web services in the same way as an inventory is managed. Whenever, the last service of a particular category from the Potential Service table is replaced with a service in the Active Service Table, it will inform the Service Manager module to retrieve more services, matching the criteria, from the external repository. Therefore the Potential Services Table will always have some services ready for replacement. However, if the Service Manager could not find any matching candidate services, then the Potential Services Table will not have options. In such cases, as the active service becomes unavailable, the application may have to be terminated.

4   Implementation Aspects

This section presents the results of experiments to quantify its effectiveness and efficiency. A prototype tool of framework is implemented in Java EE. The Abstract Composition, Workflow Manager, Service Manager and Service Repair are implemented as
single components for simplicity. The Workflow Manager and Service Manager are
exposed as RESTFUL web services. Service Repair module is implemented as an agent.
Client Monitor Agent (CMA) is implemented as a mobile agent.

The configuration of experiment environment for client and provider is done on an
i5 processor with 4 GB RAM using Tomcat server and JADE 7. The external service
registry and web service database is implemented using SQL server. The client request
is taken from an android phone.

For the implementation of the framework, an emergency hospital finder scenario is
used as an example. An execution model of *SearchHospital* service composition
scenario is taken to help a user to find a nearest hospital with particular disease diagnosis
and bed availability in an emergency. A user sends a request from his Android phone
with search string related to any disease such as 'heart attack'. The composition offers
services to find the current location of user using GPS system, to find nearest hospital
with specialization of disease and availability of bed and doctor, to provide the route to
be taken, the total time duration of reaching the hospital and to even invoke cab service
if the patient has asked for cab service.

We assume an abstract service composition is available before execution of the
workflow starts. We further assume that each service is *atomic*. That is, behavior of a
service is independent of other services. Network connection between services is error
free, even though individual atomic services may be problematic.

In order to evaluate the framework, the focus is on following two cases as described
below:

Case 1: Effectiveness of the framework through demonstration
Case 2: Demonstration about the framework when the availability of web services is
0 %, 30 %, 60 % and 100 %.

We used an environment with following different machines namely

(a) Client machine responsible to create simultaneous requests to the service compo-
     sition simulating several concurrent requests.
(b) Workflow manager is connected to different service providers. Each service
     providers contains different web services for the execution.

Case 1: In this case we compare three different scenarios: (a) the best case scenario,
(b) the proposed framework, and (c) a normal reactive solution. The best possible
scenario is the static execution of web services that are all available when a client
requests is handled. Best case scenario gives the optimistic lower limit on the performance. There is no monitoring overhead involved. All the services are available in this
case, so no service replacement issues arise.

A normal reactive solution involves the following steps- i. on client request, it
searches and discovers for the web services needed in the service registry, ii. It makes

a composition plan for execution of the required web services and iii. It executes the plan with the web services till the situation does not arise when a web service becomes unavailable. As the particular web service becomes unavailable, the execution process halts for the selection and discovery for the candidate web service to be replaced with the alternative web service from service repository in composition plan, and then execution resumes again.

We compare these three scenarios on the basis of execution time of the complete process. Execution time is defined as the difference of completion time and start time.

Figure 3 shows the results of this experiment. As shown in the figure for every 50 client requests, for case (a) the time to execute the composition without any adaptation in best case is two times better than our framework. The results also show that for case (b), the time to run our framework for proactive adaptation of web services has added the overhead for the very first client request that is the time taken by the framework as the startup time but the average execution time is 0.5 s and for case (c) execution time is increased even further, not using our framework that is reactive case. It verifies an improvement in execution time while using our proactive approach over non-proactive approach in the given situation.

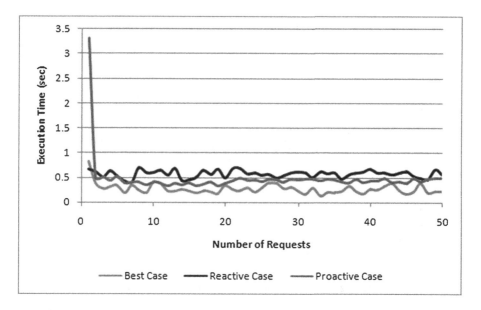

Fig. 3. Comparison of best, reactive and proactive approach

Case 2: In this case we analyze the execution time taken by the framework and the reactive case in four different cases with i. 0 %, ii. 30 %, iii. 60 % and iv. 100 % availability of web services. Figures 4, 5, 6 and 7 shows the four cases defined with the execution time and the experimentation time. In all the four cases proactive approach is better than the reactive approach with a clear demonstration that unavailability of web services does not affect the framework, but in reactive approach it varies according to web availability ratio. The performance of the framework is not affected by the unavailability of web services. In all the four cases the execution time taken by the framework is on average 0.5 s while it increases in reactive case.

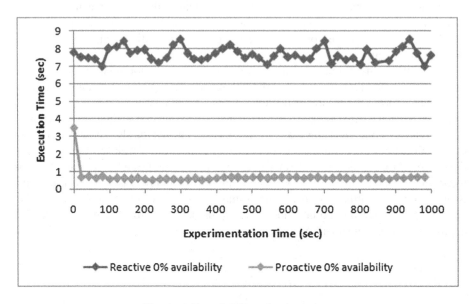

Fig. 4. 0 % availability of web services

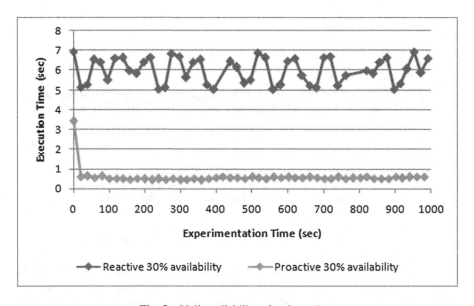

Fig. 5. 30 % availability of web services

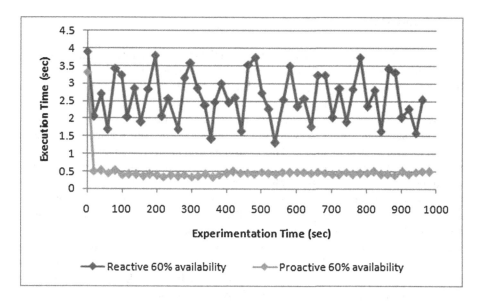

Fig. 6. 60 % availability of web services

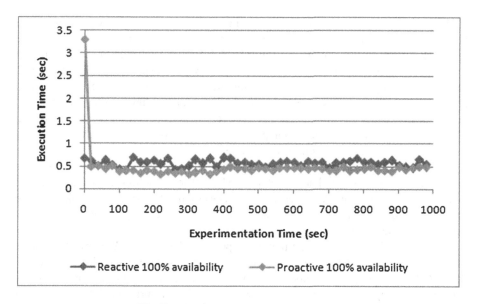

Fig. 7. 100 % availability of web services

Overall, the results are very positive which shows that proactive framework can be supported for execution of web services in order to save the time which would be wasted in non-proactive cases. The performance of the adaptation is very good and the solution does not cause any penalties for changes.

5   Related Work

Basically two types of solutions are proposed in the research literature to deal with this issue. These solutions are (1) Reactive (2) Proactive. In reactive solutions which mostly use monitoring, a web service is monitored either by client (client side monitoring) or by provider (provider side monitoring), or both (hybrid).

When a service becomes unavailable, it is replaced with another (similar) service. In provider side monitoring, service provider monitors the web service and replaces whenever it becomes unavailable. This replacement remains transparent to the client. In client side monitoring, a client collects status information of the web service [7]. Regarding the unavailability issue, it has to replace the service with a service from some other provider. Monitoring, of any kind, involves overhead. Some optimizations solutions to reduce this overhead also exist [8]. Psiuk *et al.* [16] observe that monitoring of interactions between clients and providers is important to ensure QoS.

In proactive solutions, mostly prediction based approach is used to deal with the issue. To adapt dynamically to composition environment, reinforcement policy is used [11] to get optimal workflow. ProAdapt, is a framework that uses proactive adaptation of web services using exponentially weighed moving averages based upon prediction [1]. It determines the unavailability at three levels: operation (a service method), service, and (service) provider.

Self adaptation of web services at runtime is known as self management or self healing of web services. Self healing, self configuring, self optimising and self aware approach [3, 15] is also known as runtime or autonomic adaptation. It can prevent disruption of web services by monitoring the QoS parameters, analyzing, planning, executing, and by following recovery techniques. The errors and exceptions [9] that arise in web service processes can be handled using error-handling mechanisms that can automatically detect errors and can take recovery actions accordingly. A self-healing technique based upon model-based approach [4] is used to repair the faulty process by taking appropriate recovery actions at runtime.

In [14] QoS management of web services is done using self healing web service based framework that uses Hidden Markov Model for prediction. It uses substitution and duplication for recovery of web services. The composite service replanning is done at execution time [2] if there is Service Level Agreement (SLA) violation of a web service or service is unavailable.

Harney and Doshi [7] suggest that a composite web service (CWS) must be aware of the latest information regarding its component services during execution. They opine that a CWS should query component services for their latest information. They use selective query approach to reduce overhead involved in this process. They assume that service providers mention the time period through which service parameters remain stable.

Zisman *et al.* [18] also deals with availability issues of web services availability. But they suggest a solution for service discovery only. The prototype is implemented using pull and proactive push mode in parallel to execution of web services. Their solution is proactive as it uses the push mechanism for informing the service oriented application regarding the availability of better services in the repository.

6   Conclusion and Future Work

Due to the dynamic nature of the service oriented solutions, status of web services is unpredictable most of the times. Information about change in the status of a web service (e.g. when it becomes unavailable) should reach the service user as soon as possible, lest a lot of time and resources are wasted which results in performance degradation of the user application. Most of the existing solutions are reactive in nature. Action is taken to replace a service, only when the invoked service does not respond. This paper proposes a proactive approach in which service replacement takes place as soon as a service becomes unavailable. This is asynchronous with the invocation requests of a client. The solution is implemented in J2EE and JADE. Experimental evaluation shows that the proposed solution is effective as well efficient. A comparison of proposed solution with a reactive solution, and a best scenario shows difference in results. Though this paper discusses from availability of web service perspective, in future we want to extend the framework by incorporating more QoS properties.

References

1. Aschoff, R., Zisman, A.: QoS-driven proactive adaptation of service composition. In: Maamar, Z., Motahari-Nezhad, H.R., Kappel, G. (eds.) Service Oriented Computing. LNCS, vol. 7084, pp. 421–435. Springer, Heidelberg (2011)
2. Canfora, G., Penta, M.D., Esposito, R., Villani, M.L.: QoS-aware replanning of composite web services. In: Proceedings of the IEEE International Conference on Web Services (ICWS 2005) (2005)
3. Frei, R., McWilliam, R., Derrick, B., Purvis, A., Tiwari, A., Serugendo, G.D.M.: Self-healing and self-repairing technologies. Int. J. Adv. Manuf. Technol. **2013**(69), 1033–1061 (2013). doi:10.1007/s00170-013-5070-2
4. Friedrich, G., Fugini, M., Mussi, E., Pernici, B., Tagni, G.: Exception handling for repair in service-based processes. IEEE Trans. Softw. Eng. **36**(2), 198–215 (2010)
5. Ghezzi, C., Guinea, S.: Run-time monitoring in service oriented architectures. In: Baresi, L., Nitto, E.D. (eds.) Test and Analysis of Web Services, pp. 237–264. Springer, Heidelberg (2007)
6. Gorbenko, A., Romanovsky, A., Kharchenko, V., Tarasyuk, O.: Dependability of service-oriented computing: time-probabilistic failure modelling. In: Avgeriou, P. (ed.) SERENE 2012. LNCS, vol. 7527, pp. 121–133. Springer, Heidelberg (2012)
7. Harney, J., Doshi, P.: Selective querying for adapting web service compositions using the value of changed information. IEEE Trans. Serv. Comput. **1**(3), 169–185 (2008)
8. He, P., Yu, K., Wen, J., Xu, J.: Monitoring resources allocation for service compositions under different monitoring mechanisms. In: 2011 International Conference on Complex, Intelligent, and Software Intensive Systems. IEEE (2011)
9. Jannach, D., Gut, A.: Exception handling in web service processes. In: Kaschek, R., Delcambre, L. (eds.) The Evolution of Conceptual Modeling. LNCS, vol. 6520, pp. 225–253. Springer, Heidelberg (2011)
10. Liu, X., Bouguettaya, A., Wu, J., Zhou, L.: Ev-LCS: a system for the evolution of long term composed services. IEEE Trans. Serv. Comput. **6**(1), 102–115 (2013)

11. Moustafa, A., Zhang, M.: Towards proactive web service adaptation. In: Ralyté, J., Franch, X., Brinkkemper, S., Wrycza, S. (eds.) CAiSE 2012. LNCS, vol. 7328, pp. 473–485. Springer, Heidelberg (2012)
12. Maximilien, E., Singh, M.: Agent based architecture for autonomic web service selection. In: 1st International Workshop on Web Services and Agent Based Engineering, Sydney, Australia (2003)
13. Peltz, C.: Web services orchestration and choreography. IEEE Comput. 36(10), 46–53 (2003)
14. Pegoraro, R., Halima, R.B., Drira, K., Guennoun, K., Rosario, J.M.: A framework for monitoring and runtime recovery of web-based applications. In: 10th International Conference on Enterprise Information Systems (2008)
15. Psaier, H., Dustdar, S.: A survey on self-healing systems: approaches and systems. Computing 2011(91), 43–73 (2011). doi:10.1007/s00607-010-0107-y
16. Psiuk, M., Bujok, T., Zielinski, K.: Enterprise service bus monitoring framework for SOA systems. IEEE Trans. Serv. Comput. 5(3), 450–466 (2012)
17. Verma, K., Sheth, A.P.: Autonomic web processes. In: Benatallah, B., Casati, F., Traverso, P. (eds.) ICSOC 2005. LNCS, vol. 3826, pp. 1–11. Springer, Heidelberg (2005)
18. Zisman, A., Dooley, J., Spanoudakis, G.: Proactive runtime service discovery. In: Proceedings of IEEE 2008 International Service Computing Conference (SCC 2008) (2008)

Author Index

Printed in the United States
By Bookmasters